THE GUY YOU LOVED TO HATE

THE GUY YOU LOVED TO HATE

CONFESSIONS FROM A REALITY TV VILLAIN

SPENCER PRATT

GALLERY BOOKS

New York   Amsterdam/Antwerp   London
Toronto   Sydney/Melbourne   New Delhi

Gallery Books
An Imprint of Simon & Schuster, LLC
1230 Avenue of the Americas
New York, NY 10020

For more than 100 years, Simon & Schuster has championed authors and the stories they create. By respecting the copyright of an author's intellectual property, you enable Simon & Schuster and the author to continue publishing exceptional books for years to come. We thank you for supporting the author's copyright by purchasing an authorized edition of this book.

No amount of this book may be reproduced or stored in any format, nor may it be uploaded to any website, database, language-learning model, or other repository, retrieval, or artificial intelligence system without express permission. All rights reserved. Inquiries may be directed to Simon & Schuster, 1230 Avenue of the Americas, New York, NY 10020 or permissions@simonandschuster.com.

Copyright © 2026 by Pratt Productions Inc.

Some names and identifying characteristics have been changed. Some dialogue has been re-created.

All rights reserved, including the right to reproduce this book or portions thereof in any form whatsoever. For information, address Gallery Books Subsidiary Rights Department, 1230 Avenue of the Americas, New York, NY 10020.

First Gallery Books hardcover edition January 2026

GALLERY BOOKS and colophon are registered trademarks of Simon & Schuster, LLC

Simon & Schuster strongly believes in freedom of expression and stands against censorship in all its forms. For more information, visit BooksBelong.com.

For information about special discounts for bulk purchases, please contact Simon & Schuster Special Sales at 1-866-506-1949 or business@simonandschuster.com.

The Simon & Schuster Speakers Bureau can bring authors to your live event. For more information or to book an event, contact the Simon & Schuster Speakers Bureau at 1-866-248-3049 or visit our website at www.simonspeakers.com.

Interior design by Jaime Putorti

Manufactured in the United States of America

10 9 8 7 6 5 4 3 2 1

Library of Congress Cataloging-in-Publication Data has been applied for.

ISBN 978-1-6682-1176-2
ISBN 978-1-6682-1178-6 (ebook)

 Let's stay in touch! Scan here to get book recommendations, exclusive offers, and more delivered to your inbox.

For Heidi

CONTENTS

NOTE TO THE READER   xi

PROLOGUE: **PARADISE LOST:**
When the Palisades Burned   xiii

PART ONE: THE THIRST AWAKENS

CHAPTER 1 **SPENCER: ORIGINS:**
AKA How I Got This Way   3

CHAPTER 2 **DEAD MAN'S CURVE:**
Near-Death and Other Formative Experiences   13

CHAPTER 3 **HUMMINGBIRD PROPHECIES:**
When I Decided to Live Life at 1,200 Beats per Minute   24

CHAPTER 4 **INITIATION CEREMONIES:**
My First Movie, the Olsen-Twin Photo Deal That Paid for It, and How I Accidentally Became the Youngest Executive Producer in Hollywood   35

CHAPTER 5 **THE PRINCES OF MALIBU:**
When I Went from Producer to Product   54

CHAPTER 6 **A SPEIDI IS BORN:**
Two Players, One Game   60

CHAPTER 7 **WHIPPED:**
How to Lose a Girl in One Dance   72

CHAPTER 8 **PLAYING DOUBLES:**
When the Main Characters and the Sidekicks Date
One Another   84

CHAPTER 9 **TWO BIRDS, ONE STONE:**
How I Abandoned My Own Show to Infiltrate *The Hills*   89

CHAPTER 10 **WELCOME TO THE PUPPET SHOW:**
The Science of Frankenbiting and Professional Assholery   94

CHAPTER 11 **OPERATION UPSTAGE AND OTHER DARK ARTS:**
How MTV Turned Us into Monsters, One Edit at a Time   103

CHAPTER 12 **I KNOW WHAT I DID:**
The Sex Tape Scandal That Ruined Us   112

PART TWO: THE VILLAIN EDIT

CHAPTER 13 **FUCK AROUND AND FIND OUT:**
Survival Strategies for the Despicable   129

CHAPTER 14 **BIRTH OF A SHE-PRATT:**
When Blood's Not Thicker Than Water   134

CHAPTER 15 **TABLOIDS AND TUNES:**
Reclaiming Narrative Control   140

CHAPTER 16 **THE WEDDING NO ONE EXPECTED, INCLUDING US:**
Elope Now, Explain Later: Our Nuclear Option   145

CHAPTER 17 **WEDDING REBOOT:**
'Til Fake Do Us Part   152

CHAPTER 18 **MAYDAY IN THE JUNGLE—PART ONE:**
When Our Dry Shampoo Commercial Turned
into *Tropic Thunder*   155

CONTENTS ix

CHAPTER 19 MAYDAY IN THE JUNGLE—PART TWO:
Inside the Lost Chamber   *168*

CHAPTER 20 SHELTER FROM THE STORM:
Crystals, Plastic Surgery, and Other Safe Spaces   *176*

CHAPTER 21 VISION QUESTS IN A WORLD OF ILLUSION:
Gurus, Psychic Protection, and the Search
for Something Real   *191*

CHAPTER 22 SWAT TEAM SERENADE:
From Chart Flops to Cop Raids   *199*

CHAPTER 23 HEEEERE'S SPENCER!:
Our Last Days on *The Hills*   *207*

CHAPTER 24 THE GOLDEN BACKPACK:
Why a Trail of Dead Bodies Made Us Pack
Our Crystals and Run   *216*

CHAPTER 25 THE SOUND OF SILENCE:
How We Went Broke in Paradise   *226*

PART THREE: NEW DAWN

CHAPTER 26 CRYSTAL VISIONS:
Manifest, Receive, Release   *235*

CHAPTER 27 RULE BRITANNIA:
Speidi in the Shire   *243*

CHAPTER 28 PRATT DADDY:
Wait, People Actually Like Me?   *249*

CHAPTER 29 BRING BACK *THE HILLS*:
Reunions, Regrets, and the Confession You'll Never See   *260*

CHAPTER 30 **WHEN THE PALISADES BURNED:**
Our House Went Up in Smoke, and Heidi
Went to Number One   *268*

CHAPTER 31 **TRUE CRIMES:**
When the Villain Has Receipts   *276*

EPILOGUE **HOLLYWOOD ENDING:**
The Director's Cut   *281*

ACKNOWLEDGMENTS   *283*

NOTE TO THE READER

If, following the publication of this book, anything happens to me—heart attack, "suicide," slip in the shower, brakes go out, fall on my head, choke on deli meat . . .

KNOW THAT IT WAS MURDER.

AND YES, PLEASE SEEK REVENGE.

Love,

Spencer Pratt

PROLOGUE

PARADISE LOST

When the Palisades Burned

You know what's cool about your house burning down?

Nothing. Obviously.

After the fire, I stood in what used to be my driveway, touching the air where walls used to be, searching for a silver lining. A reason for this. Some philosophical lesson, or profound realization about impermanence. Whatever people say when a tragedy happens.

But no. Sometimes there isn't a silver lining. Sometimes you just lose everything.

And it wasn't just us—the entire Pacific Palisades and eastern Malibu neighborhoods had been incinerated.

Twenty-three thousand acres.

Seven thousand homes.

Twelve people who woke up the morning of January 7, 2025, with no clue their time was up.

Across town, Altadena was mourning its own dead, too.

These were the biggest wildfires ever to hit Los Angeles. Apocalyptic. An absolute catastrophe of mismanagement and governmental failure, corruption, and incompetence. They want to call it a natural disaster? No, this was negligence dressed up as an act of God. This was decades of budgets cuts, ignored warnings, and politicians who cared more about their careers than our lives.

But in those first days, I wasn't ready for that anger yet. I was just another guy wandering through what used to be our neighborhood, picking through toxic ash, like an idiot.

I searched for anything I could salvage from my crystal collection. The chunk of moldavite that turned my meditations into time travel. That first piece of sugilite that healed the pain of my wife, Heidi. None survived. All reduced to the same gray dust.

I did find the remains of my hummingbird feeders. Sixty of them, which had been strategically placed where my tiny angels could always find sweetness. Just the copper frames survived, their glass hearts melted. I knew instantly my bird friends were gone.

My phone buzzed. A text from the producer who'd first convinced me to step in front of a camera, who'd helped birth "Spencer Pratt, the character" into existence.

"I'm so sorry, Spencer," he wrote. "Life sure takes some interesting turns. Who would have thought this would be your path?"

I stared at the text. My path had *always* been on fire. I just never imagined it would get this literal.

The truth is, I'd already burned my life down years before this wildfire. Torched relationships for storylines. Nuked my reputation for ratings. Set my soul ablaze and called it entertainment. Back then, I called it success.

But I'd walked away from all that. Killed the character, buried Spencer Pratt the villain. It hadn't been easy. You can't just turn off a persona that made you famous. You have to learn to exist without it. You have to find out who you are when nobody's watching. The emptiness is terrifying. But somewhere in that silence, you figure out what's left when no one is paying you to be terrible.

Tomorrow there would be insurance adjusters, FEMA forms, the paperwork Olympics. I'd wake up without any physical proof, aside from our beautiful sons, that Heidi and I had built a life worth anything. But at least I'd still be myself. Not the villain they'd paid me to play. Just a man who'd survived everything, including himself. Including this.

Not a silver lining, exactly. But I'd take it.

PART ONE
THE THIRST AWAKENS

CHAPTER 1

SPENCER: ORIGINS

AKA How I Got This Way

To understand how I got here, you have to go back to the source. Back when the chaos was just potential energy, waiting for the right moment to ignite.

August 14, 1983. A lightning storm lit up Los Angeles the night I was born—summer thunder rolling over the city like the universe announcing something it would later regret. MTV had already detonated into the culture, and in two years, the first reality TV show would air. The world didn't know it yet, but it was getting hungry for people like me.

In the maternity ward at Saint John's hospital in Santa Monica, I appeared lifeless. Blue, silent, the umbilical cord wrapped around my neck. They cut the cord, but still I lay limp. Unmoving. My debut was almost my finale.

Suddenly, I filled the air with a scream. A newborn's battle cry. It wouldn't be the last time I looked death in the eye and said, *Not today*.

The doctor held me up like I was Simba in *The Lion King*. "He's *perfect*!" my mother sobbed, gazing at her ten-pound baby boy, who would unfortunately grow up to be America's second-most-hated person, according to a Reuters poll.

God bless my mom. She's never seen a red flag she couldn't paint white.

• • •

Looking back, I can see the pattern was already there, some sort of compulsive need to make every moment a story.

Take a look inside my brain. Actually, don't. It's like *The Matrix* in there. Epiphanies and apocalyptic visions. Sacred symbols and master plans. Zeros and ones, pixels and dollar signs. Neurons firing like it's the Fourth of July.

Pew! Pew! Pew!

So much noise, just to avoid sitting in silence with myself.

This restless, relentless energy would eventually collide with a culture that monetized attention, that turned personality disorders into personality brands. Back then, I thought it was a superpower. Now I know where that energy can lead when it's not channeled right.

My natural disposition doesn't come with an off button, by the way. It just sits in my chest like a nuclear reactor, keeping me moving, keeping me scheming, keeping me launching myself into the sky. Sometimes I'll land to a standing ovation. Sometimes I'll face-plant in front of everyone. Either way, I'm fun to watch. At least, that's what they keep telling me.

My first full sentence was "THAT'S MINE!" Straight to property rights.

It started small—some kid's sippy cup at Mommy & Me? Mine now. The sick tricycle at the park? Obviously mine. My half sister, Kristin—seven years older and who believes herself infinitely wiser—loves telling this next story at family dinners, because she's sure it explains everything about who I came to be.

Picture a perfect summer afternoon by our pool. Kristin's floating in our Zodiac inflatable boat, probably lost in *Sweet Valley High*. Then here I come—angelic toddler Spencer, surveying my domain.

"MINE," I said, pointing at the boat. "Get off." No "pretty please."

No negotiation. Just the certainty that wanting something made it mine.

Kristin looked toward our parents, poolside. "Mommy, Spencer thinks everything belongs to him!" she said.

"Oh, it's just a phase," Mom called back, absorbed in a *People* article about Princess Di.

"No," Kristin insisted, "he literally believes everything is his. The boat. The pool. My room."

My dad, Skip, said, "Kristin, don't you see? Our boy's gonna be a CEO!" And there it was—every land grab reframed as cute, entrepreneurial spirit. That level of unconditional validation from my parents hardwired something dangerous into my developing brain. A sense of weapons-grade confidence, combined with the belief that desire equaled entitlement. Meaning, if my parents believed I could have whatever I wanted, then yeah—sounds legit to me.

One day, during my second year on planet Earth, I received some devastating intelligence: My brief reign as the youngest and allegedly most powerful ruler of House of Pratt was about to end. "You're going to have a sister!" my mom announced, hand resting on her expanding belly. "Her name is Stephanie."

I didn't like the sound of this Stephanie character.

"Can you send it back?" I asked.

"No, you can't return babies, sweetie."

WHAT KIND OF SCAM IS THAT? I thought. You can return everything else in America!

After Stephanie's birth, my parents sensed my unease and tried their best to convince me that I remained their crown jewel. They were trying to prevent sibling rivalry by inflating my ego to dangerous altitudes. The result was a small person who believed his mere existence deserved constant recognition.

Every minor developmental milestone was a national event. A tooth fell out? Parade. First soccer goal? Fireworks. Every wobble forward in life was met with the kind of fanfare usually reserved for returning war heroes.

For my sixth birthday party, they rented the *Ghostbusters* car. Not some weak replica. The ACTUAL car. Imagine twenty sugar-high kids losing their minds, screaming "WHO YOU GONNA CALL?" in our driveway; meanwhile, I'm sitting by myself, proton pack on my back, staring into the void. Why? A gaggle of moms had crowded around Stephanie, cooing over her supposed cuteness. I was the birthday boy; why was *she* the main attraction?

I was learning something important about attention—that love felt most real when it was focused directly on me. This wasn't malicious; it was just how my young brain processed the world. If people weren't looking at me, were they thinking about me? And if they weren't thinking about me, did I really exist?

Nana Joan, my maternal grandmother, wandered over, margarita in her hand, instinctively sensing my distress. She sat down next to me, put an arm around my small shoulders, and sighed. "I told your mother to stop at two kids, but she wouldn't listen!" she whispered in my ear. "Anyway, having a younger sister could be a blessing, Spencer. Look at Warren Beatty and Shirley MacLaine—that's a dynasty. And don't forget, your mom and dad love you to the moon and back. Nothing will ever change that."

She was right. Mostly. Years later, when the whole world would turn savage and my life became a cautionary tale, everyone's faith in me would be tested. Even my devoted parents wavered—not in their love, but in their certainty that I was making the right choices. Friends disappeared, as if my toxicity might be contagious. But Nana Joan never flinched. Not once. What others would interpret as self-destruction, she always recognized as the inevitable expression of a personality that was always going to burn bright, for better or worse.

Ah, Nana Joan. She always understood me. We were cut from the same cloth. Even her license plate could have told you that. It said DEVIOUS 1. Not BLESSED 1. Not GRAM 1. DEVIOUS 1.

Nana Joan should have been a star. She had the looks, the walk, probably could've charmed her way to a three-picture deal at MGM. But life's full of surprises. At seventeen, she fell pregnant by some guy with "nice teeth and fast hands." His name was Billy or Bobby or something.

Her mom, my great-grandma Mimi—who was on husband number four and had married into the Chicken of the Sea tuna empire—couldn't allow Nana Joan's scandal to contaminate her reputation in canned-fish circles. So she orchestrated a hasty Mexican wedding that solved the scandal but doomed young Joan to a life she never wanted.

Three months later, Nana Joan lost the baby. She stayed in the marriage nonetheless. Cooked meals for a man she barely knew. Made Jell-O in molds and watched her Hollywood dreams die slowly while Billy/Bobby drank Coors and listened to Dodgers games on the kitchen radio.

But domestic servitude was never Nana Joan's destiny. A few years later, she got a divorce and moved back home with her mom in La Cañada Flintridge, about thirteen miles northeast of Hollywood. She'd sit on the porch of her mom's ranch house in her robe, searching for the Hollywood sign across the canyon, longing for the martinis at Musso & Frank.

Being so close and yet so far from the action was torture. So she coped by reading celebrity tabloids. The *National Enquirer*. The *Star*. The *Globe*. *Midnight*. She just loved losing herself in celebrity gossip. Years later, when I made it into her favorite magazines, she couldn't have been prouder. She wore a button with my face on it everywhere. To the bank. The doctor. Probably to funerals. When *Today* host Al Roker called me and my wife "everything that's wrong with America," Nana Joan hugged me like I'd just won an Oscar. "Everyone knows who you are, and that's all that matters," she declared. Through my fame, even my infamy, I guess she finally got what she'd always wanted—a connection to the celebrity world she'd spent decades reading about from the outside.

Nana Joan had always had admirers. After her divorce, she burned through boyfriends until meeting my grandpa Stan, a military engineer whose career appealed to her lifelong hunger for anything that glittered with importance. When I was a teenager, I asked my grandpa Stan to explain exactly what he did for the government. He just handed me a book called *Skunk Works*, about an engineering firm—Lockheed Martin—that builds stealth bombers and spy planes for the Pentagon.

"What *are* these things?" I asked, flipping through pages full of diagrams that looked like flying saucers. That's how I learned about JANET Airlines—the government's secret shuttle service to Area 51, where the American military stashes alien tech in underground bunkers. JANET was an acronym for Just Another Non-Existent Terminal.

Janet is also my mother's name. Coincidence? I don't believe in those.

Looking back, I can see how these two forces shaped me. From Joan, I inherited the conviction that being known mattered more than being understood. From Stan, I learned that reality was negotiable—that with enough vision and audacity, you could engineer your way into existing on your own terms. These weren't just family traits I observed from a distance. They were my genetic inheritance, the psychological DNA that would eventually drive me to build my own impossible thing: a career based on nothing but the raw force of wanting to be famous.

My mother, Janet, the older of Grandpa Stan and Nana Joan's two daughters, was eighteen when she left Los Angeles to follow her high school boyfriend up Mammoth Mountain. Family meant everything to her, so they got married quickly, had my half sister, Kristin, and posted up at eight thousand feet. He ran ski patrol. She ran the bar at Whiskey Creek and made what people said were the best margaritas in three counties.

But after a few years, the mountain began to feel less like adventure and more like a cage. The thin air, the snowbound days, the way she could feel herself disappearing into fleece and small-town resignation—this wasn't the life she'd imagined. She was Nana Joan's daughter, after all, born with the same hunger for something larger than what she'd been given.

That's where my dad comes into the picture. William "Skip" Pratt, a surfing dentist who embodied the California dream.

Skip had grown up in Inglewood, a neighborhood in South Los Angeles. He was the son of William Chauncey Pratt III, my grandpa Bill, a WWII battleship veteran and Golden Gloves boxer at UCLA, who said things like, "You call that a handshake?" I was supposed to be named William Chauncey Pratt IV, after him, but my mom shut that down fast. "You don't name someone 'the Fourth' unless you own a yacht or a university building," she said. True.

Grandpa Bill was notoriously frugal. He was so tightfisted he'd charge my dad quarters to use the phone in his own house. "You think money grows on trees?" he'd say, holding out his palm.

My dad was built different, though. Where Grandpa Bill saw limits, Skip saw opportunities. He wasn't just buying into the American dream—he was convinced it was written for him. Sports seemed like his obvious path to glory. He possessed genuine talent—shone as his high school's pitcher, earned a legitimate USC tryout. But his first day on campus delivered a brutal lesson.

He walked onto the field and heard a *crack*. The sound of a freshman's fastball breaking the sound barrier. My dad stood there, watching this prodigy Tom Seaver—future Hall of Fame Major League Baseball pitcher with the New York Mets—knowing he could never compete. Ten minutes later, he walked off that field and changed his major to pre-dental. If you can't be the best, be the guy who fixes his teeth.

I inherited that adaptability from him—the ability to pivot, to reinvent, to find new angles when the first plan doesn't work. When one door closes, we just find another one to kick open. The difference is people light up when they see my father coming. They trust him with their mouths, their kids' cavities, their family dental emergencies. He's the guy everyone wants at their dinner party.

Me? Well, I'm guessing you've read the title of this book. *The Guy You Loved to Hate.* Yeah. Different skill sets.

When Dad graduated from USC, he opened a practice in Santa Monica and rented himself a surf shack in Malibu so he could wake up at 4:30 a.m. and paddle out before driving forty-five minutes to stick his hands in people's mouths. His whole blueprint for how to live came from this dentist he met at the beach once—surfboard tucked under one arm, Porsche keys dangling from the other. This guy would catch waves at sunrise, then spend his day fixing teeth while bumping the Beach Boys and charging rich-people prices. My dad saw that setup and said, "That's literally the dream right there." Back then, Malibu wasn't the billionaires' playground it is today. It was still ramshackle beach shacks rented to burnouts and artists. No private security, or Nobu, or influencers. Just fish tacos from Carlos & Pepe's, empty waves, and the kind of California sunshine that made you understand why people traveled west and never left.

Skip had found his perfect rhythm: waves at dawn, dental work by day, enough money to sustain the lifestyle he'd envisioned. But he possessed the restless hustle that runs through our family—the compulsion to turn every opportunity into a bigger opportunity, every success into a launching pad for the next conquest.

One day, my dad was working on some patient's molar when the guy casually dropped that dental gold was undervalued by 30 percent. Within a month, Dad had unlocked a whole new revenue stream. He'd be up at 5 a.m. driving downtown, pulling up behind Mahmoud's Gold Exchange on Hill Street with a briefcase full of dental gold, then walking out with straight cash.

This wasn't just entrepreneurial hustle; Skip was building something larger than a dental practice. Constructing a life that would prove his father's scarcity mindset wrong. Stacking money for a beach house dream and family goals. All he needed now was the right partner. Someone who understood that dreams weren't meant to remain theoretical—they were blueprints waiting to be built.

That's where Stevie, my mom's little sister, comes in. She was dating a very colorful character who lived at the end of Dad's cul-de-sac. This guy looked like what might happen if Tom Selleck banged a key of cocaine. Gold chains living in his chest hair ecosystem. Silk shirts with a permanent open-to-the-navel policy. "Solid neighbor," my dad still says. "Fixed my board once."

Anyway, Stevie called Janet up one day, all hyped. "Janet! You need to get down here ASAP! I want you to meet our neighbor Skip! He's perfect for you!" My mom, knee-deep in divorce proceedings and mountain-life recovery, wasn't exactly in the market for romance.

"He looks like Don Henley . . ." Stevie said, and that's when my mom, being completely obsessed with the Eagles, decided maybe a beach trip wasn't the worst idea after all.

Janet showed up for her blind date with Skip at a restaurant called Trancas overlooking Zuma Beach in Malibu, surf central. After dinner, they walked down to the sand to check out the waves, where my dad revealed his life plan—dentistry was just the day job. He was going to be rich one day. "How?" my mom asked. My dad leaned in, his eyes lighting up. "Oil, Janet. My buddy, he's got these geological surveys of the Permian Basin in West Texas. There's an ocean of black gold under that desert, and one day, it's gonna be mine!"

My mom felt giddy hearing him outline his mad, far-fetched plans to become an oil baron. They were both California kids, after all, born with those restless pioneer genetics, raised on the mythology that the horizon wasn't a boundary but an invitation, that every sunset is just the warm-up act for tomorrow's possibilities. It's the same optimism that built Silicon Valley, that powers the entertainment industry, that turns every failed venture into a "learning experience."

"You're so cool, Skip," she said, making him feel like a god.

"I wanna be rich, Janet," he said, "but I also wanna be happy. No bad vibes. No kooks in the lineup. No bosses, no clocks, no polyester ties. Just beautiful summers and enough coin to keep the good times rolling. And margaritas. The real ones. With good tequila."

In that moment, Janet knew she'd found the one. Here was someone whose optimism matched her own, whose dreams were big enough to include her in them.

And that's what my parents taught me about love—it's about finding someone who doesn't think your dreams are batshit, even when they probably are. And when that connection clicks—when your stoke recognizes their stoke on a beach in Malibu—that's the universe showing you your future. That's when you know you've found your person, your partner in whatever beautiful madness comes next.

CHAPTER 2

DEAD MAN'S CURVE

*Near-Death and Other
Formative Experiences*

When we moved to the Pacific Palisades in 1992, it felt like my dad's victory lap. This was where all his hard work had led, a finish line that meant his children's lives could begin. For Skip, moving to the Palisades wasn't just about real estate—it was validation of his entire worldview, everything he'd been trying to prove to Grandpa Bill: that optimism could be converted into assets, that charm and hard work could buy you into the big leagues, that a guy from Inglewood could give his kids what he'd never had—a beach house in paradise.

And what a paradise it was. Perched on bluffs overlooking the Pacific Ocean about twenty miles west of downtown Los Angeles, the Palisades sit where the Santa Monica Mountains meet the sea, in a perfect microclimate where ocean breezes keep everything 72 degrees year-round. You can hike mountain trails in the morning, surf in the afternoon, and watch the sunset paint the sky orange and pink from your backyard every single night. The air smells like jasmine and salt water. The light is always golden. When you wake up to ocean views, fall asleep to the sound of waves, and live in perpetual early summer weather, every day feels like a gift.

The neighborhood was built by Methodists in the 1920s as their version of paradise on earth—a wholesome beachside community with tree-lined streets winding down toward the sand—and in the 1990s, it still carried that original family-focused spirit. Public school teachers could afford modest homes just blocks from where entertainment executives lived on huge estates. Firefighters, small-business owners, and middle managers all mixed together at Little League games and neighborhood barbecues.

I was around nine years old when Dad moved us into this 120-year-old Spanish Colonial sitting right on the bluffs—one of the original Palisades estates with a submarine-deep swimming pool. He'd bought it for $400,000, discounted because three people had allegedly been killed in it. I never saw a single ghost, but hey, maybe we were the happy, chaotic spirits that the house had been waiting for all along.

We filled those walls with happiness at maximum volume—three kids who knew we were absolutely, unconditionally loved, living in paradise with parents who had made their wildest dreams come true. Skip would come home from long days of dental work and gold-tooth schemes to find Janet in the kitchen, chocolate chip cookies cooling on the counter, perfect margaritas with the good tequila waiting. Stephanie, Kristin, and I would run wild through rooms that seemed designed for childhood adventure. At night, the underwater lights would make our pool glow, and me and my sisters would dive to the bottom, holding our breath until we almost passed out, pretending we were deep-sea explorers discovering some sunken civilization.

As a kid, I spent a lot of my time in what we called the Library—which sounds fancy, but it wasn't actually a library. Zero books, just an ancient big-box TV, Mom's photo albums, and my entire Lego empire. I'd dump whole buckets of Lego pieces onto the rug and disappear for hours, building my own universes—skyscrapers, space stations, whatever my brain could imagine. Just me, my imagination, and thousands of tiny plastic possibilities.

Usually, I'd have a 007 film playing in the background. I ran those James Bond VHS tapes relentlessly. I memorized every frame, every suave one-liner, downloading what I thought was a blueprint for how to be a man in the world.

"You do realize James Bond is a made-up character, right?" my older sister, Kristin, once asked me, catching me practicing my Bond face in front of the mirror.

"The name's Pratt," I said, pointing my imaginary Walther PPK into an imaginary camera. "Spencer Pratt."

But even more than Bond himself, I was fascinated by the villains. Dr. No chilling on his own private island. Jaws with his steel teeth. Oddjob turning a bowler hat into a weapon. These guys had vision. They weren't afraid to dream big, to say what everyone else was thinking while stroking a white cat. Sure, they always lost in the end, but for two hours they were the most interesting people I'd ever seen on-screen. Their confidence was absolute, their ambitions limitless—world domination, gold monopolies, underwater cities. Sometimes, it seemed like being the bad guy might be even more interesting than being the hero.

I was twelve when I first put my 007 training into practice. It was a summer afternoon, and I was kicking a soccer ball around the living room. Kristin strolled in just as I unleashed this rocket, and *bam*, the ball smashed into her face.

She immediately called our parents, who were out at the Jonathan Beach Club. "Spencer broke my nose!" she wailed. (Her nose was, in fact, fine.) She hung up.

A few minutes later, the phone rang. No one answered it. The machine clicked on—one of those old-school boxes that announced your family drama at full volume to everyone in a three-room radius. It was Dad, and he wasn't just pissed. He was DEFCON 1.

"SPENCER PRATT! WHAT IN GOD'S NAME HAVE YOU DONE?! YOUR SISTER'S NOSE IS BROKEN, YOU LITTLE SHIT! WHEN I GET HOME, YOU'RE GOING TO WISH YOU WERE NEVER BORN!"

He said other things that would definitely violate his Hippocratic oath. My chill surfer-dentist dad had transformed into Jack Nicholson in *The Shining*, and it was all on tape. That's when my twelve-year-old brain experienced its first devious epiphany. On my *Home Alone 2* Talkboy cassette tape recorder, I made twelve copies of Dad's meltdown. Then I waited until the time was right. For when I really needed them.

Weeks later, I deployed. Standing in front of my parents like a tiny mob boss, I cleared my throat, showing them just one copy of the tape. I popped it in my Talkboy, hit play, and smiled.

"What if Grandpa Bill heard this? What if your patients heard this? The dental board? What if I accidentally left this at school?"

"Give me that, Spencer," my dad said, furious.

"Sure, but there's more where this one came from."

His anger soon gave way to amusement as he realized his preteen son had unlocked his first hustle.

I milked that tape like a dairy farm. New bike? "Remember the recording." Movie tickets? "About that tape . . ."

Every time, a glint of pride in my dad's eyes. Game recognizes game. Chip off the old block. His approval wasn't for my being good or well-behaved; it was for my being clever, strategic, effective.

That tape became my first master class in power—not the kind you're born with, but the kind you create. Or, as Dr. No once said, "World domination. Same old dream."

Like many parents who'd worked their way up, mine believed education was everything—so they enrolled us in the best private school Skip's money could buy. From kindergarten through senior year, my sisters and I were students at Crossroads, an artsy-progressive temple in Santa Monica where the children of Oscar winners and studio bosses learned alongside regular kids like us. Crossroads was where Hollywood royalty sent their children to learn that the world belonged to them. I was there to learn it didn't *quite* belong to me, yet. The difference was subtle but absolute, like the gap between first class and business class: close enough to see what you're missing, far enough away to know your place.

Every week we had "Council," sitting in a circle with a talking stick, sharing feelings. Once, a Native American student brought actual peyote for show-and-tell. At any other school, bringing a Schedule I psychedelic to campus might have created complications. But at Crossroads, it was just a beautiful teachable moment about Indigenous spiritual practices.

The school itself was an IMDb dream: Your lab partner might be a Spielberg, your study group could include a Streep. Alumni were Jack Black, Kate Hudson, Gwyneth Paltrow. Jonah Hill was in my orbit, quick and ruthless with jokes. Maya Rudolph, Liv Tyler, Jason Ritter—every pickup looked like a red-carpet event.

For a dentist's kid from the Palisades, this was both paradise and purgatory. I was surrounded by children who had never questioned whether they deserved attention, who assumed the world would bend toward their desires, because it always had. I became a student of what made people magnetic, because I understood that in a room full of stars, you either shine brighter or disappear.

I worked not just on my grades but on my personality, my passion, my sense of humor, my ability to talk to anyone, my curiosity, and my positive energy. If there was an adventure to be had, I'd be there. The irony wasn't lost on me: Here I was, this hyperactive, somewhat OCD kid who refused to use the bathroom at school and couldn't use a towel twice, throwing myself wholeheartedly into every fun situation like my life depended on it.

Because, in a way, it did—my social life, anyway.

One day when I was around fifteen, I was chilling at my friend's house when her older brother grabbed his dad's keys and said, "Who wants to take the Porsche for a ride?"

"ABSOLUTELY!" I said.

I hopped in the passenger seat of this 911 Turbo convertible and immediately started nagging this senior to buckle up—classic me, saying yes to adventure while obsessing over safety protocols. My mom had drilled "Put on your seat belt" into my brain since day one, and even in my desperate-to-be-cool moments, I couldn't turn off her voice in my head. He rolled his eyes like *Seriously?* but clicked it in anyway. That decision saved his life. He still hits me up to thank me for it.

There we were, top down, Nine Inch Nails blasting, flying down Sunset. Dead Man's Curve came up fast—an infamous turn where Sunset Boulevard hooks a sharp left near Will Rogers State Park. People died there regularly. We knew that. We didn't care. We were teenagers. Invincible.

We hit the curve fast. Way too fast. Started spinning. Time did something strange. It slowed and stretched. I could see the world breaking apart frame by frame. I felt strangely calm, like I'd slipped outside of the moment and was just watching. Then the airbag hit me, hard, like a fist from God. Everything went white, then nothing.

Am I dead? I thought.

I opened my eyes and looked around. The Porsche was accordioned against a steel guardrail. I could hear Nine Inch Nails still playing from the miraculously functioning stereo, Trent Reznor screaming about control while I sat in the wreckage realizing I had none. The only salvageable thing in the end was that twelve-disc CD changer worth $1,000. And us, somehow.

An ambulance pulled up, and the paramedics started checking us out, asking the usual questions. We were both okay, just bleeding and concussed. My friend's brother was getting loaded into the ambulance with a neck brace. That's when I spotted this car slowing down to rubberneck. A senior from my school was driving, and in the passenger seat I recognized Natalie Cross, a girl from Pali High. A model who looked like Jennifer Connelly.

I waved them down.

"Hey, can you give me a ride home?" I asked, completely focused on Natalie.

"Bro, just get in the ambulance," the senior said.

"Nah, nah, the paramedics said I'm fine. I just need a ride home. Can I hop in?"

Even with double vision and blood literally on my shoes, I wasn't about to miss the chance to be in a car with Natalie Cross. *This is how you die, Spencer*, a voice in my head said. *Refusing medical attention because there's a pretty girl nearby.*

I was bleeding, and when we got to my house, Natalie insisted on coming inside with me, to make sure I was okay. As she gently cleaned the blood off my forehead, I found myself wondering if I'd actually died and this was heaven. Maybe this was my reward for forcing everyone to wear seat belts?

Natalie and I ended up together, and when the Pali High guys found out their dream girl was dating some random Crossroads kid, they completely lost it. Started egging my house. Making threats at parties. Such Neanderthals.

Three months after the Porsche incident came my next brush with death. This time was way less glamorous. Over-the-counter medicine. My mom had given me some for a minor ailment, and instantly, my throat closed like a fist. Anaphylactic shock. This wasn't like the car crash—no cinematic slow-motion moments. Just pure, unfiltered terror as I gasped for air.

Instead of calling 911, my dad decided to drive me to the hospital himself. This man was stopping at yellow lights while I was turning blue, puttering along like Morgan Freeman in *Driving Miss Daisy* as I was dying in the passenger seat. *My obituary will say I was killed by grandma medicine and my father's safe driving*, I thought, imagining people laughing at my funeral.

To this day, I'm deathly scared of any medicine or drug whose exact ingredients I don't know. When my peers began experimenting with street drugs, pills, and powders of vague origin, I steered well clear. I had one rule when it came to drugs: It better be FDA approved with a pharmaceutical label listing all ingredients, or I will not touch it. (Actually, I did try a sketchy powder once, only once. A very sleazy media mogul pulled out a white brick while some buddies and I were in Puerto Vallarta when I was twenty-one. I immediately said no, but he kept insisting what he had was "pharmaceutical grade," totally pure. Against every instinct I had, I tried it. Verdict? Meh. I don't need blow. I am blow. My natural state is already dialed to eleven.)

At the hospital, after that medication put me in anaphylactic shock, they put me in an induced coma so as to minimize the risk of brain damage from oxygen loss. I was in that coma for days. And when I regained consciousness, the first thing I felt was a sense of profound clarity.

So this is how death happens, I realized, staring at the hospital ceiling. *Not in some blaze of glory. Not doing something that matters. Life just ends, and we have no idea when or how it might happen.*

I promised myself, from that moment on, I'd squeeze every drop out of every second God gave me. We don't get to choose when it ends—only how brightly we burn while we're here. What's my headstone gonna say? "Here Lies Spencer Pratt, He Kept It Low-Key"? No. I realized that when God hands you a second *and* a third chance, you don't zen out on life—you wring it like a dishrag and shotgun every last drop before the credits roll.

After that, my ambition became supercharged. I always needed to be the final boss at everything I did. Soccer—I was determined to go pro. Trained like I was preparing for the World Cup. Then I discovered golf and became hell-bent on getting on the PGA Tour one day. Scuba diving, too. I got my advanced rescue license, doing night dives while my classmates were playing Xbox. When I decided investment banking was my destiny, I enrolled in UCLA night-school business courses while still in high school. Had my whole path mapped out: USC Marshall School of Business, then Wharton, then Wall Street domination. Even back then, I never, ever did anything halfway. I was relentless, like the Terminator. I could not be bargained with, could not be reasoned with, and absolutely would not chill.

Ever.

I spent my whole high school era collecting mentors. Successful people whom I could study for intel. Their habits, their connections, their mindsets. In the Palisades, surrounded by so many players who'd already won the game, I had a front-row seat to the workings of some of Hollywood's most iconic minds. They were right there, doing carpool duty after soccer practice—legends who could green-light or murder a hundred-million-dollar movie with a phone call. The last icons of the Hollywood studio system, rulers of three networks and six studios who basically controlled what the entire planet watched. The last of their kind.

Now? That world's gone. Streaming said "Your time is up" to old Hollywood, and the people running studios today are more like corporate CEOs who could just as easily be selling insurance or breakfast cereal. But back then, in the '90s, Hollywood was run by actual pharaohs. They didn't report to shareholders. Only their egos. And there they were, going absolutely feral on the sidelines of the Crossroads soccer field, with me taking notes.

Take Jon Avnet, who directed *Fried Green Tomatoes*, produced *Risky Business*. This absolute legend who literally created Tom Cruise's whole career would pull up to every single soccer game with director-level attention to detail and a lawyer's understanding of FIFA regulations. Same with Joe Roth, chairman of Disney Studios. He'd referee from the sidelines like he was trying to keep a blockbuster from going off the rails. These weren't just helicopter parents—they were control freaks who'd spent decades having everyone worship their every opinion. Actual certified geniuses who'd pause billion-dollar business deals to watch their kids chase a ball around. They showed zero mercy, even to the kids. Everyone got the full Hollywood executive treatment. But to be fair, they were usually right.

I was absorbing everything like a sponge. Watching, learning, taking notes. Then I tried to channel that same energy in my senior year, during playoffs—the first time I ever completely lost my composure in public. I knew that I was right, that I was fighting the good fight. But people talked about that moment for *years*, and not as a compliment. Even Mary-Kate Olsen—who was definitely in the stands watching her boyfriend, Max Winkler, my teammate—would weaponize that incident against me when she was feeling petty. (I have a whole messy story about Mary-Kate later, don't even worry.)

Anyway, here's how it went down: In the most important match of the season, Team Crossroads was getting demolished. Why? Because our coach had benched all his best players, me included, apparently to punish us for ghosting a meeting the night before playoffs.

Finally, he put me in, and I scored immediately. Then again. And again. Three goals, and suddenly we're up 3–2, the crowd going insane. Then this idiot coach tries to sub me out, and I said, "Absolutely not," and refused to leave the pitch. Obviously, he wasn't about to physically drag me off himself, so this man really chose violence and subbed out our goalkeeper instead—putting some nervous freshman in goal. Immediately, the other team scored. Tie game.

The Crossroads parents were screaming like villagers with pitchforks. Me? I went full Hulk. I sprinted toward the coach, bellowing, "ARE YOU FUCKING INSANE?" To me, it seemed obvious that this coach was tanking us with his ego and terrible decisions, and I couldn't let him get away with it. Not on my watch.

This is probably a good time to mention I was fully amped on this legal strawberry-flavored energy supplement called Ripped Fuel, having mixed it into my water bottle. It had insane levels of ephedrine in it, a stimulant drug that was commonly found in over-the-counter weight-loss and energy supplements in the 1990s and early 2000s. Side effects included anxiety, irritability, or straight-up paranoia. Later, ephedrine would be banned, but when we were kids, you could just grab it at GNC like it was a protein bar. So yeah, maybe that's why I was acting less like a teenage soccer player and more like a raccoon on bath salts. We wound up losing the match 4-3. Total fiasco.

A few days later, my parents and I got hauled into the principal's office. "Spencer, you can't scream at school staff like that," the principal said. "This is serious."

"Sir, I apologize for embarrassing Crossroads," I said. "But that coach is a saboteur!"

He squinted at me. "Spencer, I need you to be honest. Were you on something? You didn't seem . . . yourself out there."

I reached into my backpack and pulled out the Ripped Fuel container, sliding it across his desk like evidence in a crime drama.

"Sir, I bought this at GNC. But I may have had too much—I usually do one packet in my water, but I think I had three because it was the playoffs."

I watched his expression change as he read the ingredients: ephedrine, caffeine, enough stimulants to wake the dead.

"Listen," I said solemnly, "I'm the captain. This team is my whole life. Of course I wanted us to win. I'm sorry I lost my temper. But I hope you can understand where I was coming from."

He did not understand where I was coming from. I was kicked off the team and barely escaped expulsion. Still, walking out of that office, I felt vindicated. I knew I was right. Perhaps I could have expressed myself more calmly.

But there's nothing like the rush of being right when everyone else is wrong, of speaking truth to power. I'd found my gift. Some people are born to keep the peace. I was here to disturb it.

CHAPTER 3

HUMMINGBIRD PROPHECIES

When I Decided to Live Life at 1,200 Beats per Minute

Crossroads gave me many things, but the most fateful was my friendship with Brody Jenner—the so-called Prince of Malibu and my future partner in adventures through Hollywood.

Brody's family tree was absurd. His parents: Caitlyn Jenner—Olympic gold medalist, Wheaties box hero, American icon—and Linda Thompson, the songwriter who'd dated Elvis and lived at Graceland. When Brody was three, his parents divorced. Caitlyn (then known as Bruce) later married Kris Kardashian, who became the mastermind behind America's biggest reality TV empire. Meanwhile, Linda married David Foster, the Grammy-winning producer behind every power ballad that ever made your mom cry—"All By Myself," "I Have Nothing," all the classics.

Brody called it elevator music.

Brody and his family lived at Villa Casablanca. Twenty-two acres of pure Malibu flex. The house was twelve thousand square feet, which is bigger than many people's high schools, plus tennis courts, a full spa, and three recording studios. The absolute crown jewel was the funicular—literally a mini train that carried guests from the mansion down to the pool.

To me, Brody was the teenage James Bond—untouchable, half real. Most of what I knew about him came from other kids who'd been invited to Casablanca and returned with stories about riding the funicular like they'd just been to Disneyland, except this was one rich kid's backyard.

Was I jealous? Obviously. I mean, I was still the dentist's kid from the Palisades, which sounds fancy until you meet someone whose house has its own train. And there I was, pressing my face against the glass like a kid at a candy store.

Not that Palisades kids ever got Malibu party invites anyway. Sure, we all went to Crossroads together, but the moment school ended, Topanga Canyon turned into the Berlin Wall. You were either Team Malibu or Team Palisades—no switching sides, no visiting privileges. The beef was real. Cross into enemy waters, and suddenly it's *West Side Story* with surfboards instead of switchblades.

Malibu had its own crew, MLO, which sounds like a homeowners' association but actually stood for "Malibu Locals Only." They'd throw up their hand sign, like the West Side symbol flipped upside down to make an *M*. In the Palisades we had PTL ("Palisades Town Locals") and PIE ("Posse in Effect"), which pulled graffiti and skater kids from all over West LA. Not on a Bloods or Crips level, but not exactly pillow fights either. Then there was PLB—Palisades Local Boys—mainly surfers claiming their piece of coastline. The rivalry got legitimately intense sometimes. I remember kids getting ambulance airlifted off Little Dume beach parties because the fights had gotten completely out of control.

Remember the '90s movie *Point Break*? Yeah, it was like that. These weren't just high school cliques; they were decades-old surf crews with real hierarchies and codes. Salty older guys who'd been surfing these breaks since the '70s passing down rules about who could paddle out and where. Dawn patrol was sacred. The lineup had an order. And if you didn't respect it, you'd learn fast why you should.

When I was coming up, we Palisades kids had an edge over the Malibu guys thanks to our secret weapon—the Gracies, a legendary martial arts family that invented Brazilian jiujitsu, who just so happened to live in our neighborhood. I started training with them because my neighbor was dating the son of Rickson Gracie, the most famous *vale tudo* fighter on the planet. *Vale tudo* means "anything goes" in Portuguese, which is basically Brazilian for "We're going to fuck you up with science."

When Rickson Gracie invited me to join the Gracie Academy, it felt like I'd found my spiritual home. *This is actual power*, I realized, watching Rickson absolutely dismantle someone twice his size. Funny story: At a beach party once, Dustin Hoffman's son begged me to show him a choke hold. Acted like it was a party trick. "Make me go to sleep!" he kept saying. So I did. That's the thing about jiujitsu; it just looks like adult Twister until someone takes a nap. Hoffman was out in seconds and woke up fine a few minutes later, saying, "Wow, that was amazing!" like I'd just pulled a rabbit out of a hat instead of temporarily cutting off the blood flow to his brain.

For a kid who'd always felt like he had to prove himself, jiujitsu was a revelation. Finally, something that couldn't be bought or inherited—just earned through getting your ass kicked. Before long, half the kids in the Palisades were training at the academy, becoming known as the Jitz Mob. Which brings me back to Brody Jenner, who was about to discover what happens when Malibu royalty tangles with kids who'd learned that the best way to win a fight is to hug someone really, really hard . . .

I was sitting on the soccer bus, waiting for Sarah, a talented soccer player around my age whom I definitely had a crush on but was pretending was just a friend because that's how teenage boys handle their feelings.

She walked on with Brody, and they were full PDA, whispering to each other like they were the only two people in a world populated by seven billion extras. My stomach dropped like someone had cut the cables. Not just because she was with someone else—I could handle regular rejection—but because she was with *him*. The Prince of Malibu. The nepo kid who'd never had to work for anything, including, apparently, the girl I'd been too chicken to ask out. It was like watching a billionaire win the lottery with a ticket they found on the ground.

Then Brody bumped me, straight up on purpose, with this smug little smirk that said, *What are you gonna do about it?* So I bumped him right back. Then he bumped me one more time, and we fell to the floor for like ten seconds of the least-impressive combat in school bus history. Then it was over.

Somehow, our pathetic little shoving match became legend. Middle-school gossip turned it into *Mortal Kombat*, and by Monday, people swore I'd unleashed some Palisades Jitz Mob black-belt fury on the Prince of Malibu, when, in reality, I'd completely blanked on every single BJJ move I'd ever learned—it was just two kids aggressively hugging each other to the floor while Sarah stood there wishing she'd taken a different bus.

But here's what that bus fight actually proved: I didn't take disrespect from anybody, not even Brody. Didn't matter that he had twenty-two acres and a personal train. Didn't matter that he was dating the girl I liked. The second he decided to test me, I showed up. Sure, it was the world's most embarrassing fight, but sometimes the principle matters more than the execution.

That principle would be tested again soon enough, because apparently the universe wasn't done throwing Brody Jenner at me.

This girl Amber and I had been hanging out for a couple of weeks—flirting, making plans, hooking up. Then, plot twist: Amber wasn't talking just to me. She was Brody Jenner's girlfriend. And she'd been running game on both of us.

By then, Brody and I had half squashed our beef. Summer school had thrown us together, and we'd bonded the only way teenage boys in the late '90s could—by battling for Snake high scores on a Nokia brick with twelve pixels. Still, to say we were "friends" would be a stretch. It was more of a ceasefire. Except now, thanks to Amber, we were sharing a girlfriend.

I could have ghosted her. I could have pretended I didn't know, let Amber keep playing us both. The smart move, probably.

Instead, I sent word through the beachside bro network for Brody to meet me at Don Antonio's, my favorite Mexican spot on Pico in West LA. If you're going to wreck someone's day, at least do it over chips and guac. "Brody, I hate to be the bearer of bad news," I said, "but I've been hooking up with your girlfriend for two weeks."

I watched Brody's face cycle through the stages of betrayal—confusion, realization, fury, then devastation. The Prince, the untouchable golden boy, had been played. "She lied to me, too, Brody," I continued. "Never mentioned your name once." Brody shook his head, and for the first time in my life, I actually felt bad for this guy.

We sat there for a minute, neither of us knowing what to say. The silence was weird—not hostile, just . . . honest. Like we'd finally found something we had in common that wasn't about who had more or who was cooler. In that moment, we were both just regular teenage dudes who'd fallen for the same trick.

"Brody, maybe it's payback time," I said, dipping my chip in that absolutely delicious guac.

For a few glorious weeks, Brody Jenner and I ran psychological operations against Amber that would've impressed the CIA. We'd each make plans with her, then cancel last minute. Back and forth, keeping her perpetually dizzy, like she was dating two malfunctioning pagers. The coordination required actual teamwork—we had to text each other updates, synchronize our stories, time our moves. It was the most collaboration I'd ever done with someone I'd previously wanted to destroy.

Finally, the kill shot. We both locked in plans with her for the same night, same exact time. When she called to untangle the double booking, I patched Brody into the line. "GOTCHA! HA HA!" we shouted in unison. The silence on the other end? Absolutely gorgeous. The sound of pure justice being served.

Here's what I didn't expect: Somewhere between coordinating our revenge plot and watching Amber squirm, I realized Brody was actually . . . cool. Like, genuinely cool, not just rich-kid cool. No wonder everyone wanted to be around him. The guy had actual charisma. He was funny, he was loyal to his friends, and he'd just proven he could take a hit and bounce back. Plus, he was surprisingly good at psychological warfare, which I respected.

Yeah. We made a pretty good team.

Our friendship leveled up just in time for that one last epic summer—the golden window between high school ending and college starting. That weird limbo where you're not kids anymore but you're definitely not adults either. Basically free-range teenagers with driver's licenses. That summer was totally unmatched. Endless barbecues at my parents' spot, the whole Palisades crew turning our backyard into budget Coachella. Everything felt like it could last forever, like we'd cracked the code on life.

Brody and I had no idea we were about to take that code and rewrite it in the most spectacular way possible.

One afternoon, I cruised home with one sacred mission: get astronomically stoned and float in my parents' pool until I became one with the multiverse. Brody rolled through, and we commenced the ritual. I packed the Jerome Baker mothership—this legendary glass bong that was practically an art piece. Always with ice, never without. We hit that thing until our faces went numb, courtesy of the freshest OG Kush from our dealer, Goose Blackfinger. (Yes, that was his real government name. Yes, he would later become my assistant. LA career paths are wild.)

Twenty minutes later, we were chilling by the pool, so faded we could see through the fabric of reality. Every single thought felt like the most epic philosophical breakthrough in human history. Which is how I ended up having what would turn out to be the most important stoned conversation of my life.

"Brody?" I said, watching the sun hover over the Pacific.

"Yeah?"

"You know that Paris Hilton chick?"

"What about her?" he mumbled.

"Well, my little sister's obsessed with her, and I'm trying to understand why."

It was true. Stephanie had turned her entire bathroom into a Paris Hilton crime scene investigation board. Posters everywhere, photos overlapping photos, like she was trying to solve the mystery of how to become *that girl*.

"So here's my question," I continued. "Paris Hilton's cool. She's loaded. Obviously a total boss. But, like, she does nothing. She just exists, and gets paid for it. How is that even possible?"

"Bro, we've mastered doing nothing," Brody yawned, adjusting his position to maximize tan coverage. "We could get Pulitzers in the art of nothing. We're like the founding fathers of doing fuck all."

"Speak for yourself, Brody. I work my ass off. But I'm not getting paid. That's the difference. Paris is getting rich; meanwhile, we're out here being equally charismatic for free." I stared at the endless sky, my brain connecting dots that probably shouldn't be connected. "Maybe that's the future, Brody," I said. "Maybe being yourself IS the product."

It sounded profound in the moment, the kind of revelation that only makes sense when you're high enough to think hummingbirds are trying to communicate with you. Which, coincidentally, is exactly what happened next.

I must have dozed off, because I woke up to buzzing inches from my face. A hummingbird was hovering there, wings beating at warp speed, staring at me like it had something important to say. Its black eyes locked on to mine for what felt like an eternity, then it zipped away.

All of a sudden, I didn't feel stoned anymore. I felt clear. Antsy. Like I'd just received some kind of download about my future, even though I had no idea what it meant. I just knew something was about to change.

I sat up, stretched. "I'm going inside to get sodas," I told Brody. "Want one?"

"Whatever," he grunted, still napping.

In the kitchen I found Mom, Dad, and Nana Joan huddled around the island, looking like someone had just delivered bad news. Mom's eyes were red-rimmed. The energy in my house had been heavy all summer—serious family stuff that made even Nana Joan, who'd survived multiple earthquakes and the Cuban Missile Crisis, look genuinely worried.

Walking into that kitchen, seeing my family's pain, something shifted in my brain. Maybe it was the Kush wearing off, maybe it was that hummingbird encounter, but I suddenly felt this overwhelming need to fix things for the people I loved. To be a solution instead of just another problem floating around the house.

"Yo, yo, yo!" I said, trying to flip the vibe. "You guys, I have a major announcement!" I grabbed the latest *Us Weekly* from Mom's stack and held it up next to my face. "One day, you're gonna see me right here, on this cover." Brad Pitt stared back at us from the magazine. And in that silence, something crystallized. This wasn't just stoned rambling—it was a promise. To my family, to myself, to whoever was listening—though at the time, I'm sure they just assumed I had sunstroke.

I watched my mom's face light up—suddenly alive again, riding my energy. "And the day you're on that cover, Spencer, I'm buying fifty copies!" she said. "I'll wallpaper the whole house with them! The bathroom, the garage, everywhere!"

"Only fifty?" I clutched my chest like I felt personally attacked. "Mom, when your son makes the cover of *Us Weekly*, you better buy out the whole newsstand. I'm talking hundreds. Thousands. We'll build a shrine."

Nana Joan shook her head, grinning. "That's my boy," she said.

"Just make sure you're getting paid, son," Dad chimed in. "Fame doesn't pay the mortgage. And buy gold. Physical gold."

For the first time all summer, my family was laughing instead of crying. All it took was me being ridiculous enough, confident enough, entertaining enough, and suddenly the heaviness lifted. Mom stopped looking like she was carrying the weight of the world, Dad cracked his first smile in weeks, and even Nana Joan looked proud instead of worried. I was good at this—at being the bright spot, the comic relief.

I noticed my fourteen-year-old sister, Stephanie, lurking in the doorway, arms crossed, studying me with that new intensity she'd been perfecting, looking like she'd just stepped out of *The Craft* and was about to hex someone. Probably me. "Is Brody still here?" she said, her voice casual.

"Yeah, he's out by the pool."

She twirled a strand of hair, all sweetness. "Tell him I say hi."

"Sure," I muttered, my stomach turning. The thought of Brody even noticing my little sister made me want to build a moat filled with sharks around our house.

"Hey, guess what, Steph?" Mom said. "Spencer just told us he's going to be on the cover of *Us Weekly* one day!"

And just like that, the spell broke. Stephanie's smile shifted into a scowl. That's all it took with her now—one wrong word and the darkness would rush in. "Oh wow, *Spencer's* gonna be famous," she said, mocking. "SUCH a go-getter. Someone call CNN; maybe they'll do a special report!" She turned and stomped upstairs, and she would have slammed her bedroom door shut if it hadn't been taken off its hinges already for her own safety.

"LOVE YOU, TOO!" I yelled. "REMEMBER—JUST SAY NO!"

"Spencer!" my mom snapped. "NOT funny."

Except it wasn't a joke. My sister, who loved Paris Hilton and ponies and pretty shoes, had been smoking crystal meth. With a glass pipe she kept in her Hello Kitty zip-up pouch in her Kate Spade purse.

The high from making everyone laugh evaporated instantly. All my talk about being the solution, about bringing positive energy—what did any of that matter in the face of what was happening to my family?

Stephanie's journey into addiction had started with prescription medication for ADHD, which then spiraled into something much darker. My parents threw everything they had at the problem—specialists, therapists, rehabs eventually. Anyone or anything that promised answers. When Stephanie was diagnosed with borderline personality disorder, it at least gave us a name for the emotional storms she'd been living through. But watching someone you love battle addiction and mental illness is like watching them drown in slow motion.

Stephanie was getting the best help money could buy—this shrink Bob Timmons, who had supposedly gotten Nikki Sixx clean, was now working with her. But apparently Stephanie was tougher to crack than the bassist of Mötley Crüe. She'd become addicted to cocaine behind our backs and was keeping clean urine in a bag in her Ugg boot so she could finesse any surprise drug tests.

At seventeen, I simply couldn't process any of this. I thought addiction was something that happened to other families. There was no ChatGPT to ask "sister on drugs with BPD what do." Just denial, school, and manifesting a better future—like maybe success could somehow fix everything that was broken. Because when your house starts feeling like a psych ward, you either get sucked into the drama or find a way out.

I chose out. I had a whole destiny to manifest. I was gonna either take over Wall Street . . . or be on the cover of *Us Weekly*. Whichever came first. *Never stop moving.* That became my survival strategy. Become a hummingbird—heart pounding 1,200 beats a minute, wings beating so fast you're just a blur. I thought I was choosing ambition over despair, but I was really choosing distraction over presence. Because maybe if I moved fast enough, achieved enough, became important enough . . . I could outfly everything I couldn't control.

CHAPTER 4

INITIATION CEREMONIES

My First Movie, the Olsen-Twin Photo Deal That Paid for It, and How I Accidentally Became the Youngest Executive Producer in Hollywood

My dad had always drilled it into me: Real power lives in hedge funds and investment banks. The guys who lunch with Warren Buffett and move billions with a single phone call. Those are the real puppet masters. With that in mind, after high school, the plan was simple. Step One: USC's Marshall School of Business. Step Two: Wharton for an MBA—golden ticket, handed the keys to the global economy. Step Three: world domination.

The first wrinkle in my plan: USC made me a spring admit. They'd accepted too many students for fall semester, so some of us got bumped to January, like passengers on an overbooked flight. Watching everyone else start their lives while I sat in limbo was brutal.

Thankfully, Brody, who had already dropped out of CU Boulder, refused to let me spiral, and our endless summer just rolled straight into fall. Our goal was to infiltrate the USC social scene, whether we belonged there or not. So we hit the Row parties, crashed at sorority houses, acted like we were supposed to be there, rolling up to parties with a bottle of Patrón each.

What I learned fast was that USC had its own brutal hierarchy—if you weren't in a frat or sorority, you were socially dead. It was training wheels for the LA club scene, all about who you knew and who knew you. The connections mattered more than grades, more than talent, more than anything else.

Luckily, Brody and I had those connections. We could walk into any party like we belonged because, in a way, we did—our Crossroads network had tentacles everywhere. But watching other kids get frozen out was a reality check. Smart, cool people who just didn't have the right last names or zip codes, relegated to the social margins.

This whole system should have disgusted me, but instead it fed my competitive spirit. I wasn't just relieved to be on the inside—I was energized by it. Every party we crashed, every door that opened because of a name we dropped proved I was winning at a game most people didn't even know they were playing. The unfairness wasn't a bug; it was a feature. It meant that being good at the game mattered more than being good at anything else.

January finally arrived, and I threw myself into college life with desperate intensity. I pledged Beta, the same fraternity my dad had been in, which birthed a secret society known as "Stumpo's Raiders." Hazing week was truly unhinged. They dragged us out to a ranch in the Ojai mountains and humiliated us for sport. I spent most of that week shut in a basement closet doing wall sits until my legs went numb. My pledge master was a USC football player named Owen Hanson. Check out the doc series on Amazon *Cocaine Quarterback*. Future international drug-and-gambling kingpin. He tried to beat me with a paddle until I finally snapped and used my Gracie jiujitsu on him to get away.

Looking back, it was all perfect training for reality TV—the psychological willingness to be debased for a shot at winning. The Greek system taught me status was worth any price, that you could transform suffering into social currency if you were smart about it. I was already practicing to become Spencer Pratt™, even if I didn't know it yet.

Then, at the end of the first semester, disaster struck—my whole world-domination investment banking dream got wrecked when I got a D-minus in business trigonometry. I tried to retake it using something called Freshman Forgiveness, but—surprise—spring admits didn't qualify for that. One grade literally nuked my entire life plan. My chances of getting into Wharton without a perfect GPA were nonexistent.

I sat in my student apartment at the Medici in downtown LA, staring at that D-minus. Everything I'd planned, everything my father expected, everything I'd built my identity around—gone. But what hit me hardest wasn't the academic failure. It was the realization that for the first time in my life, effort hadn't been enough. My chest felt tight with something I'd never experienced before: the possibility that wanting something desperately, believing you deserved it completely, wasn't enough to make it happen.

What terrified me wasn't just losing the business school dream. It was discovering that I had no idea who Spencer Pratt was if he wasn't the guy who was going to conquer Wall Street. My entire sense of self had been built around future achievement rather than present reality. Without that narrative, I was just another college kid who couldn't handle math.

That said, getting that D-minus was probably the universe doing me a solid. My destiny was never Excel models at 3 a.m. and worshipping at a Bloomberg terminal. I was meant for something that didn't fit on LinkedIn. I switched to political science, convincing myself that if I couldn't master the language of money, I could at least learn the grammar of power—the way empires rose and fell. Still, in the moment, it felt less like liberation and more like an obituary for the person I thought I was supposed to be.

For my second semester, I moved into this massive loft at Fourth and Spring in downtown LA with my friend Spencer Gilbert, an architecture student. My Brazilian jiujitsu sensei Wander (pronounced

Vonder) lived nearby and was always around. We installed mats that took up half the space and turned the place into part dojo, part party headquarters, part creative sanctuary—high ceilings, concrete floors, the kind of space that made you feel like anything was possible. Sort of like my very own Mojo Dojo Casa House—yes, like in the film *Barbie*—which was weirdly prophetic in that the actual future Ken, Ryan Gosling, lived next door. Pre-*Notebook* Gosling. Just a Canadian guy drifting the halls shirtless at 3 a.m. with a ukulele, working on some character or just being beautifully weird. I'll never forget the night he hit our three-foot glass bong and was catapulted fully into the stratosphere.

Around this time is when I started using Xanax. Some sketchy downtown doctor was handing out prescriptions for cash. It had a proper label, which fooled me into thinking it was civilized. I told myself it was healthier than alcohol. Pop a Xan bar, skip the fifteen beers, enjoy the chill vibes, no hangover. "Winners work smarter," I told myself. (Real talk: Do not mess with Xanax. It is addictive. Withdrawal can kill you. I'm glad I haven't touched it since my freshman year. Not counting that one time in the jungle, which I'll tell you about later. Chapter closed.) I think what I really liked about it, though, was how it quieted the noise in my head. All that relentless ambition, the constant need to be moving toward something, the anxiety about not being special enough—Xanax just turned the volume down.

But even medicated, I couldn't stop scheming. I'd inherited something from my mom—this compulsion to document everything. Growing up, she was always at family gatherings with some huge clunky camera on her shoulder, preserving every moment like it might be historically significant. Now, with my investment banking dreams dead and reality TV exploding everywhere—*The Osbournes, Newlyweds, The Simple Life*—I'd started carrying a camera around campus and filming a professional surfer in my frat who, at the ripe old age of twenty-seven, was somehow a USC freshman.

This guy was living like *Van Wilder* meets *Point Break*—showing up to business classes in board shorts, talking about wave conditions during economics lectures. I started filming him, seeing the absurdity through my lens. Here was a grown man with sponsors and magazine covers sitting in freshman orientation, and nobody seemed to think this was insane. Except me. Every keg party he attended, every lecture he slept through, every time he showed up to a study group talking about Bali surf breaks—it was all content waiting to be monetized.

Brody and I started drifting apart that semester—probably because I was deep in my downtown era, staying up all night editing footage, rolling around on jiujitsu mats, and keeping little bowls of Xanax around like breath mints. Meanwhile, he was living his fantasy life at Casablanca: golf cart drag races down to the beach, endless Nobu dinners, parties that started at sunset and ended with sunrise over the Pacific.

We'd gone from daily scheming partners to occasional texts. "What's up, bro?" "Not much, you?" The kind of exchange that keeps a friendship technically alive but emotionally vacant. I missed him. Chalked it up to different zip codes, different dreams.

It didn't bother me too much, though. The camera had become my new obsession—my replacement addiction for the business dreams I'd lost and, if I'm honest, for the friendship with Brody. If I couldn't conquer Wall Street, maybe I could conquer Hollywood instead.

One day, Wander told me he was heading back to Brazil for the World Jiu-Jitsu Championship. "Come compete," he said. "And bring your camera. Film something."

Portia, our new roommate, was shamelessly eavesdropping from the kitchen. She was this flirty British party girl from Laguna Beach I'd met in the math class that had murdered my business career. According to her carefully constructed mythology, she was loaded—she'd told me her dad was in the English royal family. Sure, okay. "You should absolutely make a film in Rio," she declared, inserting herself into the conversation, and my destiny. "Starring me, obviously!"

"No way, Portia," Wander said, shaking his head. "You'll get kidnapped. Where the competition happens is not a joke place."

"I don't care," Portia shot back, that reckless gleam in her eyes that I was starting to recognize. "I want to go. And I won't get kidnapped if I'm with you and Spencer, right?"

Wander looked at me like I was supposed to be the voice of reason. "Spencer, tell her this is crazy."

"It is crazy," I agreed. "But crazy makes great art."

The idea of spending a month in Brazil competing in jiujitsu and shooting an indie film with Portia sounded like salvation. This could be it—my breakout project, the thing that would prove Spencer Pratt was more than just another college washout with a D-minus and a reality show concept that seemed to be going nowhere.

But making a real film meant real money and serious equipment—not the handheld camera I'd been using all year. I did the math: Canon GL2 camera, batteries, tapes, accessories, two tickets to Rio, a month of hotels, bribes for locations, plus a chaos fund for whatever went wrong. Twenty grand, minimum. I had maybe $2,000 in my bank account. The gap between my cinematic ambitions and my financial reality seemed insurmountable. But that had never stopped me before—when you're hell-bent on mattering, you find a way to bend the universe to your will.

That's when it hit me. A solution emerging from the depths of my scheming mind, terrible and perfect in equal measure.

My Crossroads buddy Max Winkler, son of Henry Winkler, aka the Fonz, had a photo shrine to his ex, Mary-Kate Olsen, in his bedroom from when they had dated. Young love documented in European hotels, Hollywood parties, stolen moments. This, I realized, was a wasted resource.

It was 2004, the golden age of tabloid voyeurism. One exclusive—"Mary-Kate's Teen Romance!"—could fund my entire Brazilian expedition. I'd never monetized my proximity to fame, but desperate times, desperate measures. So I asked Max if I could take the photos off his wall—you know, for his healing process. Wouldn't it be better, I suggested, if those photos weren't staring at him every night? He didn't say no, so I took that to be a yes. Rolled up to his house in Brentwood, waved to the Fonz, who was posted on the porch smoking cigars, iconic and oblivious.

"Hey, Mr. Winkler!" I called out.

"Spencer! How's college treating you?"

"Great! Just picking up some stuff from Max's room!"

"That's nice. You boys stick together. Max needs good friends right now."

I nodded. "Absolutely. That's what I'm here for."

"Have Ricardo make you a sandwich before you leave!"

While their personal chef made me a sandwich, I went upstairs. In Max's bedroom, I started peeling photos off his wall. Each image was currency waiting to be converted. It was hard not to grin. All that teen gossip, just sitting there on his wall collecting dust. I tucked them into my jacket, went downstairs, and grabbed my mozzarella sourdough sandwich. The Fonz was still on the porch when I left, completely clueless that I'd just walked out with a small fortune in celebrity candids.

I sat in my car on one of those leafy Brentwood streets where every house costs more than most people make in a lifetime, staring at the photos spread across my passenger seat. Next to them sat a copy of *Us Weekly*. This was it—the moment of no return.

I flipped through the magazine until I found the masthead, ran my finger down the staff directory until I spotted "Photo Editor." My hands were steady as I dialed, but my heart was hammering against my ribs.

"*Us Weekly*, this is Peter Grossman."

"Hi, this is Spencer Pratt of Pratt Daddy Productions," I said, trying to sound like I had business cards and everything. "I have some exclusive photos of Mary-Kate Olsen you might be interested in."

There was a pause. "What kind of photos?"

"The kind that show her being a normal teenager. Partying."

Grossman told me to contact a photo agency called White Bronco (yes, like O.J.'s getaway car). I called them from my car, still parked on that leafy Brentwood street, and within minutes had arranged a meeting. The British voice on the other end was all business—no names, just location and time, like we were arranging a drug deal instead of trading teenage romance pics.

We met at Brentwood Country Mart, an upscale marketplace where everything was curated to look effortless and expensive. The whole scene felt surreal—Westside moms pushing strollers past the café where I was about to sell my friend's private moments to strangers.

A black S-Class rolled up, and my pulse quickened. This was really happening. I showed him the prints. The buyer stepped out, took one look, and whistled. "Christ. No one's ever seen the Olsens like this. Real teenage stuff, not posed bullshit."

"So we're in business?"

"Yes, Mr. Pratt. Fifty-fifty split."

I handed the photos over, trying to look like a seasoned photo dealer, impressed with my own hustle. Here I was, twenty years old, turning my buddy's romantic misery into startup capital. Who knew heartbreak could be such a growth industry?

Less than a week later, there it was, evidence of my entrepreneurial genius staring back at me from the *In Touch* cover at a gas station: "TEENS GONE WILD!" across the cover. A shot of Mary-Kate with a constellation of empties—"LOOK AT ALL THE EMPTIES!"—and there I was in the background, frozen mid-shaka. I hadn't sold that frame. Someone else was shopping photos, and now I wasn't just the seller, I was part of the merchandise. My face was now forever linked to Mary-Kate Olsen's supposed wild phase, displayed in grocery store checkout lines across America.

An hour later, the guy from White Bronco dropped an envelope at my door. "Pleasure doing business," he grinned, handing it over. I waited until he drove away before tearing it open. A check for $50,000. "Holy shit," I whispered to the empty loft. "I'm rich."

Fuck business school—this was where the real money was! Not in understanding markets and derivatives, but in understanding what people craved and finding ways to feed that hunger. America was starving for celebrity intimacy, and I had access to the kitchen.

When you really think about it, it was a win-win. Mary-Kate got her rebel rebrand, Max got closure. And soon, cinema would get my masterpiece.

Sorry, guys, I thought, not feeling sorry at all. *Sometimes you have to break a few hearts to make great art. That's just the price of genius.*

Portia, Wander, and I landed in Rio with a solid plan: First, I'd compete at the World Jiu-Jitsu Championship, and then we'd start shooting our film. Alas, the jiujitsu part got derailed approximately thirty seconds after I walked into the tournament venue and nearly passed out from the smell. "Oh my God," I said, covering my nose with my shirt. "What is that?"

"That's the aroma of champions," Wander said proudly. The stench came from thousands of unwashed kimonos—those heavy cotton uniforms that jiujitsu practitioners wear, like karate outfits but thicker—fermenting in humid air.

Here's the deal: Some jiujitsu guys treat their unwashed kimonos like a secret weapon. They'll go weeks without washing it, convinced that the accumulated funk gives them a psychological edge—that opponents will be so disgusted they'll lose focus before the match even starts. And honestly? They're not wrong. Until it was banned in 2025, it was a legitimate strategy, just a revolting one.

I'd faced plenty of stinky kimonos during my training at the Gracie Academy, but Rickson kept that place at hotel levels of cleanliness. This tournament was different. Every breath was a gamble with your gag reflex.

Not to mention, I'm a Howard Hughes–level germophobe. Every instinct I had was screaming, *Get out. This is not safe. This will make you die.*

"Spencer, you need to get used to this," Wander said. "This is normal."

"*Normal?*" I was breathing through my sleeve, trying not to gag.

Portia stepped up behind us, took one whiff, and immediately backed away. "See?" I pointed at her. "She gets it."

"But you trained for months!" Wander protested. "You cannot give up because of smell!"

"Watch me," I said, already following Portia toward fresh air.

After I withdrew from the competition, Portia and I went straight into production on our untitled movie—a gritty mockumentary shot in the favelas, like *City of God* meets *The Blair Witch Project*. Handheld, found footage about an American filmmaker and his British girlfriend who venture into the unknown.

Thanks to Wander's local connections, we had unprecedented access to Vidigal, one of Rio's most notorious favelas—a crime-ridden neighborhood stacked like Jenga blocks against the mountainside. Wander had grown up training with guys from there, and his reputation opened doors that would have usually been welded shut to random foreigners with cameras.

He'd put the word out that we were hiring local talent and paying everyone well—within record time, we had a crew of people eager to be part of our insane project. I rented a white Sprinter van—apparently the vehicle of choice for tourist-kidnappings—and hired two uniformed police officers to block streets with their car. Our fixer was Vinnie, this Michael B. Jordan look-alike who became our star, playing a hotel worker who orchestrates Portia's kidnapping.

When we shot the abduction scene and the van screeched up with masked guys grabbing Portia, her terror looked so genuine I panicked and yelled cut. "KEEP ROLLING, YOU IDIOT!" she screamed from inside the van, fully committed to the performance even while being dragged away by strangers with real guns.

Standing there watching my fake girlfriend get fake-kidnapped by people I'd met twelve hours earlier, I felt either this was the most authentic filmmaking ever captured or I was about to become a cautionary tale about dumb Americans who confused reckless endangerment with artistic vision.

Before long, Portia began hooking up with our local contact, a guy they called Lagarto—the Lizard Man. I figured it out after one jungle scene turned into twenty minutes of *Where's Portia?* She came back with leaves in her hair and the "Who, me?" face that means exactly what you think it means. Did I care? Not really. We'd hooked up, sure, but we weren't in love. I was married to the shot list.

Look, I was never a "relationship guy" anyway. My eyes were always on the prize—success, fame, stacking cash. Love? That sounded like a distraction from my goals. In fact, in my high school yearbook they literally voted me most likely to become a tempter on *Temptation Island*: the flirt, the charmer, the guy who'd be cast just to mess with other people's relationships. In fact, my plan was to stay single forever. Keep things fun, keep things light. Nothing that might slow down my momentum. So if Portia wanted to make love to a lizard, more power to her.

A month later, we wrapped shooting and I flew home with thirty MiniDV tapes of pure madness. Footage that felt like it could make my career as a director. Portia had gone back to Laguna Beach, so I decided to drive down and visit. We needed to talk next steps, editing, our distribution strategy.

I was expecting some sprawling beachfront estate based on all her royal family stories. Instead, GPS led me to a prefab trailer next door to a power transformer on the side of a hill. Hmm. This wasn't poverty, but it definitely wasn't royalty either.

She led me inside and left me alone in her bedroom while she made tea or whatever. That's when I spotted the half-finished letter on her desk, practically begging to be read.

My Lagarto . . . it began. *I'm torn between staying with Spencer so he can make me rich and famous, or following my heart back to you.* Leaving the letter out like that wasn't an accident—it was either unconscious cruelty or conscious manipulation. Either way, it told me everything I needed to know about how she saw me.

I didn't bother with a confrontation. What was the point? She hadn't broken my heart because we'd never gotten deep enough for that. But she'd definitely bruised my ego. I thought we were creative partners. Turns out I was just another candidate for sugar daddy, and apparently I hadn't even gotten the part.

On the drive back to LA, I called Brody. I needed to completely switch up my environment, get away from the loft and all its complicated energy.

"Yo, Brody, can I come crash at your place for a minute?"

"Mi casa, su casa," he said, and I could hear the smile in his voice.

The beach has always been my reset button. When the city burns you, the ocean rinses out the smoke.

The next morning, I set up my laptop in the living room at Casablanca, ready to show Brody my Brazil footage.

The voice of Brody's stepdad, David Foster, exploded from down the hall.

"WHO KEEPS EATING MY FOOD?!"

Brody's favorite thing to do was eat David's chef-prepared meals out of the fridge.

Brody's mom, Linda, floated by in tennis whites like an angel. "The boys were hungry, David!" she said, softly defending us as always.

I turned back to Brody with supreme confidence. "Okay, buddy, prepare to have your mind blown."

I hit play, and for fifteen minutes, Brody watched in complete silence. I kept glancing at his face, waiting for that inevitable moment of recognition—the dawning realization that he was witnessing the birth of a filmmaking genius. Instead, his expression grew increasingly horrified.

Then he hit pause.

"What are you doing?" I asked.

"Spencer," he said slowly, like he was talking to someone who might be genuinely dangerous. "You can NEVER show this to anyone."

My stomach dropped into my shoes. "What do you mean? It's raw, it's real, it's—"

"It's a snuff film!" he interrupted. "Seriously. Like someone's going to find this footage and use it as evidence in a murder trial. Is Portia even alive?"

"Of course she's alive!" I protested, but suddenly I was seeing the footage through his eyes—shaky cameras, masked men, a terrified girl screaming as she gets dragged into a van in one of the world's most dangerous neighborhoods, head and face entirely duct-taped.

I stared at the frozen frame on-screen: Portia's face, twisted in terror, as hands reached for her from the shadows. What I'd envisioned as cinema verité now looked like . . . well, exactly what Brody said it looked like. CCTV footage of a terrible crime.

Dammit. I'd spent $50,000 of Mary-Kate Olsen's heartbreak money. Not to mention, I had zero release forms from Portia, whom I was definitely no longer speaking to. My cinematic masterpiece wasn't just unusable—it was the world's most expensive, most problematic home movie.

"Turn it off," I said, watching my artistic dreams crumble in real time.

On TV, they were rerunning an episode of *The Osbournes*. I loved that show—and so did the rest of America. Reality TV in 2004 was a gold rush. Networks had figured out you could score huge ratings without paying writers or building sets. America wanted "real." Or at least "real enough." I'd heard the Osbournes were getting paid insane money just to be their dysfunctional selves on camera—something like twenty million dollars per season.

Suddenly, I had an idea. I'd spent weeks in Brazil chasing some verité nightmare about kidnapping, convinced I needed to manufacture drama and danger. But I was about to discover that sometimes you don't have to chase a story. It's already there, in the pure, ridiculous comedy of life swirling around you.

The next morning, I pulled out the battered Canon I'd taken to Brazil and a single MiniDV tape.

By 8 a.m., I was shoving the lens into Brody's sleepy face. "Dude, what are you doing?" he mumbled, still half asleep.

"Making you famous," I said, following him to the kitchen, where he immediately started eating David's chef-prepared lunch with his hands, like some kind of caveman.

David walked in as Brody was mid-bite: "BRODY! GET YOUR HANDS OFF MY FUCKING LUNCH! AND SPENCER, TURN THAT CAMERA OFF!"

"Spencer, what are you doing?" Linda asked, floating through. "That looks exciting."

"It is," I said, not lowering the camera for a second. "I'm going to sell a show about you guys to Fox."

Brody paused, his mouth full of something gourmet. "Wait, what?"

"GET OUT OF MY HOUSE, BOTH OF YOU!" David screamed.

I grabbed Brody's arm, pulling him aside while keeping the camera rolling. "Dude, your family is *The Osbournes* on acid," I whispered to him. "The only thing missing is a camera."

Brody stared at me for a long moment, and I could see him processing the idea. "That's either genius or the dumbest idea you've ever had," he said, grinning.

What I was really feeling, but couldn't articulate yet, was this: I'd finally found something I was genuinely gifted at. Not math, not jiujitsu competitions I was too germophobic to enter, not art films that looked like evidence in murder trials. But this—seeing the entertainment value in chaos, turning dysfunction into content—this felt like discovering my superpower.

I spent the next few hours in a manic editing session, cutting together a sizzle reel in iMovie. David yelling, us existing, Linda apologizing, all set against the backdrop of the most expensive house in Malibu. It wasn't artistry; it was accuracy. I balanced my laptop on David's Steinway to show the family. David watched himself yell for three minutes straight. I braced for the laptop to become airborne. Instead, he smiled. "You're a little shit," he said, and I could hear the grudging respect in his voice. "But this looks good."

"I know," I said. "I told you, I'm going to sell this show."

Because I was twenty with zero credits, David recruited a grown-up to help me: Brant Pinvidic, a Canadian producer who David had done some pilots with, trying to sell his own shows. Brant took one look at the footage and got it immediately. His stroke of genius was cutting the whole thing to "The Final Countdown" and titling it *Battle in Malibu*—an epic father-stepsons cage match.

Brant wanted to shop it the standard way, but I went straight to my old childhood buddy Dave Chernin. His dad was Peter Chernin—president and COO of News Corporation, which owned Fox. I handed Dave a DVD of the sizzle reel. "Would love your thoughts," I said, all casual.

Sunday night, my phone rang. "Spencer, it's Peter."

"Peter who?"

"Chernin," he said. "You have a meeting at nine tomorrow with Gail."

"Uh, who's Gail?

"Gail Berman. She runs Fox Television. She knows the deal." Click.

I called David Foster with the news right away. "Fox is interested!"

Ten minutes later, unbeknownst to me, David called Brant, who called his agents. They were all intending to gate-crash my meeting. When I rolled up to the Fox lot, they'd already taken my parking spot, and I had to park six blocks away, sprinting to the meeting in a purple surf-shop button-down (my best shirt at the time), sweating like a busted sprinkler.

I walked into the elevator and there was Brant, flanked by agents. One, a superagent named Sean Perry, lit a cigar. "Just here to support you, buddy," he said, grinning at me like I was an adorable pet. That's when I realized they'd totally jacked my parking pass.

In Gail Berman's office, before I could talk, the Cigar said: "Our friend Benjamin has a show—"

"His name is Spencer," Gail snapped. "And put that cigar out." Then she looked at me. "We love the sizzle, Spencer. We're ordering six episodes. Three-point-seven million."

The words hit me like a freight train. Three-point-seven million dollars. For my idea?

For a three-minute video I'd cut together in iMovie?

"What?" was all I could manage. My mouth felt like it was full of cotton.

"We have meetings today at ABC, CBS, and NBC," the Cigar said. Oh. The agents were trying to engineer a bidding war. Gail coolly said, "Sean, we already have a deal, so I don't know what you're talking about. Peter bought it. We're done here."

The meeting wrapped, and I stepped into the hallway and ran into Peter Chernin himself. He clocked my purple shirt with disgust. "Never wear that in my building again," he said. "Buy a real outfit."

That day, despite Gail's assertion that Fox already owned the show, we met with every other major network in town. NBC offered us $4.5 million, but Peter Chernin wasn't having it. He called me that night.

"What the hell are you doing, shopping to other networks, Spencer? We have a deal."

That was that. Fox it was.

David Foster hooked me up with his lawyer, Peter Lopez, who represented Michael Jackson and Dr. Dre—basically the most connected entertainment lawyer in Hollywood. When the contracts arrived, I asked him to walk me through them.

"Where's my name?" I asked, scanning the credits section.

"You're listed as co-creator," he said.

"What does that mean?"

"It means you get credit for the idea, but minimal ongoing control."

Meanwhile, Brant was getting an executive producer credit—the real power position. Even though I had zero experience in television, I wanted that title, too. Not because I understood what it meant, but because I understood what it represented: respect, control, the ability to shape my own creation.

This was my idea, my footage, my friends that I'd convinced to participate. Yet the adults were positioning themselves as the real creators while I got pushed to the margins. It felt unjust to me.

So I did what any reasonable twenty-year-old with access to unprecedented power would do: I bypassed every layer of Hollywood hierarchy and called Peter Chernin direct.

"Peter, it's Spencer Pratt."

"Spencer, why are you calling me?"

"Because they're not giving Brody and me executive producer credit, and it's not fair. This is our show, our idea."

I could practically hear him calculating whether this conversation was worth his time.

The silence stretched so long I thought he'd hung up.

"I'll look into it. Don't call me again." Click.

I sat there staring at my phone, wondering if I'd just nuked my entire television career before it started. Had I pushed too hard for a twenty-year-old kid with no television experience? Demanded too much?

An hour later, Brant called.

"Spencer, I don't know what kind of voodoo you just performed, but whatever you said worked. You're getting executive producer credit."

And just like that, a kid with a D-minus and a dead Brazilian snuff-not-snuff feature became the youngest executive producer in network

TV. Not because I understood the system, but because I sprinted at it like a golden retriever who heard the word *ball* and refused to stop barking until someone threw it.

If there's any moral to the story, here it is: The universe rewards action. Not always the *right* action—just action.

Step One: Get denied.

Step Two: Build your own door.

Step Three: Walk through it like you were always invited.

Pick up the camera. Pick up the phone. Get told no. Call again. Get told "never wear that shirt." Buy a new shirt. Keep rolling.

I'd started the year planning to conquer Wall Street. I ended it green-lit on network TV because a guy who hated my outfit liked my sizzle reel. The first check hit my account: $90,000. More money than I'd ever seen with my name on it. Did I save it? Invest it? Put a down payment on a condo? No. I drove straight to the nearest BMW dealership and dropped the entire check on a brand-new 6 Series. Black on black, executive producer style.

Was it financially idiotic to blow my entire first payment on a car? Maybe. But I had a Fox deal. More checks were coming, I knew that. Big, juicy, yummy checks. Not to mention, Peter Chernin had given me a side quest—*Dress the part*—and in my mind, that extended to vehicles. No more pulling up to meetings in my soccer mom car. Exec producers drive coupes. That's not even a flex, that's science.

The Princes of Malibu was scheduled to drop alongside the return of *Family Guy* on Sunday nights, right before *The Simpsons*—prime real estate in Fox's lineup. Our sponsors were Coca-Cola and McDonald's, the kind of major league advertisers with massive budgets that meant this wasn't some late-night experiment. This was Fox betting serious money on my ability to turn family dysfunction into appointment television.

Was this world domination? Not yet. But I'd found my arena: the space between reality and entertainment, where other people's drama becomes your opportunity, and the willingness to cross lines that others won't determines who gets to write the rules. This wasn't the game I'd planned to play. But it was definitely the game I was built to win. Now came the hard part: actually making television. Time to see if the kid could deliver.

CHAPTER 5

THE PRINCES OF MALIBU

When I Went from Producer to Product

The first day of filming rolled around, and I was in my element, strutting around with a walkie-talkie that wore a strip of masking tape with the words EXECUTIVE PRODUCER scrawled on it in Sharpie. My badge of honor. My crown. My Excalibur. My whole personality.

Then, out of nowhere, Sean Travis—the showrunner we'd hired—came up to me. "Spencer, you should be in this scene. Just hop in front of the camera and say you're moving into the pool house."

Sean Travis was a seasoned showrunner type who'd been around the unscripted block, brought in to wrangle Brody, his brother Brandon, and, yeah, me.

"Yeah, great idea, Sean," Brant chimed in immediately.

Producers always come at you in pairs. I'd learn that later.

"Me? On camera? Why?" I asked, freezing up. Up to this point I'd been the gremlin behind the camera, the Dennis the Menace voice-over snickering at the chaos. Why mess with a formula that worked?

"Trust me," Sean said. "This show will be way funnier with you in it."

I clutched my walkie with the EXECUTIVE PRODUCER label.

"Do I get to keep the walkie?" I asked.

"Yes, yes, keep the walkie," Brant sighed. "Just get in front of the damn camera and do what comes naturally."

And that's how I went from boss mode to unpaid clown in a single conversation. Nobody mentioned talent fees. Nobody explained that the $3.7 million Fox check went straight to Brant's company while I got $90K to create, produce, AND star in my own show.

If this were today? I'd keep the IP, hire a production company for a flat fee, and eat the back end. But I was young, dumb, and high on my own walkie-talkie. I had a lot to learn. Plus, what I didn't know—what NOBODY told me—was that crossing from behind the camera to in front of it was career suicide back then. Before Kim K proved you could do both, there was an unwritten law in Hollywood: Once you become "the talent," you're trapped there forever. And "talent" in reality TV? That's Hollywood speak for "circus freak." You're not Timmy Chalamet. You're a dancing monkey.

I DID NOT KNOW THIS.

REPEAT:

I HAD NOT BEEN WARNED.

This was my red pill moment. Two paths lay before me: Stay in the shadows, end up a suit yelling at assistants about kale salads, or . . . step in front of the lens and become "Spencer Pratt™." I chose wrong. Or maybe I chose destiny. Hard to say.

That first night, we shot a party scene where Linda and David return from vacation to find we'd turned Casablanca into Studio 54. Wall-to-wall hotties, bass shaking the windows, pure chaos. I was living my best life, puppet-mastering the mayhem, when I clocked this girl moving through the crowd like she owned the future.

"Who's that?" I asked Brody.

"Oh, that's my stepsister Kim. That's my other stepsister Kourtney with her."

Before the sex tape, before the empire, before the *internet literally collapsed under the weight of Kim's butt*, the Kardashians were background extras at our *Princes of Malibu* rager. Just a couple Valley girls, radiating billionaire energy like they'd already read the script of their lives. Kim caught me staring and smiled. Not the desperate *please-put-me-on-TV* smile I was used to seeing at Hollywood parties. This was the smile of someone who knew something you didn't.

"Great party," she said, and even that felt loaded with meaning I couldn't decode.

Years later, I'd understand. They were studying us. Watching us so they could run the *real* game later.

The storyline for that night's shoot was simple: David walks into the party; loses his mind; tries to kick Brody, Brandon, and me out of his house . . . fails. Textbook reality TV. This was our inciting incident, the dramatic engine meant to power six episodes of chaos and comedy.

What we didn't know was that, hours earlier, Linda had busted David in his studio, pants down in a full-on Bill Clinton situation. Unbeknownst to us, their marriage was done. But Linda—gangster mom of the century—made a decision. For her boys. For their shot at TV glory. She swallowed the betrayal, fixed her smile, and played house on camera while her real house was collapsing. She said nothing and made David vow to do the same.

Linda and David walked into that party and delivered their Oscar-worthy performances. David's fury was real. Linda smiled through her heartbreak. I thought we were making a goofy reality comedy about spoiled rich kids. Turns out, we were filming the trailer for a divorce.

As our premiere approached, I went into publicity overdrive. We needed something nuclear to launch our show into the culture. "We should do a low-speed chase through LA," I announced to the production team. "Like O.J., but with PRINCES OF MALIBU banners streaming off the car. We get arrested live on TV. Front page of every newspaper. Instant fame."

Thankfully, Brody chickened out. Something about not wanting a criminal record. So I pivoted: "How about a sex tape?! Look what *One Night in Paris* did for her. She went from hotel heiress to global icon overnight. We could call it *Bonin' with Brody* or something."

We actually had footage. During filming one night, Brody had forgotten about the night-vision cameras in his room while entertaining a Guess model.

"LEAK IT," I said.

"Spencer, NO," said Brody, rolling his eyes.

I couldn't understand his resistance. To me, scandal was just smart marketing, and I had zero boundaries when it came to making our show successful. I would've done that car chase solo, waving at the news helicopters while the cameras rolled. I would've dropped a sex tape without hesitating, if only I'd had one. I was so obsessed with making a splash that I'd lost all sense of consequences.

Turns out I wasn't the only Pratt with that competitive gene.

One shoot day, my sister Stephanie stumbled onto set, clearly on one, and without any invitation or discussion marched straight to the edge of the Casablanca pool and cannonballed into the water fully clothed. Obviously, she knew how to make a splash. Maybe she was trying to win something—our attention, a spot on the show—or just upstage her brother.

When she climbed out, dripping and disoriented, she glared at the crew with the fury of someone who'd just made a play and wasn't getting scored.

"Why aren't you filming this?" she slurred. "I thought this was *reality TV!*"

Brant pulled me aside. "We can't put your sister on television like this."

"I know. Of course not," I said quietly. Though part of me understood her frustration. In the Pratt family Olympics, I'd found my event, and she was still searching for hers.

Not long after this, as documented in her book, Stephanie overdosed. On purpose. Meth, Xanax, OxyContin, alcohol—whatever she could get her hands on. Thank God my mom has this almost supernatural ability to sense when her kids are in danger. She was across town when something—call it mother's intuition, call it divine intervention—told her to check on Stephanie right then.

She found her just in time. My sister was still conscious enough to whisper what she'd done. Then came the ambulance, the stomach pump, the sleepless night in the ER—my parents sitting beside her bed, watching the heart monitor, praying it wouldn't flatline. My mom and dad must have aged ten years that night.

And me? I did what I always did. I built a wall. On one side was Real-Life Spencer—the brother, powerless. On the other was TV Spencer—the executive producer with a show to deliver. I threw myself into production like it was a life raft. I was everywhere on set—storyboarding drama in my head, nudging castmates into confrontations, sweet-talking the crew into bending the rules. Every hour focusing on the show was an hour I didn't have to think about what was happening at home.

Looking back, maybe Steph and I weren't so different. She ran toward the darkness. I ran toward the Hollywood lights. Same instinct: get out of our own heads, chase a different reality.

On July 10, 2005, the first episode of *Princes* premiered on Fox. An hour or so after it aired, Peter Chernin called, sounding like the Grim Reaper.

"It's over, kid."

OVER? What? We hadn't even gotten to the episode where I try to auction David's Grammys on eBay!

"Don't take it personally," he said. "We loved what you and Brody did, but it's not going to work out. We bought a family-friendly four-quadrant show, not a divorce with cheating allegations. We'll run Episode Two next week, then we're pulling the show."

He hung up without explaining himself any further.

I was so confused. This made no sense! Until, of course, I found out what had really happened.

Turns out, Linda had watched the premiere and was upset at how the edit made her look: like some delusional enabler who'd raised two sociopaths while her husband suffered nobly. After everything she'd just been through, she wasn't about to let America watch her and her offspring get character-assassinated for another five episodes.

The moment the premiere ended, she called Chernin and dropped the nuke: She was filing for divorce. Boom. Show's over. No Season 2, no continuation of our television empire, all because Linda Thompson caught David Foster getting a private concert in the same studio where he'd produced "I Will Always Love You."

If I'd been smarter—if I'd actually been the savvy producer I thought I was—I would've had Linda in all the edit sessions. Made sure she felt good about every frame. Instead, she had to watch herself and her sons look stupid on national television—the final insult after spending weeks smiling for cameras while her husband was cheating behind her back.

No wonder she shut us down.

After receiving the news, I sat in my childhood bedroom in the Palisades, staring at the BMW keys that now felt like evidence of my stupidity. Ninety thousand dollars blown on a car I couldn't afford, for a Hollywood career that didn't exist anymore. But here's the thing about the Pratt family—we don't quit.

"Son, this is just the beginning," my dad said when I told him the news. "You got on network television. That's not luck—that's talent."

My mom was even more direct: "Spencer, you're going to get it all back. I know it." But it was Nana Joan who really sealed the deal. She had this way of seeing the future that was almost supernatural. "Honey," she said, squeezing my hands, "this is just an intermission. Your second act is going to be even better."

With that kind of support system, how could I not keep fighting to be the success story I was obviously supposed to be?

CHAPTER 6

A SPEIDI IS BORN

Two Players, One Game

I went back to USC, surrounded by kids melting down over midterms. I wanted to shake them. You think Writing 140 is life or death? Please. Try pitching to Gail Berman. While everyone else was stress-eating Cheetos in the library, my brain was cooking up a resurrection. Nana Joan was right—failure wasn't my ending, it was my origin story. Every closed door, every no was just material for the eventual yes that would make it all worth it.

I could feel my next chapter building, that familiar electricity in the air that meant something big was about to happen. The universe was lining up the pieces again. And when the next great opportunity of my life came calling, you'd think I would have recognized it immediately. You'd think I would have grasped it with both hands and never let go.

Not so much.

I was riding shotgun in Brody's Escalade with twenty-four-inch spinners when his phone started buzzing. He peeked at it and got this confused look.

"It's my stepmom. That's . . . random. Why is she calling?"

It seemed like they barely had a relationship. He chatted with Kris Jenner for a minute, then slid the phone over to me.

"She wants to talk to you, Spencer. This is weird."

Kris Jenner's voice purred through on speaker.

"Spencer, honey! I want to do what you boys did with *Princes*, but with my family in Calabasas. What do you think? Wanna team up, make TV magic?"

"Uh, a reality show . . . in the Valley?" I asked, genuinely confused.

"Yes! About my daughters and Bruce—they're dying to do it!"

Here's the thing: Bruce Jenner had been showing up to *Princes* shoots as Brody's parent. Fox editors said "absolutely not" to every single scene. This person had the on-screen charisma of drywall. So why would we center a whole show on that energy? And don't even get me started on the Valley. The Valley was where dreams went to die in a cul-de-sac. Strip malls, wine moms, Chili's happy hour. It was the anti-Malibu. Who the hell would want to watch that?

Spoiler alert: Everyone. Literally everyone. For twenty seasons and counting.

I ended the call with Kris. Brody and I burst into laughter.

"Yeah, we're gonna have to pass on this one, prince," I said with the kind of confidence only available to people about to make the worst decisions of their lives. "The only thing they film in the Valley is porn."

I have replayed that moment in my head probably forty million times. That "choose your own adventure" moment when we picked the path that definitely wasn't a billion-dollar empire. Kris Jenner ended up linking with Ryan Seacrest. He had *American Idol* clout, a first-look deal with E!, and—not to mention—the ability to recognize a huge opportunity when it was handed to him on a silver platter. If only I'd said yes, I would have been an executive producer of *Keeping Up with the Kardashians*. I'd own a yacht. I'd have fuck-you money. Instead, I have fuck-me money. Which is to say: no money. Which is exactly what you get when you think you're too good for the Valley.

I guess the universe was pushing me toward something else. Obviously.

• • •

It was midsummer 2006. Nearly a year since *The Princes of Malibu* had ended. The media landscape was mutating into something unrecognizable. Twitter had just launched as "Twttr," because apparently vowels cost extra? YouTube was exploding with user-generated content that was somehow more entertaining than anything on TV. And everyone was living on MySpace, where your Top 8 was basically your social credit score. Social media and digital culture were blowing up alongside the reality TV boom, and I was studying it all like my life depended on it.

I was still at USC part-time, taking whatever classes, but my real major was Hollywood. People were actually taking my calls. I was constantly pitching. I wasn't some wannabe anymore. I had actual credentials. I could deliver the goods. I even looked the part now. Still had the BMW, plus full access to Brody's designer closet. I was rocking head-to-toe Chrome Hearts before anyone knew what Chrome Hearts even was.

The meetings kept coming. Remember Sean Perry, the superagent/partner at William Morris who deadass called me *Benjamin* in that meeting with Fox's Gail Berman? I pitched him a military-style reality competition where celebrities did extreme challenges. Years later, *Special Forces* premiered with basically the same concept. Then I pitched a talent show eerily similar to *America's Got Talent*. Looking back, it's insane how close I came to breaking through with concepts that ended up making other people stupid rich. But that's Hollywood—timing is everything. Also, there's a difference between having an idea and having the ability to fully execute that idea.

Of all the concepts I was pitching around town, the one that came closest to actually taking off was "Banking on Brody." Brody, Brant Pinvidic, and I had cooked up this comedic reality show—the premise was I'd be Brody's hustler manager, orchestrating fake celebrity situationships for him that would dominate the tabloid gossip cycle. Picture this: Cameron Diaz exits her yoga class. Suddenly, Brody "randomly" bumps into her. They chat for maybe thirty seconds—just long enough for it to look natural. Meanwhile, I'm already blowing up my paparazzi contacts. Within hours, every gossip site is running "EXCLUSIVE: Brody Jenner's Secret Romance with Cameron Diaz!" We'd pull this operation with a different A-lister every single episode. By Season 1's finale, Brody would be Hollywood's most eligible bachelor, and I'd be the evil mastermind who orchestrated his reign.

Rod Aissa, MTV's West Coast head, was absolutely obsessed with the concept, and when he green-lit our pilot budget, I knew this was it. I was officially back in the game. "Phase One: Domination" was in full effect, and I had the checklist to prove it:

Executive producer credit ✓
Designer everything ✓
Black BMW looking clean in the parking lot ✓
MTV pilot that could actually change my life ✓

Looking at my list of accomplishments, there was one glaring omission. Something that most people my age considered pretty fundamental to a happy life.

Love. It wasn't even on my radar.

I'd mapped out my entire life like a hedge fund portfolio: grind relentlessly until fifty, accumulate massive wealth and power, then maybe—and I mean *maybe*—consider a relationship. I had empires to build, deals to close, concepts to sell. Love was a luxury for people without that ambition grindset, as far as I was concerned.

Marriage? Children? No thank you! I'd watched my parents pour everything into raising us—the late nights, the financial stress, the constant worry. They'd sacrificed their own dreams to build ours, and while I respected the hell out of that, I was going to make a different choice. Which, of course, is exactly when the universe decided to test my commitment to staying emotionally unavailable for the rest of my life.

• • •

One day, I came home to the Palisades and found my mom and her best friend, Lucy, glued to the TV, completely mesmerized.

"What are we watching?" I asked.

"Just this cute MTV show with these adorable girls," Lucy said, eyes never leaving the screen.

The show was called *The Hills*.

The star was Lauren Conrad—LC from *Laguna Beach*, the reality show that proved Orange County high schoolers were richer, tanner, and far more dramatic than the rest of civilization. Now Lauren had her own spin-off, moving up the coast to Hollywood to chase her fashion journalism dreams with her bubbly best friend, Heidi, in tow. Blond hair, perfect smile, energy that reached through the screen and grabbed you.

"That blond one's absolutely precious," Lucy said from the couch. "You should marry her, Spencer."

Those. Were. Her. Exact. Words.

"Heidi's your type," my mom agreed, studying the screen like she was reading tea leaves. "She's got that sparkle."

"Y'all are insane," I said, posting up to watch and do some market research. Reality TV was my job now, so I needed to stay informed. First impression? *The Hills* was aggressively boring. Like watching paint dry, except the paint was really pretty and had perfect lighting.

Lauren Conrad. Eye rolls. Fashion internship. Ambien in human form. SKIP.

Heidi Montag. Party girl. Firecracker waiting to go off. Doesn't.

Audrina Patridge. Staring off into space receiving transmissions from another planet.

Whitney Port. Human beige sweater. (I actually knew her from Crossroads. She was dating Dave Chernin and desperately trying to get him cast on the show, apparently, but he wanted zero to do with it. Understandably.)

Plotlines were also giving me nothing:

- Heidi ditches class to play computer solitaire.
- Lauren does fake gossip sessions with Whitney at *Teen Vogue*, where they're both pretending to intern.
- Audrina just . . . exists near a pool. She's got this rock musician boyfriend called Justin Bobby who wears beanies. His actual name is Justin, but he wants everyone to call him Bobby for literally no reason so . . . PLEASE MAKE THIS STOP.

Where's the conflict? The stakes? Why was this even on TV? Because it looked pretty, I guess. The lighting *was* superb. (The cinematographer, Rachel Morrison, later shot *Black Panther* and became the first woman nominated for an Oscar in cinematography. Even then, you could tell she was slumming it, making these girls look like Renaissance paintings while they discussed which outfits to wear that night.)

When the credits rolled, I saw it: *Executive Producer: Sean Travis*. MY showrunner. The guy we'd brought in for *Princes*. That guy had never said a word about landing an MTV deal.

I called him immediately.

"Sean, what's good? I'm watching *The Hills* right now."

"Spencer! Hey!"

"So let me get this straight—we hook you up with that Fox gig, you use that to secure this MTV show, and you don't even think to put me and Brody on it? Where's the loyalty, bro?"

"Listen, it's not that kind of narrative, it's all girls—"

"Even better! You've got four girls and zero interesting dudes. Brody and I would kill on this show."

Sean let out this sigh. "Listen, the creator, Adam DiVello, doesn't want—"

"I don't care what this Adam DiVello wants. You owe us, Sean.

You're EP'ing a show about young people living it up in Hollywood. THAT'S US, dude. We ARE the Hollywood scene. If you won't put us on . . . well, I guess we'll just have to handle this ourselves."

And then, for maximum drama, I added:

"I'll see you in the club."

I hung up. Annoyed.

Then I hit up Brody. "We're getting on that new MTV show. *The Hills*."

"Huh? We have our own show, brother."

"Yeah, but I'm not letting Sean Travis use the connections we gave him while we're just sitting here watching him cash checks."

"Uh, okay, Spencer. Sure!"

Sure was right. Once I see an opportunity, I'm like a shark in the water, a dog with a bone. I see what I want. I take it.

That's mine.

Later that summer, Brody and I pulled up to this new club in Hollywood called Privilege, where Brody was meeting his girlfriend, Kristin Cavallari, who just happened to be Lauren Conrad's sworn nemesis on *Laguna Beach*. The drama between those two was already MTV canon. Where Lauren was carefully constructed California pretty, Kristin was raw magnetism, switching from flirty to lethal in 0.5 seconds. She had this tiny frame, but she moved through the world like she was six feet tall and bulletproof. She wasn't performing wildness; she WAS wild.

And Brody was completely gone for her.

When we walked in, Kristin was sitting at a table with a beautiful blond girl.

It was Heidi.

Kristin brought Heidi over and introduced us. Heidi's energy was dialed to eleven, and not just from the vodka Red Bulls. Her aura was radiating FUN! PARTAY!! WELCOME TO *MY* WORLD! She also happened to be absolutely stunning, wearing this mini jean skirt from

Ralph Lauren and a Forever 21 halter top—details she still remembers. What I remember is that she had these bright eyes that seemed lit from within, cheekbones that could cut glass, and this smile that made me feel like I was the only person in the room, even though the place was packed.

Here's what's crazy—I didn't even realize who she was at first. Didn't connect this glowing party goddess with the girl I'd been watching on MTV. Between the club lighting, the vodka, and the fact that she looked completely different when she wasn't playing Lauren Conrad's sidekick, my brain just was not computing.

Then the DJ dropped "SexyBack," which is exactly when I knew the gods were on my side tonight.

"Want to dance?" I asked her.

We hit the floor at that perfect level of tipsy where you're willing to bust out your best, most lethal dance moves because you think you're in a music video. When Heidi spun around and pressed her back against my chest during the "take it to the bridge" part, I thought I might spontaneously combust. When Timberlake got to "dirty babe," she did this little shimmy that should probably be banned in multiple states.

The crowd around us had basically formed a circle, like we were putting on a show, and honestly, we kind of were. Sorry to Channing and Jenna in *Step Up*—this wasn't just dancing. This was full-contact seduction by two halves of the same soul, finally colliding after light-years apart. All we needed was rain to come down on us in the middle of the club.

Brody and Kristin appeared at the edge of our circle, took one look at us, and just laughed. They knew. Everyone knew. Spencer Pratt, the guy with the rock-solid anti-love strategy, was done for.

When the song ended, Heidi slid her hands onto my shoulders, holding my gaze while the next track kicked in.

"So what's a nice girl like you doing swimming with the sharks?" I yelled over the bass, trying to sound slick, even though my brain was short-circuiting from how close she was.

She smirked. "Who says I'm not one of the sharks?"

Ohhhh. This wasn't just some random party girl. This was *Heidi. The Hills* Heidi. The one my mom's psychic friend Lucy swore I'd end up marrying.

"Wait, I know who you are," I said, pulling her closer.

"Oh yeah? Who am I?" Her voice was teasing, but there was something else there—a challenge, maybe.

"You're definitely a player," I said.

She grinned. "Well, I'm writing a book—"How to Play the Player." Maybe you should read it sometime."

"Yeah? Did your boyfriend read it first?"

"Which one? I've got three." She let it hang there, watching my face glitch. Then she laughed. "Actually, not boyfriends. Just . . . friends. I have a lot of friends."

She was playing with me, and we both knew it. The question was whether I minded.

I didn't.

Kristin and Brody approached, like party referees calling time.

"We're going back to Casablanca!" Kristin announced. "Let's go!" She grabbed Brody's arm with the casual ownership of someone who knew she was the main event. He looked at her like she'd hung the moon.

I turned to Heidi.

"You wanna drive with me?"

She didn't even blink. "Yeah!"

That was it. No fake hesitation, no checking her phone for other invites, no "Who else is going?" Like—girl was down, full-send energy. Just "Yeah!" like it was the most obvious answer in the world.

Next thing I know, we're flying down the Pacific Coast Highway in my BMW, windows down, ocean air whipping in, and I learn Heidi's number one hobby in life: kissing. Every stop sign, every red light, she's climbing across the console like the seat belt's optional. My hands are on the wheel, my brain screaming, *Don't crash,* but also, *What a way to go.*

"You're trouble," I told her at a red light in Santa Monica.

"The best kind," she said, kissing me like she was trying to prove it.

Somewhere around the Getty, my entire plan for staying single began disintegrating in real time. This girl was rewriting my operating system with every mile.

By the time we got to Duke's, the Malibu beachfront restaurant, I had to pull over. Couldn't even pretend to focus. Somewhere between Hollywood and here, I'd lost the plot entirely. And honestly? I didn't even want it back.

We stumbled onto the shoulder, ocean roaring below, stars overhead, headlights sweeping past us. I lifted her onto the hood, heat still rising from the engine, and kissed her like it was my last meal.

"I like you, Spencer," she said between kisses.

A cop car drove by, slowed down, then kept going. Even the Malibu sheriffs knew better than to interrupt this kind of chemistry.

By the time we finally rolled up to Casablanca, Brody and Kristin probably thought we'd either crashed or gotten arrested for PDA on PCH. We found them in the lounge, sprawled on the giant couch like the king and queen of Malibu.

"Well, look what the cat dragged in!" Brody said, grinning.

"Your friend's house is ridiculous!" Heidi whispered to me as Kristin jumped up to hug her.

"Babe, we thought you died! Don't tell me what took you so long—I already know."

The four of us basically had the house to ourselves—after the divorce, David Foster had sold the property to media mogul Larry Ellison. Larry wasn't moving in straightaway, and David had said we could just chill there whenever we wanted. Translation: Brody and I had free rein of a Malibu mega-mansion for almost a year, which, looking back on it, is insane. We were just kids playing in someone else's castle.

We sank into the cushions beside Brody and Kristin, and Brody didn't waste a second—out came the ROOR German designer bong.

Our old ritual. How many nights had we sat right here, passing it back and forth, convinced we were fixing the world one hit at a time?

I took a hit and held it out to Heidi with a grin.

She wrinkled her nose. "Ew. Weed's for losers."

Brody and I looked at each other, then at the premium German bong, then at the panoramic Malibu ocean views.

"Losers?" I said. "This is six-hundred-dollar-an-ounce OG Kush in a forty-million-dollar mansion."

"Where I'm from, only losers smoke weed," Heidi explained.

Brody exhaled a cloud and shrugged. "Well, we're from Malibu, and you're missing out."

Heidi just laughed at us, shaking her head. "You guys are ridiculous."

"Come on, Heidi," I said. "Wanna take the train to the pool?"

We hopped on the funicular, gliding down the hillside in slow motion. When the doors slid open onto the pool deck, I caught Heidi's face—it lit up like she'd just stepped into a dream. She slipped off her heels, kicked them into a corner, and dipped her toes in the water, the pool lights painting her skin in electric blue.

"You and Brody are quite the duo," she said, watching me.

"Brody? He's basically my brother," I told her.

Before I could elaborate, she was already tugging at her clothes. "Come on, let's swim!"

Seconds later we were in the water, stripped down and weightless. I kissed her because I couldn't not. Then again. And again. Somewhere in the back of my mind I was praying Brody and Kristin weren't upstairs glued to the security monitors, watching us turn their pool into a late-night pilot episode.

Heidi swam up to the edge and took a long pull from the champagne bottle we'd stolen from Brody's kitchen, looking like everything I'd ever wanted without knowing I wanted it—wild and grounded, beautiful and real, someone who could call bullshit on Hollywood's games while playing them better than anyone.

This wasn't supposed to happen. I was supposed to be the ultimate player, a tempter on *Temptation Island*. And here I was, dismantled by a girl from Colorado who thought our $10K bong was tacky.

We went deep that first night. All the way deep. Not just physically—though yes, that, too, in ways that made me understand why people wrote poetry and started wars—but something else. Recognition. Like we'd been looking for each other without knowing it.

Most girls I'd dated in LA were always running an angle, playing a game just like me, trying to level up. Heidi was just . . . herself. She didn't need me. She had her own hustle, her own show, her own ambitions.

We even had the same job description: professional sidekick. She was Lauren's wingwoman, I was Brody's wingman. The supporting cast. The extras who made the stars shine.

Here's the thing, though. You know what happens when two sidekicks get together? Sometimes they steal the whole damn show.

CHAPTER 7

WHIPPED

How to Lose a Girl in One Dance

Heidi was on summer hiatus from *The Hills*, which meant no cameras, no call times, no meetings—just pure, unfiltered access to each other. For the first time since I'd started chasing Hollywood, I had something I wanted more than my next career move. Suddenly there was this whole other dimension to existence that didn't involve pitch meetings or networking or calculating my next strategic move. Just me and this girl, figuring out whether what we had was real or just really good chemistry.

Early on, Heidi brought me around to meet her bestie and *Hills* queen bee—Lauren Conrad. I'd been mentally preparing for this introduction like it was a job interview, because in a way, it was. Lauren's approval would determine whether I was Heidi's boyfriend or just some guy she was seeing.

First impression: Lauren had that effortless California-girl thing down to a science. Sun-streaked brown hair that looked like she spent every weekend at the beach, wide-set eyes that gave her this perpetual "Wait, what?" expression.

She seemed chill enough at first. Sweet, a little type A, but nothing alarming. What I didn't recognize then was the specific energy of someone who'd been the main character since birth and couldn't conceive of being anything else. In her world, she's always center-frame.

And she would NOT leave us alone. We'd be trying to chill in

Heidi's room and here'd come LC, sliding onto the bed like she was part of the package deal. She had this way of inserting herself—leaning against Heidi, brushing her arm, tossing me side-eye like, *Just so you know, I was here first, Spencer.* It wasn't overt. It was more like subtle territory marking.

"Oh my God, Spencer, you HAVE to meet my parents!" she said one day, smile stretched wide. "My dad is going to love you! You're perfect boyfriend material!"

The words hit strange. Not flirting exactly, but something weirder—like she was shopping for Heidi, picking out accessories for her friend's life. Or maybe testing me, seeing if I'd blush under the attention of the show's star.

I remember thinking how exhausting it must be to be her. To never be able to turn off that main-character energy, to treat every interaction like a scene that needed directing. Even in her own apartment, she couldn't just exist. Everything was staging, angles, control.

Even Heidi bought into this idea that Lauren was the untouchable, ordained star of the friend group, the sun everyone else orbited. It drove me insane—this gorgeous, vibrant, one-of-a-kind girl standing right in front of me, convinced she was someone else's supporting cast.

I wanted to shake her sometimes. "You realize you're the most magnetic person in any room, right? You realize people light up when you walk in?" But she'd just laugh it off, deflect back to Lauren's latest drama or outfit or whatever.

Despite our growing closeness, Heidi was still keeping her options open. She had other guys circling—not just casual flirting, but actual contenders. Texts at all hours, invitations she'd consider, backup plans she wasn't hiding. Part of me respected the honesty. She wasn't playing games or pretending I was her only option. The other part of me wanted to hurl her Sidekick into the Pacific and maybe follow it with a few of those other guys.

Still, I told myself I wasn't sweating it. Spencer Pratt doesn't chase—Spencer Pratt conquers. I had my own game, my own rules. I'd built my entire identity around being the guy who stayed in control, who never needed anyone more than they needed me.

That delusion lasted about a week.

One night, Heidi and I rolled up to the club. VIP section, bottles flowing, everything perfect. Kristin Cavallari was there doing her whole thing, working every corner of that place. Heidi ducked into the bathroom, and Kristin swooped in with that evil little smirk.

"So word is you're completely whipped for Heidi," she purred. "Like . . . *obsessed* obsessed."

My whole body went rigid.

There it was—my worst nightmare exposed under the club lights. That people could see it written all over my face. The Spencer Pratt who never needed anyone, never cared too much, never got played—that guy was gone, replaced by some lovesick idiot.

"Kristin, shut the hell up," I said quietly.

The truth was I'd never felt anything this intense before, and it terrified me. Every other girl had been a game I could win or lose and walk away from. With Heidi, losing felt like it would actually destroy me. So when Kristin called me "whipped," she wasn't just teasing—she was exposing the thing I was most afraid of: that I'd become the kind of guy who needed someone more than they needed me.

"Oh my GOD, you ARE in love!" Kristin giggled. "This is so cute! Spencer Pratt is totally pussy-whipped! Heidi's got you acting like her little lost puppy!"

When she said that, I felt my soul leave my body. I could practically see the brunch table. Heidi and her friends, mimosas flowing, dissecting my desperation. "He's in LOVE! After ONE night! Can you believe it?" Cue laughter, eye rolls, the whole *Mean Girls* chorus line.

Twenty minutes later, Heidi tracked me down at the bar, looking all worried.

"Babe, where'd you go? I was looking everywhere for you."

"Nowhere, babe," I said, but the words came out sharp, defensive.

"You seem off. Want to find somewhere quieter?" She reached for my hand.

"Nah, I'm good right here," I said, jerking away from her touch like it burned. "Actually, your girl Kristin's over there, if you want to go gossip some more."

The confusion that crossed her face should have snapped me out of it. She looked genuinely lost, like I'd started speaking a different language. But my ego had taken the wheel and was driving us straight off a cliff.

Heidi walked away, and within seconds, this blonde in a skimpy dress, an acquaintance, appeared next to me like she could smell my emotional breakdown from across the room.

"Wanna dance?" I asked her.

I could see Heidi standing there watching us, probably trying to figure out what the hell was happening. But I was committed to this self-destruction now.

"Of course!" my acquaintance giggled, already wrapping herself around me, an extra in my one-man show called "Watch Spencer Destroy His Own Happiness."

So I put on a show. Not just with her—that would've been too subtle for my wounded pride. I went full scorched earth. Six different girls in thirty minutes. A rotating cast of backup dancers for my pity party. A brunette who laughed too loud at nothing. A redhead who pressed too close. Another blonde who looked enough like Heidi in the strobe lights that, for a second, I forgot what I was doing. None of them mattered. They were just bodies to put between me and my feelings.

I caught Heidi's face in the crowd—the confusion melting into understanding, then hurt, then something worse. Disappointment. Like she'd thought I was different, better than this, and I was proving her wrong in the most spectacular way possible.

Good, the wounded part of me thought. *Let her see that she doesn't own me.*

Of course, I was lying to myself. She did own me. Had owned me since "SexyBack" started playing. And that's exactly why I was doing this—because being owned by someone, caring that much, feeling that vulnerable, was the scariest thing I'd ever experienced.

As Heidi started cutting through the crowd toward me, my heart rate spiked. Part of me wanted to run. Part of me wanted to drop everything and apologize. Instead, I just kept dancing, pretending I didn't see her coming.

It's showtime, I thought bitterly.

She tapped my shoulder.

"Spencer, what the hell are you doing?"

"Dancing. Is that okay?"

The sarcasm in my voice made her flinch. I watched it happen—the way she physically recoiled from this version of me.

My dance partner vanished into the crowd like smoke, probably sensing the nuclear fallout about to happen. The music was too loud, the lights too bright, everything was too much.

"So Heidi," I said, my voice getting louder, needing to hurt her the way Kristin's words had hurt me, "why are you going around telling everyone I'm obsessed with you?"

"Because you ARE!" she shot back. "And if that bothered you so much, maybe you should've talked to ME about it instead of . . . whatever this pathetic display is supposed to be!"

The light in her eyes—the one that had been shining just for me all night—went out. And I knew, with the kind of certainty that makes you sick, that I'd just destroyed something beautiful.

"I don't know why I expected different," she said, shaking her head.

"Heidi, wait, you're right, I'm being an idiot . . ."

But it was too late. She walked away, said something quick to Kristin, and headed for the exit without looking back. Not once.

I stood there in the middle of that dance floor feeling like the biggest piece of shit in Hollywood. The music was still pounding, but it sounded muffled now, like I was underwater. The lights kept flashing, but all I could see was Heidi's face when she'd realized I was just another asshole who couldn't handle his feelings.

The next morning hit me like a freight train. My head was pounding, but that was nothing compared to the sick feeling in my gut when last night's highlight reel started playing in my brain.

Six different girls. Jesus Christ, Spencer.

Now I was alone, reeking of failure and other girls' perfume.

Call her. Fix this. Apologize until she believes you.

I reached for my phone. Dialed Heidi's number. One ring, then: "The number you have dialed is no longer in service."

She'd actually changed her number. Within HOURS.

I sat up, suddenly completely awake. This wasn't a normal ghosting. This wasn't blocking someone on MySpace or avoiding their calls. This was the nuclear option—calling your carrier in the middle of the night and saying, "I need a new number. Now."

The finality of it knocked the wind out of me. No chance for drunk texts at 3 a.m. No possibility of apology voicemails. No way to explain that I'd ruined everything because I was scared of how much she mattered.

Days, weeks passed, and still, I couldn't stop thinking about Heidi. Every minute of every day, she was there in my head like a blond poltergeist. The way her face had crumpled when she saw me doing *Dancing with the Stars* with Random Girl #3, throwing her in the air and catching her with her legs wrapped around my waist. The way she'd looked at me before I'd decided happiness was for the weak.

DAMMIT, SPENCER.

Almost two months later, I still woke up, stared at my phone like it was a Ouija board, and hoped Heidi's name would magically appear. It never did. By now, the ache had started to rot into something else—not full-on bitterness, but close. She wanted to ice me out? Cool. I'll act unbothered. *Spencer Pratt doesn't chase—Spencer Pratt conquers.* That had always been my mantra. Girls were supposed to be interchangeable. One exits, another enters. Circle of life in LA.

It was October when I found myself third-wheeling with Brody and Nicole Richie at Chateau Marmont. Brody and Kristin's yearlong fireworks show had finally blown itself up. And honestly? I'd never seen him so wrecked.

Enter Nicole Richie, Kristin's polar opposite. Kristin was fire, Nicole was ice. Kristin was chaos, Nicole was control. She was the perfect antidote. We had a lot of fun, hanging out as a trio. A brief and beautiful moment in time when Nicole and I were cool. (Later, *Details* magazine ran a profile of Brody where they quoted me saying he "only dated Nicole Richie to become a celebrity." Brody was mortified by the article, *Details* stood by it. Either way, that article blew up whatever friendship Nicole and I had. Understandable.)

Nicole's friend Sophia Rossi—the talent coordinator for *The Hills*—joined Brody, Nicole, and I at the Chateau that night. Sophie's job was texting the cast their call times, which meant she had every girl's number, schedule, and current drama status. For weeks after Heidi ghosted me, I'd begged Sophia for her new number. Each time, Sophia shut me down cold. "She made her feelings very clear, Spencer. Move on."

Move on. Like it was that simple. Like I hadn't spent two months trying exactly that and failing spectacularly. Every day I'd wake up telling myself today would be different—today I wouldn't think about her, wouldn't check if she'd called.

And every night I'd fall asleep knowing I had failed again.

By now, I'd given up on the possibility of fixing what I'd broken. But some petty revenge? That was still on the table.

"So, what's up with the show?" I said to Sophia, trying to sound casual while my brain was already calculating angles.

"Actually, we're filming tonight at this new club, Area."

Hmm. I could feel the gravitational pull of *The Hills* circling closer. I'd been bugging Sean Travis to get me on there, but he kept giving me the runaround. Maybe tonight would be the night I forced my way in.

"I'm coming."

"Well, no, you can't, Spencer. Heidi's working there tonight."

Perfect. That's exactly why I needed to be there.

Then Audrina Patridge walked into Chateau—Sophia's friend and a *Hills* cast member. Olive skin glowing under the low light; sleepy, half-lidded eyes that made her seem permanently unbothered. She wasn't giving Laguna Beach sorority princess. She was giving *rock star's girlfriend who only smokes on the balcony at 3 a.m.*

I learned that Audrina and Heidi weren't talking right now—some summer drama about Audrina hanging out with Lauren's ex, a rich Orange County kid named Jason Wahler.

And Heidi, ever the loyal soldier, had naturally chosen Lauren's side in the conflict.

"Yo, Audrina," I said in front of everyone. "I hear you and Heidi aren't talking. Well, ditto. Heidi changed her number on me. You should bring me to the club with you. It'll drive her crazy."

I was too far gone to care about dignity. I wanted Heidi to see me, to feel something, even if that something was anger or jealousy or hurt. Anything was better than indifference.

"Sure," Audrina smiled, 10,000 percent on board with whatever this might unleash. "This should be interesting." I appreciated her commitment to chaos, I must say.

Brody was watching this whole scheme unfold with barely concealed amusement. The idea of infiltrating Lauren Conrad's little scene probably felt appealing to him, too, on some level. Like indirect revenge on Kristin for cheating on him. The vibe back then was incestuous: Everyone had either hooked up with everyone, hated everyone, or both. And Brody knew the second his name hit LC's guest list it would travel back to Kristin like wildfire. Half the game wasn't even dating, it was making sure the *right people* saw who you were standing next to.

We pulled up to Area, by now the most popping spot in LA. Unless you were dropping serious cash on a table or had your face on a billboard, you weren't getting past the rope.

"There's the film crew," Audrina said, pointing to the MTV vans. "You ready for this?"

"Yep. Let's go ruin Heidi's night," I said.

This wasn't how I'd imagined seeing Heidi again. In my fantasies, I'd run into her somewhere neutral, with someone else on my arm. She'd realize what she'd lost. We'd have some moment of recognition. Maybe she'd even want me back. And I'd blow her off, of course.

This wasn't that. This was me showing up to her workplace with her enemy, trying to cause maximum drama because I couldn't handle being ignored. Different vibe. Maybe a little toxic. Whatever.

As we walked the carpet, I saw her. Heidi standing at the velvet rope, earpiece in, clipboard clutched like a weapon. Professional. Put together. Living her best life as a coordinator for Bolthouse Productions. (Back then, Bolthouse ran Hollywood nightlife like the mafia ran Vegas in the '70s. If you were young, hot, and trying to make it in LA, you wanted to be inside one of their clubs—Area, Privilege, Les Deux, Hyde. They controlled the velvet ropes, the bottle service, the gossip pages. Paris, Lindsay, Britney—if they weren't stumbling out of a Bolthouse club, were they even alive?)

And Heidi was at the epicenter of it all. Sorta. I mean, the *actual* job was fake AF—she only worked there for the cameras—but she owned it like an Oscar role. Her real gig was actress, and the part was "Heidi Montag," a heightened, polished, reality-TV version of herself. It was fake, but it was her. And she was absolutely killing it.

Seeing her knocked the wind out of me. Two months of imagining this moment, and I wasn't prepared for how good she looked. How natural she seemed in her element. How absolutely fine she appeared to be without me in her life. *I'm gonna get you*, I thought. *Ha ha. Changed your number, now here I am with Audrina.*

Yep, here I was again, being exactly the asshole she'd decided I was when I spontaneously combusted our relationship.

I strolled straight up to Heidi at the entrance. For a split second, her eyes widened—genuine surprise before the professional mask slammed down. I'll give it to her, she handled me like a pro. That smile never wavered, even as her eyes promised murder.

"You're not going to show us to our table?" I said with an evil grin. Her smile got sharper.

"No. Sorry, that's VIP only. Bye."

The way she said "bye," like I was a telemarketer calling during dinner. Like I was gum under her shoe.

BURN.

What did I expect? That she'd see me and melt? That two months of silence would evaporate because I'd orchestrated some reality TV moment? No, not my girl. Like I said earlier, Heidi's a player. The worst part was that behind her professional smile, I caught something in her eyes. Not anger. Not hurt. Just . . . nothing. Like I was already forgotten. That's what killed me. Not the rejection. The sense that she didn't care.

WHY DID THIS MAKE ME LIKE HER MORE?

I walked inside, alone. Brody and Nicole were probably still outside on the red carpet posing for the cameras. Audrina went off somewhere. I noticed the MTV cameras were set up everywhere, cables snaking across floors, lighting rigs turning the VIP section into a TV set.

I still didn't understand the full scope of the beef between Heidi and Audrina. Sure, Heidi was pissed at me—but the way she'd glared at Audrina outside? That was on another level. She didn't even acknowledge her existence. Finale-level rage, about to pop. I could feel a showdown coming the way dogs feel an earthquake before it hits.

I went to the bar, ordered a drink, and noticed Heidi storm over to Lauren and Lauren's friend Jen Bunney at their table, her whole body tense. She said something, then marched over to me.

"Why would you come here with Audrina?" she demanded.

She was cool and collected—she was trying to solve a puzzle. Like, what was my angle? She knew Audrina and I didn't even know each other.

"Oh, I just walked in with her—" I said, trying to play it smooth.

"I HATE her," Heidi spat.

"Why do you hate her?"

Before she could answer, Audrina appeared, wrapping her arms around me. The timing was perfect. I felt Heidi recoil like I'd slapped her.

"Oh wow," I said, seeing Heidi's face crumple, trying to defuse with humor. "We got beef in the streets!"

But Heidi was already gone, disappearing into the crowd. She couldn't stand to be in the same zip code as Audrina and me, let alone the same conversation.

I started massaging Audrina's shoulders—pure performance, zero feeling—telling her I was sorry she was caught in the crossfire. "Let's dance," I suggested, but my heart wasn't in it.

I never did dance with Audrina. Couldn't do it. She'd served her purpose—gotten me in the door, made Heidi notice me.

Later, I found Heidi at the bar, white-knuckling her vodka cranberry. The fact that she hadn't left felt like a miracle I didn't deserve.

"Two months, Spencer. Two months of nothing, and you show up here with her? Are you trying to humiliate me, or are you just that pathetic?"

I told her everything. How I'd only shown up to annoy her. Each word made me sound even more like exactly the kind of guy who deserved to have his number blocked. Suddenly, I saw myself through her eyes: a grown man so terrified of his own feelings that he'd orchestrated this elaborate scheme just to . . . what? Prove he didn't care? Make her jealous? Get her attention?

"Well, I figured even if you hated me forever," I said, in my closing statement, "at least it would make for good TV."

She looked so stunned, she actually started laughing. Not happy laughing—more like "I can't believe this is my life" laughing. The kind of laugh that meant she was either going to forgive me or have me thrown out. Maybe both.

"Spencer, you're insane."

"I know. Wanna hang out again?"

She studied me, shaking her head, like she was cataloging all the ways this could blow up in her face.

"Could I at least get your new number?"

She held out her hand. I gave her my phone, triumphant.

"If you ever pull any shit again, I'll change my number AND my name," she said, with steel in her voice. "Maybe my whole identity."

And I believed her. When Heidi said something, she meant it. She'd already proved she could cut me out of her life without a second thought.

Don't fuck this up again, I told myself as I saved her number. *You won't get a third chance.*

CHAPTER 8

PLAYING DOUBLES

When the Main Characters and the Sidekicks Date One Another

It was early October 2006, and Brody was single again. Nicole was too sharp, too self-possessed, too aware of her own worth . . . Basically, all the qualities that make for a healthy relationship, which was the exact opposite of what you needed to date Brody Jenner in 2006.

The timing was perfect—Heidi and I were "hanging out" again (her words, not mine, delivered in that very specific tone that translated to *Don't get any ideas, buddy*). And now that Brody was on the market again, maybe we could orchestrate something strategic. Get Brody with Lauren. See what happened.

On the surface, it seemed like simple matchmaking. But this could be perfect for both of us.

If Brody started dating Lauren Conrad, and I was with Heidi, suddenly we weren't outsiders trying to break into their world—we were the boyfriends. Essential to every storyline. The girls' drama would become our drama. Their show would become our show. And Brody and I had always been a team—from crashing USC parties to building *The Princes of Malibu* together.

I started doing reconnaissance. During one of my "casual hangouts" with Heidi, I nonchalantly steered the conversation toward Lauren's love life. "So what's the deal with Lauren and dating?" I asked Heidi as we grabbed coffee. "She seeing anyone?"

Heidi shook her head. "She's still getting over Jason. It was messy."

Jason Wahler was her on-and-off boyfriend from *Laguna Beach* who'd followed her to *The Hills*. They'd been the golden couple of Orange County reality TV, but Jason's struggles with addiction had made their relationship increasingly difficult to sustain, especially with cameras documenting every fight and breakdown. She'd finally kicked him out during a filming break, gave him seventy-two hours to collect his Abercrombie polos before she changed the locks.

Now she was casually dating Greg Carney, who had a show with Frankie Delgado called *Twentyfourseven*. But she wasn't locked into anything. And she knew exactly who Brody was: Hollywood royalty with a dating résumé that read like a CW casting sheet. Every It girl in town had a guest-starring role—including, of course, Lauren's *Laguna Beach* nemesis, Kristin Cavallari.

Seeing Kristin's name in Brody's history wasn't a red flag, it was like dangling a championship belt in front of her. If Kristin had dated him, Lauren wanted him more. The fact that Kristin got there first didn't make him off-limits—it made him the prize.

"She keeps asking about him," Heidi whispered, lowering her voice like Lauren might somehow hear us from across town. "Like, casual questions, but I can tell she's interested."

Of course she was. Brody Jenner was the ultimate trophy boyfriend. Every girl in LA wanted to be the one who could domesticate Brody Jenner, which is like wanting your cat to do your taxes. Good luck with that.

We organized a test run double date at The Grove, this outdoor mall designed to make you feel like you're in a small European town, except you're in the middle of Los Angeles and everything costs three times what it should. But whatever, it was perfect for my little social experiment. Just a casual foursome at the movies to see if sparks flew.

We picked some forgettable horror movie, and during a jump scare, Heidi grabbed my hand. It wasn't forgiveness—I could feel it in her grip. More "I'm scared" than "I love you." Still, progress is progress.

Everything felt golden as we walked out into The Grove, past the fountain where tourists threw pennies and wished to see someone famous. The October air was perfect—seventy degrees, light breeze . . .

"Hey, everyone look left," I said, all casual.

"Why?" Heidi asked.

"Just trust me."

We turned, and—FLASH. My guy from *Us Weekly*, right on cue. I'd tipped him earlier: *Brody Jenner and Lauren Conrad at The Grove. Bring the good lens.*

By now, I had a working relationship with the tabloids, thanks to the Mary-Kate photo deal and a few other strategic tips I'd fed Peter Grossman over the months. He'd started taking my calls, trusting my intel. I was becoming a reliable source for young Hollywood gossip, which meant I could orchestrate moments like this.

Lauren lit up like Times Square on New Year's Eve, convinced the photographers were there for her *Laguna Beach* fame. Shoulders back, chin down, smile practiced to look spontaneous. She had no idea this was her first staged paparazzi moment—and I was the director.

"Brody! Lauren! Are you two dating?" the photographer yelled.

Perfect. The headlines would write themselves: "BRODY AND LC'S NIGHT OUT!" The storyline was born. This wasn't just me being a chaotic little gremlin for fun—this was strategic warfare disguised as matchmaking. Once the tabloids started speculating about Brody and Lauren as a couple, *The Hills* producers would have to address it. They'd need to show their relationship developing on camera. And where Brody went, I went. We were a package deal, like Batman and Robin.

A couple nights later, Brody was photographed partying with Lauren and Heidi at Shag. This time, I hadn't orchestrated it—the machine was running itself now, which was both thrilling and terrifying. Like watching your Tamagotchi become sentient. That's when Nicole went full scorched earth on her MySpace:

"I know there are rumors regarding my 'breakup' with Brody Jenner.

The truth is, we were never really together. We hung out, and he's a nice guy, but my heart was never in it. Anything further is just a cry for publicity."
SAVAGE.

Absolutely savage.

I laughed out loud. "Touché, Nicole."

But hey—her fury fully cleared the runway for Brody and LC. Sometimes the best plans are the ones where everyone else does the dirty work for you. The four of us would be the perfect Hollywood quartet, double-dating our way through LA's hottest restaurants while MTV filmed every second.

The American dream—sponsored by Clearasil.

What could possibly go wrong?

The next weekend, the four of us were posted up in the VIP at LAX—LAX nightclub, not the airport, though the way people were departing with strangers, it might as well have been. Those were the days when we could walk into any club and own the place before we even ordered our first bottle. The hostess would see us coming and clear the best booth, the bartenders would have our drinks ready before we asked, and the DJ would throw on something we could move to.

I was watching my little social experiment unfold in real time. Lauren kept stealing glances at Brody like he was a particularly delicious dessert she was trying not to order. Meanwhile, Heidi was three vodka Red Bulls deep, that dangerous combination that made her either want to dance on tables or tell you exactly what she thought of you.

Tonight, apparently, it made her forgive me.

She kept moving closer in the booth, our legs touching, then our arms, then suddenly her hand was on my chest and she was looking at me like maybe I wasn't the worst thing that ever happened to her.

"I missed you," she said, having to yell it over the music.

"What?" I yelled back, even though I'd heard her perfectly. I just wanted to hear it again.

She rolled her eyes, grabbed my face with both hands, and kissed me. Not a cute pecking kiss for the cameras that might be lurking. A real kiss. The kind that made the whole club disappear and reminded me why I'd spent two months pining.

"Let's get out of here," Heidi said, her lips still close enough that I felt the words more than heard them.

I looked over at Brody and Lauren. Phase One of Operation Get Spencer and Brody on *The Hills* was proceeding beautifully—her laughing at something he'd said, his hand on her knee, both of them looking like the leads in a romantic comedy about beautiful people finding love in Los Angeles.

The four of us stumbled out of LAX into the October night, two couples on the brink of something new. The air outside hit sharp and cool after the swampy heat of the club. Heidi laced her fingers through mine—no hesitation, no second-guessing. Decision made.

By the time we hit Brody's condo in West Hollywood, it was automatic. No awkward "Soooo, what now?" Just Heidi tugging me straight to the guest room like we'd already rehearsed it, like the months apart had been deleted.

She turned around, that look in her eyes that meant the talking part of the night was over. Down the hall, Brody's door clicked shut. I stepped inside and locked ours.

Best plan I'd ever had.

CHAPTER 9

TWO BIRDS, ONE STONE

How I Abandoned My Own Show to Infiltrate The Hills

After the red-carpet stunt with Audrina at Area, my phone lit up like a slot machine.

"Spencer, everyone's talking about you," Sean Travis said. I felt like I could hear the excitement in his voice—the sound of a producer who'd just discovered his next ratings gold mine.

Finally, everyone understood what I could bring to the table. My talent for creating chaos. What happened at Area, that wasn't luck. That was me. A perfect storm of drama, manufactured out of equal parts instinct and calculation. And if I could do it once, I could do it again.

Sean kept pushing for me to sign a release form so *The Hills* could broadcast the footage they got that night. "Look, I'm a thousand percent down to be talent," I told him, "but I'm not signing a release until I see a real contract." I wanted numbers on the table. I wanted to get paid like real talent. After what happened with *Princes*, I wasn't about to get played again.

One night, Heidi and I were having dinner at Blowfish Sushi in Hollywood—cameras were there, because cameras were everywhere Heidi went—when Adam DiVello, creator and executive producer of *The Hills*, materialized at our table. Slick suit, eyes glittering, looking like a Vegas used-car salesman.

It was the first time we'd met, but he had this huge smile stretched wide across his face, like we were old buddies. "Spencer! Welcome to *The Hills* family."

"Almost," I said, trying to match his slick energy. "Soon as we get the paperwork figured out, I'm ready to rock."

His handshake was firm but cold, and he had this way of looking at you that made you feel like he was calculating your exact value per episode.

"Spencer Pratt," he said, tasting my name. "You know what I love about you? You get it. You understand what we're really doing here."

"Making great television?" I offered.

"Making history," he corrected. "*The Hills* isn't just a show. It's a cultural phenomenon waiting to happen."

Looking back now, if I could hop in a time machine and warn myself what I was walking into, I probably would've tried. If I'd known how DiVello played the game—how he seemed to warp every storyline to fit his vision, how it felt like he'd own my soul for four years, as though he was sculpting me into a false character so toxic that even I'd start hating Spencer Pratt—maybe I would've run screaming into traffic.

Or maybe not. Maybe it wouldn't have mattered. Because that kid was starving. For meaning. For proof I could be somebody. For evidence that the name "Spencer Pratt" meant more than good teeth and a gift for irritating strangers. Honestly, back then I needed validation so bad I would've signed away my Nana Joan. (She'd probably have handed me the pen herself.)

After that dinner, just to get things moving, Sean Travis hooked me up with his own attorney, Dan Black from the firm Greenberg Traurig. Dan went full pit bull for me. Didn't matter Sean was also his client—Dan fought like I was his one and only. To this day, Greenberg's still my law firm, although Dan hasn't returned an email since an unfortunate jungle-based incident in 2009, which I'll get into, but maybe this memoir will get me back on his Christmas card list. (Those Hermès scarves he used to send us every holiday? Heidi still misses them.)

The paperwork came back from MTV: They were offering me $15K–$20K an episode, depending on screen time, plus Dan had worked in renegotiation clauses. Meaning: If I popped, I wouldn't be stuck making peanuts while pulling in millions for MTV. (Back then, reality stars got *paid*. Today? Not so much. People do reality shows for free these days, just for the social media followers.)

Around this same time, Brody and I were inches away from closing our completely separate deal with MTV for "Banking on Brody." We'd already shot the pilot episode, which featured scenes of me following Brody around Beverly Hills while he shopped with his then-unknown stepsister Khloé Kardashian. On-screen, Brody and I had that same magical chemistry from *Princes*, except this time it was tighter, funnier, more polished. Everyone who saw it was impressed. This was it. Proof that *The Princes of Malibu* wasn't a fluke, that we knew how to deliver a hit show.

Brody, Brant, and I had a final meeting with Rod Aissa, head of MTV West Coast, to lock in our deal.

"Before we start," I announced, "I would like to talk about *The Hills*."

Brody and Brant looked at me, then each other, confused.

Rod leaned back. *The Hills* wasn't even his department—it was an East Coast production, he was West Coast. But he was listening.

"Okay, what's up?"

"As you may or may not know, Adam DiVello already wants me on the show as Heidi's love interest. But I think it could be more than that. I think Brody and I need to create some major drama on that show—me with Heidi, him with Lauren. We become the main characters. And THEN we launch 'Banking on Brody,' as a *Hills* spin-off. That way, we're not starting from zero—we've got this built-in audience of millions of people who are already obsessed with us."

"Wait, so you want to hold off on YOUR project so you can take over *The Hills*?" Rod said, confused.

Brant was pale. "Spencer, we're here to discuss YOUR SHOW, 'Banking on Brody.' Not whatever cameo you might have on *The Hills*," he said, looking like he was watching six months of work get flushed down the toilet, which he was.

Rod was leaning forward now, and I mistook his curiosity for approval.

"So let me get this straight," Rod said. "You want to infiltrate someone else's show to launch your own?"

"I prefer *cross-pollinate*," I said, still thinking I was winning. "We'll deliver the conflict *The Hills* desperately needs. The villain every story requires. We'll be the reason people will actually tune in." I was on a roll now. "Batman needs Joker. Bond needs a psychopath plotting world domination. *The Hills* needs . . ."

"A Spencer Pratt?" Rod asked.

"And a Brody Jenner," I added.

He gets it, I thought triumphantly.

"Well, I'll pass your, uh, notes to the East Coast team," Rod said, checking his watch like he had somewhere more important to be, which he definitely did. Probably the bathroom.

As we left the MTV offices, Brant looked ready to commit murder.

"We were so fucking close . . ." he muttered.

Brody looked at me. "Spencer, what was that all about?"

"Strategy?" I said weakly.

"Strategy? You just murdered our show!" Brant sighed. "And for what? To crash someone else's party?"

"And that whole thing about me dating Lauren, you know we're just friends now, right?" Brody huffed. Yeah, it was true, in the end, there was no real spark between Brody and Lauren, they'd figured that much out already. But why should that small detail matter when it came to my genius plan for reality show domination?

"Trust me," I said, clicking my car unlocked. "By next year, everyone in America will know our names. Then we'll launch 'Banking on Brody.'"

"Yeah," Brody muttered. "They'll know us as those assholes from *The Hills.*"

Here's what Brody didn't understand yet—he'd never be the asshole. He was too likable, too careful, too aware of his image to ever truly commit to villainy.

I'd be the asshole. The Dr. No, or some guy stroking a white cat. *I'd* be the guy everyone loved to hate.

Finally, a job I was qualified for.

CHAPTER 10

WELCOME TO THE PUPPET SHOW

The Science of Frankenbiting and Professional Assholery

Remember Jaws, the fish? That hangry boy barely had any screen time, but he became one of the most iconic villains in cinematic history.

How about the Wicked Witch of the West? My kind of woman. Running monkey cartels and chasing ruby slippers. Iconic.

Darth Maul. He had maybe two lines in *The Phantom Menace* and people are still losing their minds over that double-lightsaber-wielding psychopath twenty-five years later.

Oh, and let's not forget about some fava beans and a nice Chianti—Hannibal Lecter was in *Silence of the Lambs* for maybe seventeen minutes total and we're still quoting that elegant, liver-loving son of a gun.

My point is, there is one fundamental truth in show business. Everybody loves a villain.

And reality TV was about to catch on to that.

I didn't actually invent the reality TV villain (the first was a guy named Puck from *The Real World: San Francisco* back in 1994), but I was probably the first to really lean all the way in.

It started slow, my evolution from mischievous shit-stirrer to full-blown Antichrist. Viewers may remember my debut, on Episode 1 of Season 2, with Heidi and me pulling up in my shiny BMW to Don

Antonio's Mexican restaurant on Pico—my go-to spot, the same place where Brody and I had cemented our friendship all those years earlier. This was supposedly our first date—at least, if you believed what you were watching on-screen, which you shouldn't have, because 90 percent of what happened on *The Hills* was complete lies.

We slid into a red leather booth, and I started hitting my marks like a good little actor. The producers had already texted me my talking points on my BlackBerry—specific topics I was supposed to bring up in a way that seemed totally natural and spontaneous. Basically a script disguised as improv.

Sean Travis had spelled it out: *Go full Devious Spencer*. Be the chaos agent. So I slipped into character. Wasn't hard.

My first talking point was to ask Heidi if she was excited to be working the grand opening of Area nightclub tomorrow, as part of her "job" at Bolthouse Productions. And yes, I'm using air quotes because, as I've mentioned, her job was complete nonsense, just like everyone else's jobs on the show. And as you know, the Area opening had already happened weeks ago.

So we were sitting there, pretending to be excited about an event that was ancient history, acting like it was happening tomorrow. Time travel, baby. Reality TV runs on wormholes.

Another one of the story beats texted to my BlackBerry was *Plant seeds about Audrina*. Ask about her casually, like a guy trying to hide a crush. They wanted it to look like I'd been sniffing around her all summer while also playing Heidi—sure, let's build a love-triangle setup. In my head, we were just actors at this point.

So there I was, asking Heidi about Audrina with all the subtlety of a freight train. I might as well have been wearing a neon sign that read: ASKING ABOUT AUDRINA FOR PLOT PURPOSES.

After dinner, we walked up to my apartment (fake; I was living with my parents in the Palisades at the time). Heidi thanked me for the flowers I gave her at the beginning of the date (not fake). I asked her if she was planning to stay over tonight, and she said "YEAH!" in this *duh* tone that made me fall in love with her all over again, as though the idea of her sleeping anywhere other than by my side was completely ridiculous. That was not fake.

Cut to a shot of the Griffith Park Observatory and a hummingbird. My homie. The realest, least fake of all.

The next day, it was time to fully establish me as a complete piece of shit who was trying to play both Heidi and Audrina. Sean texted me to meet Audrina at Pinkberry, and my mission was simple: flirt and invite her to the Area opening as my date. Maximum drama guaranteed.

I grabbed the roses I'd given Heidi the night before. She'd left them on my passenger seat, and I had this "brilliant" idea to recycle them. Same roses, different girl. Classic player move. The producers loved it. So did I, in that moment. I was pretty good at being bad.

I showed up with the bouquet of red roses and spotted Audrina sitting there alone, checking her phone.

"Audrina!" I called out, putting on my biggest, most charming smile as I approached her table. I handed her the recycled roses like some kind of discount Romeo, and she sniffed them with the enthusiasm of someone who'd never seen a flower before.

"These are so pretty," she said, with Oscar-winning conviction.

I was down for whatever the producers wanted, but Audrina wasn't thrilled at how this storyline was going to make her look. Unlike me, she did NOT want to be a villain, working multiple angles, making everyone jealous and angry and hurt.

Meanwhile, I was full Stanislavski method. This was my *A Streetcar Named Desire* and I was Marlon Brando, tapping into my inner toxic male on national television for real money and real fame. This shit was coming to me very naturally.

Yes, I am Goldfinger.

I am Dr. No.

I am Jaws. And I will eat this show alive, with some fava beans and a nice Chianti.

CUT TO:

The opening of Area nightclub—red carpet, the whole Hollywood circus. Footage shot months ago. Inside, Lauren was hanging out with her friend Jen Bunney, checking out guys like they were shopping for accessories at Nordstrom.

"He's CUTE," said Jen, and Lauren's face lit up with interest, as they cut to—SHOCKER—Brody Jenner, establishing Lauren's attraction to him. And voilà, the fake love story has been officially launched in Episode 1 of Season 2. My best friend, Brody Jenner, was about to become a reality heartthrob.

Yay!

Of course, that whole moment was completely fake. They weren't even talking about Brody—that was spliced together from two totally different nights. If you go back and watch it, which I did for a series of TikTok breakdowns, you can literally see that when they're supposedly talking about "this guy" and they cut to Brody, he's wearing a completely different outfit than the one he actually wore to the Area opening.

Confused yet? Good. That means you're starting to understand how this insane machine actually works. How the editors were constantly doing origami with time, making cause come after effect, aka Frankenbiting—the art of splicing together random fragments of reality to create completely fake storylines. *The Hills* was notorious for Frankenbiting. And we cast members had very little say in how they'd take our words and our images and use them to create these totally fabricated narratives. No consultation, no approval. Just pure manipulation disguised as reality TV, where chronology was a suggestion and the "truth" was whatever fit the storyline.

CUT TO:

Heidi holding her clipboard, helping out with the door—real footage from the Area opening in October. There she is, looking like the perfect professional until—moment of truth—EVIL SPENCER walks onto the red carpet with AUDRINA on his arm like she's his date.

SHOCKER.

SPENCER SUCKS!

Of course, when all this aired, the viewers had no idea that all of that footage at Area was shot months before any of my other scenes.

CUT TO:

Audrina at work the next day saying I'm a douchebag and she wants to friend-zone me.

CUT TO:

Heidi leaving work early because she feels dizzy and nauseous. When she gets home, she pulls a pregnancy test out of her purse to the saddest, most heartbreaking music in the editing bay.

OH NO, IS SHE PREGNANT BY THAT AWFUL SPENCER? TUNE IN NEXT WEEK TO FIND OUT!!!

And they did. Because that right there, my friends, is great TV.

By the end of the episode, I wasn't just the villain. I was the villain *and* the punch line. The guy recycling roses. The guy two-timing his girl. The guy who might've even gotten her pregnant—which was icky territory. Some forty-year-old producer pulling twenty-one-year-old Heidi aside, telling her she needed to pretend she might be pregnant?

The problem was, Heidi and I were young and dumb, and we didn't have anyone looking out for us. No manager reviewing storylines, no publicist saying, "This might damage my client's reputation." Lauren had a whole team protecting her image, making sure she always came off as some kind of Millennial Mary Tyler Moore. Us? We were on our own, too naive to realize we were just raw meat for the grinder.

True story: I never actually watched any episodes of *The Hills* until years later when I started making those TikToks about the show—*The Hills Spills*—where I'd watch episodes for the first time and break down all the Frankenbiting and behind-the-scenes manipulation for my followers. Heidi shut that down after a few episodes, annoyed I was even talking about these people who ruined our lives. So I've never actually watched past Season 3 of my own show. Most of what I know about what an asshole I apparently am comes from other people telling me about it—which is honestly easier than subjecting myself to the psychological torture of watching my own character assassination.

I did have the misfortune of watching one particularly cringe instance of Frankenbiting from early on in Season 2, where Brody and I roll up to Les Deux, our hangout spot. The cameras were already set up in Brody's car, filming our conversation as we pulled into the parking lot. I knew the paparazzi would be camped out by the back entrance, where all the actual celebrities went in and out. The back entrance was where the action was, so naturally, that's exactly where I wanted to be.

"Dude, let's go through the back door," I told Brody, meaning let's use the rear entrance where all the celebrities and paparazzi were.

Pretty straightforward, right?

Except when the episode aired, they'd dubbed the words onto a moment where I was talking about Heidi, and the stitched line made it sound like I was talking about banging Heidi in the back door. Which, for the record, is exactly the kind of crude thing I would never, ever say while cameras were rolling. I may be an asshole, but I'm not an idiot. But this was classic *Hills* manipulation—taking my actual words and turning me into a complete tool for entertainment value.

When I finally saw that scene, I was like: *DAMN, they really did me dirty.* You think you're in on it with the producers, that you're aware of what's happening.

Not at all.

By the way—if the camera's not directly on someone's mouth when they're talking? Red flag. That's Frankenbiting 101. They can make you say anything when they control the edit. For instance, in that same episode, there was this phone call that looked like I was talking to Audrina about our supposed relationship drama. Plot twist: I was actually on the phone with Heidi, having a completely different conversation on a completely different day about God knows what. Probably asking what she wanted for dinner.

Every week, I'd drive to this windowless building on Cloverfield

Boulevard for ADR sessions, aka automated dialogue replacement. What it really meant was: "We're going to completely rewrite what happened, and you're going to help us do it."

The sound booth was tiny. Four feet by four feet of soundproofed hell where I'd spend hours building the weapons they'd use to destroy me. A screen would show rough cuts of episodes. But half the time, we weren't even matching our mouth movements. We were recording "wild lines"—random phrases with no context, no scene attached. Just words floating in space, waiting to be weaponized.

"Say 'I can't believe she did that,'" the producer, usually Sean, would instruct through the headphones. "Now angrier. Now hurt. Now sarcastic."

Take after take after take. My throat would be raw by the end, voice hoarse from performing seventeen variations of disappointment, rage, dismissal. They were building a library of ammunition—every possible inflection of asshole they might need for their editing bay.

The booth was where I learned what we cast members really were to them: not people, but raw material. Clay. Mouths making sounds they could rearrange into whatever story they wanted to tell. Look at the credits of any episode and you'll see an army of story writers, hired to create this fictional "real world." We'd watch rough cuts where conversations happened that never occurred, where reactions from Tuesday got spliced into Thursday's drama. *The Hills* wasn't documenting our lives—it was creating new ones out of spare parts.

And that season, I was their favorite monster to build.

Viewers still want to believe it was all real—even though, if you go back and watch the episodes, it's so obviously not. But the networks were shameless about the pretense, and I guess we were so good at playing along that even now people discuss entirely fake storylines on message boards, debating if they were real or not.

By the end of Season 2, *The Hills* had found its formula. Lauren and Brody's storyline was straight out of a teen romance novel—safe, sweet, boring as hell. She'd gaze at him over dinner, and he'd deliver lines such as "You have a very nice smile" as though he was reading off the Olive Garden menu.

It was painful to watch because we all knew the truth. That first night at Brody's condo, there was zero chemistry. Nada. Lauren was playing along, too. They were both just acting. Telling the story MTV wanted to sell, after we'd sold it to them in the first place. Good-girl Lauren deserved love after bad-boy Jason. Enter reformed player Brody, ready to be tamed by the right woman. Slap some Death Cab for Cutie over two people chewing salad in silence, add some soft lighting, and suddenly you've got a love story, even though it was giving mannequin-on-mannequin CPR.

Meanwhile, I was getting the Darth Vader edit. By midseason, I wasn't just a villain. I was the toxic male moms would warn their daughters about. Moms . . . and Phoebe from *Friends*.

True story: One weekend, we were at a barbecue at Ron Meyer's place in Malibu. Ron being the chairman of Universal and cofounder of CAA, one of the biggest talent agencies in the country, aka Hollywood royalty. I'm standing there with a drink in my hand when Lisa Kudrow walks up to Heidi like she's staging an intervention.

I was standing right there. Then she said it, loud enough for people nearby to hear: "He has the eyes of a serial killer. You need to get away from him."

I wanted to laugh. I also wanted to scream. Mostly I wanted to hand her a DVD of raw footage and say, "It's called *editing*, Lisa." But how do you explain Frankenbiting to someone who just binge-watched you emotionally waterboarding your girlfriend on MTV? If it looks like you, sounds like you, and has your name in the credits—congrats, it's you. You're the villain now.

Watching America's quirky sweetheart Lisa Kudrow warn people about me like I was radioactive, something clicked. This wasn't just a job anymore. I wasn't playing Spencer Pratt™ for the cameras and then going home to be regular Spencer. The character had eaten the person—or at least that's what it felt like, because off camera, people treated me like I was that guy all the time.

But it didn't matter, because they couldn't stop watching. Every fight pulled bigger numbers. Every asshole move got more headlines. Every public blowup sent the viewership soaring. MTV didn't care that they were turning me into a monster, because monsters sell advertising space. Monsters keep people tuning in week after week, desperate to see what horrible thing Spencer and his serial killer eyes would do next.

CHAPTER 11

OPERATION UPSTAGE AND OTHER DARK ARTS

How MTV Turned Us into Monsters, One Edit at a Time

Lauren Conrad seemed unhappy. About a lot of things. Which was unfortunate, because on paper, everything was going swimmingly.

The Hills was exploding. We'd developed a cult following that was growing more obsessed with every episode. As a team, we, the cast, should have been popping champagne, counting dollar bills, and laughing all the way to syndication.

But what I think was upsetting LC was that people weren't tuning in just for her anymore. It wasn't "Lauren's love life this, Lauren's heartbreak that." It was: "Is Spencer actually Satan?" "Is Heidi brainwashed?" We were the plot twist, the chaos engine. Suddenly, the Spencer & Heidi Show was the main storyline, and it seemed increasingly obvious to me that Lauren felt uncomfortable with that. Because what's one thing Lauren Conrad doesn't do, apparently? A supporting role.

She didn't *fully* hate us yet, I think—that masterpiece was still in development. But the days of LC fangirling over me like I was Heidi's personal Jesus in summer '06? Yeah, those days were over.

Meanwhile, Heidi and I were still in beta-testing mode as a couple. Even after Season 2 started airing in January '07, she was technically still seeing other people—because we hadn't had "the talk" yet, she didn't totally trust me, and also . . . she was twenty, hot, and on TV. Of course she was keeping her roster warm.

Then I found out she'd hooked up with the twenty-seven-year-old USC freshman surfer I was trying to build a show around back in college. Of ALL the adult frat bros in LA, she had to pick MY one? Maybe it was just bad luck—LA's surprisingly small when you're all orbiting the same scene. Still. Legendary move, Heidi. Honestly, respect.

According to Heidi, things got a little messy. She remembers me having some kind of confrontation with the guy, possibly involving raised voices and wounded pride. But honestly? I've completely blocked that part out.

Bottom line, I was hurt. And I decided that meant I could "get even" by sometimes flirting on camera, because hey, that was my *job*. Eye for an eye, storyline for storyline. The truth? I was just terrified. I already knew that she was it. That she was *the one*. And knowing that scared the hell out of me, so amid the acting, I acted out.

Lauren weaponized all my on-camera missteps as proof that I was a bad guy through and through, when she knew as well as anyone that, in the end, I was just playing the role. She'd comfort Heidi after I'd mess up, cameras rolling. She got to be the good friend warning Heidi about her toxic boyfriend while simultaneously benefiting from that toxicity in the form of higher ratings and more money.

Then things escalated. It all climaxed with the infamous "He's a sucky person" scene—where she calls me exactly that because I'd encouraged Brody to hook up with her friend Jen Bunney. Never mind that, as we all know now, she and Brody were just faking their whole romance anyway—it wasn't even a real thing.

That clip is still getting millions of views on YouTube to this day. There are people in this world who know me as nothing more than "Sucky Spencer" because of that thirty-second moment. Thanks, reality TV.

February 14, 2007. Heidi and I had made plans for our first Valentine's together. Candles, roses, the whole fairy tale. But then Lauren created this codependent hostage situation where she "needed"

Heidi that night. She wouldn't let Heidi leave, basically kidnapped my girlfriend until the sun came up, while I spent Valentine's night alone, watching roses die in real time while checking my phone every five minutes, some stupid teddy bear holding a heart that said *Be Mine* mocking me.

When Heidi finally came to my house, around 4 a.m., I didn't know whether to be relieved or furious.

"How was the emergency?" I asked, and it came out colder than I intended, but I was fighting not to explode. Part of me just wanted to go to bed and pretend this night never happened.

"Lauren needed me," Heidi said quietly. "She wanted breakfast pizza."

Breakfast. Pizza. I'd spent Valentine's night alone so Lauren could have late-night carbs and an audience for her drama.

Something clicked. This wasn't about friendship anymore—it was about control.

The truth of it hung between us. Heidi had to choose—remain Lauren's emotional support human or live her own life. So at dawn on February 15, I finally said:

"Heidi, Lauren obviously thinks she should be the most important person in your life. Is that true? Because if so, I'll give you two some space." My voice cracked a little on the word *true* because I was terrified of her answer. What if she said yes? What if I'd just handed her the perfect excuse to end things? But I couldn't keep living in this triangle where I was always the third wheel in my own relationship.

"*Space?* No way, Spencer!" Heidi said immediately. "Don't EVER say that again!"

That night, Heidi and I made the call: No more games, no more "seeing other people," no more letting outsiders script our relationship. A few days later, she packed up her things from the apartment she'd shared with Lauren and hauled them into my parents' house in the Palisades. (Later, MTV staged the whole thing with a U-Haul and a teary goodbye scene.)

By choosing me, Heidi knew exactly what she was risking. Her friendship with Lauren was already hanging by a thread, and her future on the show wasn't guaranteed. She told me she hoped she could patch things up with LC, but she'd already made her peace with losing both the friendship and the show if that's what it came to. What she couldn't live with was someone standing in the way of her happiness. Our happiness.

I'd known Heidi for months before realizing she could actually *sing*. Like not "karaoke after three tequila shots" sing. Real voice, real training, real ambition.

By the time she moved in with me in February '07, she finally played me her demos—tracks she'd recorded in random LA studios—and I was shook. She already had a manager, a plan, the whole blueprint. *The Hills*? That was just the side quest. The real mission was music. Reality TV was supposed to be her launchpad, not her legacy.

Which made me fall even harder, obviously.

But when I heard her demos, something about them sounded . . . off. These songs didn't seem to reflect Heidi's authentic energy. Heidi's style was fun and sexy. This sounded like she was trying to be Ashlee Simpson on Warped Tour. "My manager says this kind of music is my best chance," Heidi said. "He thinks I should be edgy. Alternative."

Edgy? Alternative? I was trying to picture Heidi in a Hot Topic tee, eyeliner running, moshing with dudes named Travis. Nope. Did not compute.

That's when I threw out an idea: "Would you like to meet David Foster? At least just see what he thinks. He'll tell you straight up if he thinks this punk thing works."

I drove us out to Malibu to David Foster's new studio. He led Heidi to his piano, where hit after hit had been born. Heidi sat on that bench as Foster's fingers moved across the keys, finding different notes, different ranges.

"Sing this," he'd say, playing a note.

He was mapping her voice like a scientist, finding every corner of her range, every sweet spot. She nailed it, out the gate. Instant pop queen. All her nerves had disappeared. This was Heidi, raw and real, keeping up with David Foster, and it was glorious to behold.

Finally, David stopped playing and looked at her. "Well, Heidi," he said. "You've got the tone to make you a pop star. I'll set this thing up." Heidi's eyes went wide. This wasn't just lip service—he was already making calls, connecting her with Kara DioGuardi, one of the biggest pop songwriters in the game. The woman who'd written hits for Christina Aguilera, Pink, Gwen Stefani, and who would later became a judge on *American Idol*. This was real. This was happening.

I remember feeling this urgency to help Heidi with her music that I couldn't quite explain at the time. It wasn't just because she was talented—though she was, more than anyone gave her credit for. I think it was that we could both feel something shifting in the air when it came to *The Hills*. Like we needed a backup plan for Heidi, something that was all hers, untethered to Lauren.

By this point, I had begun to feel genuinely uncomfortable with some of the fake storylines the producers were force-feeding me on *The Hills*. There was this whole manufactured drama where I'm supposedly pressuring Heidi to move in with me, when SHE WAS ALREADY LIVING WITH ME AT MY PARENTS' HOUSE. It was SO DUMB. (Also: What kind of player wants to force someone to live with him? That's literally the opposite of player behavior—that's clingy boyfriend territory.)

The whole storyline resulted in one infamous scene—the "Get out of my car" scene—that still haunts me to this day. We filmed it in the alley behind Heidi's "work," the Bolthouse Productions building in Hollywood. Sean Travis had pulled me aside before we started, all serious, like we were filming *The Godfather* instead of a fake fight on a fake show. "We need Spencer at his absolute worst here. Show us that cold, controlling side."

"Jeez, okay," I said, annoyed. There's a difference between being a fun player and being provoked and then edited into some psycho who'd emotionally torture the girl he loves. Sean must have seen the hesitation on my face, a flicker of humanity. So he wheeled out the big guns.

"Want me to get Adam on the phone?" he said. "If you're not comfortable..."

"Sure."

I hadn't seen or spoken to Adam DiVello since we'd met at Blowfish. I didn't realize he was the shadow king they'd wheel in to Jedi mind trick you into doing things you were uncomfortable with, or at least that's how it feels to me in hindsight. The guy seemed to have this supernatural ability to manipulate us into doing exactly what would deliver maximum carnage. It felt like he saw us as chess pieces, not actual humans with feelings or futures beyond his storylines.

First, he'd remind you about the money. How, if the ratings hit certain targets, you'd get a MASSIVE bonus. Your dignity gets real flexible when there's that much cash on the table. He dangled other promises in front of us. He told me that they were going to get Lauren a beautiful house in the Hollywood Hills, and that they'd get Heidi and me a place in the hills, too, if we played ball. (In the end, they stuck Heidi and me in a basic apartment in the flats on Curson Avenue.) They'd use bribery to get us to do what they wanted, then bait and switch us at the last minute, once we'd agreed to do whatever.

"Okay," I said. "Just tell me what to do."

In this case: twelve takes of "emotionally abusive boyfriend."

Here's how that scene unfolded:

Spencer's BMW sits in an alleyway.

Heidi slides into the passenger seat, looking nervous because she knows what's coming.

She's about to explain to me, her controlling psycho boyfriend, for the millionth time, why she's not ready to move in with me.

First take: I'm acting disappointed, maybe a little cold. Heidi delivers her line about not being ready. I sigh dramatically, look away like I'm hurt.

"Cut! Let's go again. Spencer, I need more. You're not just disappointed—you're angry. She's rejecting your entire future together."

This was the producers' method—directing by attrition. They'd make you do the scene over and over and over again until you were so mentally exhausted that real emotion and frustration would finally break through. That's how they mined their gold.

Second take: I raise my voice, let some genuine frustration creep in. Getting warmer, apparently.

And again. And again.

Take six, and I could feel myself starting to split in two. There was Spencer playing "Spencer Pratt," and then there was me, watching from somewhere deep inside.

"Let's go again. More anger, Spencer. She's REJECTING you."

Take nine. My voice was getting harder, meaner.

Take ten. I caught myself actually feeling angry. Not fake angry. Real angry. At this stupid show for making me feel like shit about something that wasn't even real.

"Again! This is the final straw, Spencer!"

By take twelve, I'm genuinely furious. Not at Heidi—never at Heidi—but at the situation, at these manipulative producers, at myself for being stupid enough to sign up for this psychological experiment.

"My answer is no," Heidi said.

"Sweet. My answer is get out of my car."

When I said "Get out of my car," for just a moment, I wasn't acting. I was him. The asshole they'd been coaching out of me.

Bingo.

That's what they used. Of course that's what they used. This perfect little grenade of dismissive cruelty that would follow me for the rest of my life.

Heidi got out of the car, looking genuinely hurt even though she knew it was all performance. I drove away as instructed. Then I came back and the producers were like, "Can you drive away angrier? We have cameras down the street and around the corner. Drive fast, drive angry. Can you make the tires peel out?"

"What is this, *The Fast and the Furious*?" I snapped. "I don't know how to do that!"

But I did it anyway. Slammed it into gear, peeled out like I was auditioning for some kind of domestic violence PSA. The cameras devoured every second of it.

In real life, I would never have driven away from Heidi like that. In real life, we would have talked it out. In real life, we were planning to go to sushi after this nightmare wrapped, and then back to my parents' place in the Palisades.

But this wasn't real life. This was *The Hills*.

The "Get out of my car" clip has been seen and dissected by millions. The comments are exactly what you'd expect. "Abusive." "Narcissist." "Heidi should run." They're talking about a person who doesn't exist anymore—who never existed, in fact—but try explaining that to the internet.

If I could go back to that alley, I'd tell myself to run. Drive away from the cameras, not from Heidi. Choose kindness over ratings. Choose being a good man over being good TV. But I can't go back. None of us can. We're all forever frozen in MTV amber, playing out our parts on streaming services for new generations to judge. They say everyone gets fifteen minutes of fame. Nobody tells you that you'll spend the rest of your life paying for it.

Still, it was thanks to moments like "Get out of my car" that more people began tuning in, in droves. They weren't there for Lauren's fake PG romance with Brody or her fashion internship anymore. They were there for the Speidi train wreck.

Behind the scenes, production staff were calling it "Operation Upstage"—Spencer and Heidi hijacking the star's own show right out from under her. And this isn't my ego talking—the executive vice president of MTV, Tony DiSanto, personally told me that if the Speidi drama hadn't happened, *The Hills* would have been canceled.

By this point, Lauren just wanted us, this two-headed Speidi monster, off her damn territory. She knew what she was doing. She'd been playing this showbiz game at a high level far longer than me. She was no rookie—she was the handpicked recruit MTV had plucked from the *Laguna* franchise to anchor *The Hills*. That's why, to this day, I call her Keyser Söze. She's a sicario—strategic, deadly, and laser-focused on eliminating all threats to her dominion.

And make no mistake: In her eyes, Speidi was public enemy number one. She wanted us gone. Unfortunately for her, we were just getting started.

CHAPTER 12

I KNOW WHAT I DID

The Sex Tape Scandal That Ruined Us

Early April 2007, right when we'd started rolling on Season 3, I walked into my parents' house and heard Heidi's voice floating down from upstairs—urgent, almost frantic.

I wasn't trying to eavesdrop. At least, that's what I told myself as I walked up the stairs and listened to her speaking, rather loudly, in my bathroom.

"Wait, what? He said he has *what*?" Heidi's voice was sharp with disbelief. "Lauren, that's insane. Is he serious?"

A pause.

"Okay, okay, calm down. Listen to me—I'll handle this. I'll go over there. I'll literally break into his place and get the tape back if I have to. Jason's not gonna do this to you."

I listened some more. It seemed like Jason Wahler was apparently threatening Lauren with a sex tape. Whether the tape actually existed or not, I had no idea—but the threat itself was real enough that Lauren was calling Heidi in a panic about it.

Heidi emerged from the bathroom, her face flushed, eyes darting. "Everything okay, honey?" I asked, like I hadn't just overheard everything.

She waved me off, avoiding my eyes.

"I don't wanna talk about it, okay?"

Then she went off somewhere and left me with my thoughts. Always a bad idea.

They have a habit of building on one another, of circling and expanding like a galaxy. It's like *The Matrix* in there, remember? Epiphanies and apocalyptic visions. Sacred symbols and master plans. Neurons firing like it's the Fourth of July.

Pew! Pew! Pew!

Valentine's Day flashed through my mind—Lauren's "emergency" that kept Heidi out until 4 a.m. while I sat alone with dying roses. All those guilt trips whenever Heidi chose to spend time with me instead of being Lauren's emotional support animal. The way Lauren had completely frozen Heidi out after she'd moved in with me, seemingly punishing her for choosing her own happiness.

And then, there it was. A beautiful idea. Unbelievably clever. A stroke of genius, even.

I'M LEAKING THIS.

I grabbed my phone and began writing a text to Perez Hilton.

Perez, for those of you too young or too decent to remember, was Hollywood's most outrageously toxic gossip blogger at the time. Kingmaker and career killer all rolled into one, armed with a laptop and zero fucks given, working out of his local Coffee Bean. Like everyone else from that era, he's since seen the error of his ways, how our collective savagery needed to shift toward something more humane. But back then, he was at the absolute height of his evil ways, as was I. We were a match made in heaven. He needed insider information about *The Hills* and I needed allies in the media. I fed him stories, he fed the public. Everyone on the show knew about our alliance.

Me: Have you heard the rumor that Jason Wahler is trying to sell a tape of LC?
Perez: Bitch WHAT???!!!?!?!?!
Me: YUP.

Perez: how do u kno??
Me: heard some whispers . . . havent seen it (eww) but unnamed sources may have overheard her and Heidi talking about it, and what they're going to do to get it back.
Perez: TELL ME EVERYTHING!??
Me: CALL ME ;-)
Perez: Gimme five

I leaned back, satisfied. A little scandal never hurt anyone, as Nana Joan always said.

"Hey, babe!" Heidi said, walking into the room, her hair in a towel.

"Uh, hi!" I said, guiltily, as Perez's name flashed on my screen.

Heidi noticed the look on my face.

"Aren't you gonna answer that?"

"Yeah!"

"What is it, Spencer?"

"Nothing, I just think you look VERY EXTRA SPECIALLY beautiful. Okay, gotta take this call."

I rushed out of the room and told Perez what I knew. Perez said he'd have to get further confirmation before he ran anything, and that he'd be reaching out to Lauren and Jason directly to ask them if what he'd heard was true. Oh boy. The shit was about to hit the fan.

After I got off the phone with Perez, it crossed my mind that I should probably tell Heidi what I'd just done. At some point. I'd just have to find the right moment. But now wasn't the time. Heidi was going in for her first plastic surgery the next day—a nose job and breast augmentation, performed by Dr. Frank Ryan in Beverly Hills. I didn't want to stress her out with this drama.

Yeah, it could wait until after, right?

RIGHT?

• • •

Perez's post about the alleged sex tape dropped on April 5.

That same morning, Heidi had gone in for her breast augmentation surgery. She was nervous but excited—this was something she'd wanted for a long time, a decision she'd made for herself. The procedure went smoothly. When she woke up in recovery, still groggy from anesthesia, still in pain, the first thing she did was reach for her phone.

Thirty-seven text messages. Missed calls. Voicemails.

"Spencer." Her voice was weak, confused. "What's happening?"

I showed her Perez's post. Watched her face crumple as she read it.

"This is a nightmare," she whispered.

Within hours, the entire cast knew. Our whole friend group was gossiping, speculating, trying to figure out who had leaked the rumor to Perez. Fingers pointed immediately at me. And by extension, at Heidi.

Never mind that Heidi had been literally unconscious on an operating table when the story broke.

Never mind that she'd been the one person trying to *protect* Lauren.

None of that mattered.

The verdict came down fast: We were guilty.

Word traveled back to us through producers, through mutual friends, through the panicked phone tree that was our social circle. Lauren had issued her ultimatum: Lauren goes or Speidi goes. She would never film with us again. Her friendship with Heidi was over. Done. Permanent. She would never speak to either of us again.

Heidi was lying in bed recovering from surgery, and her best friend had just executed their friendship.

"I don't understand," she kept saying over and over. "I was the only one trying to protect her. How is this my fault?"

Heidi had been Lauren's loyal friend—the person Lauren turned to when things got scary and real. Heidi knew what Lauren was actually dealing with, and she'd stood by Lauren through all of it. And now Lauren was blaming *her*.

I'd watched Lauren treat Heidi dismissively for months. Like Heidi was an accessory she'd outgrown, a friend who'd become inconvenient now that she was dating me. Their friendship had been dying a slow death, and Heidi had felt it. So when Lauren reached out about the rumored tape situation, Heidi saw it as an olive branch—maybe even an apology without words. Lauren needed her again. Maybe she was finally realizing Heidi was the only real friend she had.

"I didn't do anything wrong," Heidi said, and I could hear the desperation in her voice—the need to be heard, to be believed. "I was being a great friend. And somehow I'm the one everyone hates."

"Heidi, honey . . ." I said, as she gazed at her phone. "I need to tell you something."

My throat felt tight. *Just say it. Just fucking say it.*

"I told Perez. About the . . . you know."

The silence that followed was suffocating. I couldn't bear to look at her. Waited for her to explode. To tell me she never wanted to see me again.

"Spencer." The way she said my name made my stomach drop. Not angry—worse. Disappointed.

"I'm so sorry, Heidi. I wasn't thinking—"

"You never think." She cut me off, but her voice wasn't sharp. It was exhausted. "You never think past the moment you're in."

"I know."

"She thinks *I* did it." Her voice cracked. "She thinks I'm the one who—"

She pressed her fingers to her temples, and I realized she was trying not to cry.

"We can fix this," I said, desperate. "Just tell her the truth."

"I will," she said, pulling out her phone to text Lauren.

After sending the message, she paused, waiting for Lauren's reply.

"You think she'll ever believe *you* told Perez, and I had no idea? No chance."

Ah. She was right. Of course she was right.

"Heidi—"

"It's okay," she said.

"I love you," I said, because I didn't know what else to say.

She didn't respond. Just kept staring at her phone, watching her old life disappear.

As I was writing this book, I reached out to Perez. Time can play tricks on your memory, and honestly, some of the facts still feel fuzzy, probably due to some form of PTSD. So I wanted confirmation of what had really happened.

> **Me:** Hey! Just need confirmation of one thing: It was you that broke the LC sex tape rumor, based on me letting you know, yeah?

Here's what he wrote back.

> **Perez:** I would never reveal my sources
> **Me:** Haha
> **Perez:** but if you're willing to put this out there
> Yes
> BUT . . .
> I also spoke to some other folks on The Hills
> not JUST you
> Several cast members said they believed the rumor to be true
> Told me
> So I ran with it

I didn't know until then that I wasn't Perez's only source. Turns out, I was just the first in line.

Lauren's immediate response was to deny, deny, deny in the media:

THERE WAS NO SEX TAPE. This was clearly just a vicious rumor, a terrible lie.

"Jason and I would like to make it clear that we did not make a tape with us having sex," she wrote on her website. "Jason and I are both shocked and hurt that people would say such horrible things about us. I can't believe that somebody would go to such great lengths to try to damage my reputation."

TMZ picked up the story on April 6:

IS THERE AN LC SEX TAPE?

"Lauren Conrad is denying she made a sex tape with one of her co-stars, but sources are telling TMZ a different tale. A rep for SugarDVD.com tells TMZ that they were approached by a third party claiming to have the tape—allegedly featuring Conrad with her *Laguna Beach* and *The Hills* co-star Jason Wahler."

According to the article, the porn company immediately offered $500,000 for it—sight unseen, no questions asked. They then called Jason's manager directly with the same half-million-dollar offer. When TMZ pressed Jason's manager about whether the tape actually existed, he wouldn't confirm or deny anything.

Vivid Entertainment—the company that had just released Kim Kardashian's sex tape and was basically the gold standard for celebrity porn at the time—told TMZ they hadn't been approached yet but would "certainly consider making an offer" if someone came to them.

Lauren continued to deny, insisting that no such tape existed.

"Honestly, they videotape my life five days out of the week," she told reporters. "I don't need additional footage, you know?"

She stuck to her guns: No tape. Move on. Her entire brand was built on being the good girl who made smart choices. She was the relatable everywoman whom teenage girls looked up to—not the kind of person who made sex tapes with her messy ex-boyfriend.

A few months passed, and shooting for *The Hills* resumed in August. The producers told us that they had set Heidi and me up for a showdown with Lauren at Les Deux nightclub, for Frankie Delgado's birthday. They told us to show up around 10 p.m., that Lauren and her crew would already be there.

To us it was a win, because we knew we'd get paid for the scene, and we had nothing left to lose in terms of the relationship. We were just doing our job. We knew Lauren still hated us, we just didn't realize quite how hell-bent she was on pinning the blame for everything on us.

In the club, Lauren sat holding court at a corner table. Whitney sat to her right, tall and willowy, acting as Lauren's Greek chorus, as usual. Always there with the supportive nod, the wide-eyed gasp, the "Oh my god, *totally*." Audrina was wedged in there, too, playing the role that used to belong to Heidi. She was the new best friend, the new roomie, the new person paid to orbit Lauren's drama.

I could feel Lauren's eyes on us before we even made it halfway across the room.

"I wrote you something," Heidi said, pulling a letter from her purse and handing it to Lauren. "I just want you to read it." The letter was fake, something the producers had cooked up, a supposed peace offering from Heidi to Lauren, asking if they could patch things up and be friends again. Of course, we all knew there was no chance in hell of that ever happening. But we were all playing our roles, as usual.

Lauren took the letter, her expression shifting from neutral to disgusted. She looked up at Heidi with these cold, hurt eyes—the kind that made viewers at home grab their wine and lean in toward their screens.

Heidi turned to me. "I don't know why Lauren's being so weird," she said. Heidi still didn't understand why Lauren would place the blame entirely on her. She had told Lauren in texts that she didn't do it, that I had been the one to leak the story.

"What should I do?" Heidi asked, turning to me.

"Uh, roll up on her. Just be like, *What's your problem?*" I offered.

I watched Heidi squaring her shoulders like she was preparing for battle. She walked toward Lauren, who was standing with Audrina, and for a second I felt this stupid surge of pride. My girl, handling her business.

Lauren refused to even look at her at first. Heidi stated her case, trying to understand why Lauren seemed so mad.

And then Lauren *exploded*.

"YOU KNOW WHAT YOU DID!"

The words ripped through the air.

"You guys are SICK people! You started a sick little rumor about me!"

Oh dang.

I knew how this would look on-screen. Heidi being blamed for starting the rumor. What I didn't know was how it would play out, how it would affect our entire future. The years of hatred, the way it would poison everything. No. If I'd known that, I never would have messaged Perez. I would have thrown my damn phone in the ocean.

Not long after, *Us Weekly* ran a piece quoting an unnamed source who said, "Spencer has no friends in Hollywood. Nobody wants him around." I had no proof of who said it, but at the time I instantly assumed it was Lauren, attacking my status in the only city I'd ever called home.

You've been in LA for, what, five minutes? I thought. *And now you want to act like you run the place? You're from Laguna Beach, Lauren. That's not even Los Angeles. That's Orange County.*

Ten seconds later, I was at my computer uploading to Spencer Pratt.com, my brand-new website, running on some now-prehistoric blog platform where you could just type your own posts and hit publish. Revolutionary stuff in 2007. I had no publicist to talk me down. No filter to save me from myself. Just pure, undiluted Spencer Pratt venom, about to be shot directly into the internet. Tupac's "Hit 'Em Up" blasted through my speakers as I typed "You want beef?" in the header. Straight for the jugular.

"For all you Haters . . . if you hate me because you think I ruined Lauren and Heidi's friendship . . . you have your facts all wrong! Lauren ruined Heidi and Lauren's friendship when she told Heidi that she could not be friends with her as long as she dated me . . . when those cameras turn off LC is a completely different person . . . she goes back to being the spoiled brat that made her famous on *Laguna Beach*."

I assumed maybe five people would read this. Lauren, her publicist, a few of our extended friend group. After all, this blog was brand new, and I didn't have one single follower. And I felt *good* about what I'd written. Righteous, even. Like I was some kind of warrior defending Heidi's honor. This was a warning shot. When they go low, we head for the basement. It felt like justice, at the time. Now that I'm in my forties, I think I've learned to tame the beast. But back then? When my final boss opponent was Lauren Conrad? Please. Nothing less than unapologetically toxic would do.

My blog post had been up for maybe thirty minutes when my phone rang. It was Liz Gateley, vice president of MTV, her voice tight with panic:

"You have to take that blog down. NOW."

"Wait, you saw it? How did you see it?"

"Someone reposted it, and our PR team picked up on it."

Oh. Shit.

"Spencer, I'm not asking. Take it down."

I thought about it.

"Nah," I said. Refused. Flat out, no discussion. Not when I could hear Heidi crying in the bedroom. But sticking to my guns on the blog post unleashed a whole world of new consequences.

We'd had a press tour set up to promote Season 3—radio interviews, magazine photo shoots, the whole promotional circus. Then Adam DiVello called, saying the blog post was overshadowing the entire premiere narrative, and we were being kicked off the press tour. Strangely, Adam seemed almost cheerful about it. And that's when I realized: Producers and networks don't get mad about drama. They get rich off it.

The next sign that this really wasn't looking good for us was when MTV uninvited us to the Season 3 premiere party, per Lauren's request. They threw us a bone by letting us walk the red carpet, but the second we got inside, we were treated like we had leprosy. People scattered. I half expected someone to start yelling *"Unclean!"*

"Right this way," a production assistant said, leading us away from the main party, like we were being quarantined. They stuck us in this pathetic side room—fluorescent lights, folding chairs, the kind of place where they usually store extra camera equipment.

"Are you kidding me?" I asked the PA. "You flew us all the way to New York for this?"

"I'm just following orders," she whispered, not making eye contact. "Security will be right outside, so don't do anything that will make them get involved."

"Security?" Heidi's voice cracked. "For what?"

They'd brought in extra security. EXTRA SECURITY! For a reality TV premiere party! Like I was going to flip tables and start throwing haymakers. Guys in black shirts positioned around our quarantine room, talking into their earpieces like they were protecting the president instead of protecting LC from having to look us in the eye. What a joke. The only thing I was a threat to was the open bar.

Then, twenty minutes later, another PA appeared. "Lauren's here. We're going to need you guys to exit through the back."

"You're kicking us out of our own premiere?" Heidi asked, her voice small and broken.

"Yes. I'm sorry."

TMZ had the story up within nanoseconds:

"It's her party and she'll ban Spencer and Heidi if she wants to!"

The gossip cycle was feeding on itself now, each story generating three more stories, the scandal expanding like a virus through the entertainment ecosystem.

August 13, the first episode of Season 3—"You Know What You Did"—aired. Three-point-six million viewers tuned in, already primed by the sex tape tabloid headlines that had preceded the premiere for months. It was a ratings record for *The Hills* that would stand for years. Bonus checks all around! MTV would call it their biggest success of the season. We should have been basking in the glow of being television gold. Instead, we just felt a sense of creeping dread. And rightly so.

Everything changed after that night. Speidi went from being disliked to being despised. Famous for being awful. It was a twisted bargain—wealth and fame in exchange for becoming caricatures of our worst impulses. Well, mine, mainly.

Lauren went on *Live with Regis and Kelly* the morning after the premiere, talking about "the big split" with just the right amount of wounded dignity. Never *quite* saying our names. "It's just really hard when people you trust betray that trust," she told Regis and Kelly, her voice soft and sad in a way that made America want to give her a hug and send us death threats.

Which they did.

The entire mediascape was baying for our blood. The court of public opinion doesn't do nuance. It does heroes and villains, and we'd been cast. And what my brain couldn't conceive of in 2007: The internet is forever. Back then, in my naive little world, an episode dropped, people talked about it at the watercooler for a week, and then it disappeared into the television graveyard. Next week's episode would erase this week's drama. At least, that's what I hoped would happen.

I didn't know Netflix was coming. I didn't know that Paramount Plus would package our worst moments into bingeable trauma. That iTunes would let people download our destruction for $1.99 an episode. That people in 2025 would be able to watch Lauren screaming *YOU KNOW WHAT YOU DID!* at Heidi in HD, over and over. Tik-Toks, Reels, Shorts—all these new mediums that didn't even exist when the show aired, telling the same story, over and over again.

That sex tape rumor wasn't just a storyline. It was a curse that would haunt us through every new platform, every new technology, every new way humans found to consume and judge and hate. It attached itself to us like a virus, spreading and mutating with each new generation of viewers.

To this day, people discover *The Hills* on streaming and tweet abuse at Heidi like these episodes just aired yesterday. Like she's still that twenty-year-old girl frozen in time, forever guilty. They think they're watching a villain when they're actually watching the most loyal person I've ever known.

Two days later, my phone rang. MTV.

"We need you to apologize to Lauren," the producer said. "On camera. For the next episode."

"Absolutely not."

"Spencer—"

"I'm not doing it. Heidi didn't do anything wrong, and I'm not going to make her look guilty by—"

"We're prepared to offer additional compensation."

I paused. "How much additional compensation?"

There was a number. A big number. The kind of number that makes you reconsider your principles.

"Let me talk to Heidi," I said.

I found her in the bedroom, folding laundry.

"MTV wants me to apologize to Lauren. On camera."

She stopped mid-fold. "What did you say?"

"I said no. But then they offered us a lot of money."

"How much?"

I told her.

She sat down on the bed, holding one of my T-shirts.

"What do you think I should do?" I asked.

"I don't know, Spencer. It's your call." Her voice was flat, exhausted.

"I mean, if we're going to be destroyed anyway . . ." I heard myself saying, already rationalizing. "At least we'd be getting paid for the privilege, right?"

She looked at me for a long moment. I couldn't read her expression.

"Yeah," she said finally. "At least there's that."

I called MTV back and said yes. I delivered the lines. Paused in the right places. Lauren wasn't even on the other end of the line. She later confirmed this herself on *The View*: "To be perfectly honest, I wasn't on the other line of that call. That was filmed and I wasn't on the other end."

We were both just reading our lines. Two actors in a play about reconciliation that neither of us wanted. She got her moment of vindication without having to actually talk to me. I got my check without having to actually face what I'd done.

It was perfect, in a way. Perfectly hollow. Perfectly meaningless.

That apology—along with all the other lies—became part of the permanent record. Another piece of evidence that Heidi had been involved. Another moment for people to point to and say, "See? Look what terrible people they are."

PART TWO
THE VILLAIN EDIT

CHAPTER 13

FUCK AROUND AND FIND OUT

Survival Strategies for the Despicable

The sex tape rumor was the mother of our pain—the original sin that spawned every nightmare that followed. From it, the stories multiplied like bacteria—each one more deranged than the last. For instance, someone claimed that they heard Jim Conrad, LC's dad, was sending his guys after me to break my legs, alleging that they'd heard it from someone who worked for him.

Could it possibly be true that Lauren's dad was so pissed he was gonna pull his construction crew off a kitchen remodel and send them up to LA to kneecap me? *"Hold on, boys, put down the backsplash tile—we've got a hit job to do."*

It seemed preposterous and, of course, it wasn't true. But I wasn't taking any chances, even if it was just a baseless rumor.

"We're buying guns," I told Heidi that night, dead serious.

My parents, who we were still living with, supported us exercising our Second Amendment rights. My dad was the son of a WWII veteran, and he always had a shotgun growing up, so he thought it was cool when we decided to arm up. Besides, much like us, they figured this whole thing had to blow over eventually. We'd weather the storm, people would move on to the next scandal, and life would go back to normal. Nana Joan, ever our champion, was thrilled with our infamy. Instead of one Speidi pin, she now wore two. What a legend.

We drove to Martin B. Retting in Culver City, this legendary gun shop that looked like a fortress.

The guy behind the counter clocked us immediately.

"First time?" he asked.

"Yeah," I admitted.

"What are you looking for?"

"Whatever Delta Force operators have."

"Don't worry, I got you," he said. "Follow me."

I felt safer already.

We bought two matching Wilson Combat pistols—1911s in matte green. Cold and heavy and reassuring in a way I'd never expected. And of course, we also got his-and-hers shotguns—because if someone's breaking into your house, you want them to hear that unmistakable *cha-chunk*. The universal language for "fuck around and find out."

I was in full war mode, straight up Rambo. Ready for whatever was coming. In my head I was like: *Please, Mr. Conrad. Do send your kitchen-remodel crew to take me out. I'll be here waiting—with Brazilian jiujitsu, a shotgun, and a chip on my shoulder the size of Zuma Beach. Yeah, bring your nail guns, boys. I've got triangle chokes and I'm ready for all the smoke.*

When we got home, we pulled the guns out of their cases and stared at them.

"Do you know how to load this?" Heidi asked, holding her pistol like it might explode.

"Uh, yeah? I mean . . . bullets go in there, somewhere, right?"

"Spencer, we just spent thousands of dollars on guns we don't know how to use."

"True," I said, trying to figure out which end was which. "Well, how hard can it be?"

Thankfully, we'd grabbed a flyer at the gun shop—"American Defense Enterprises," it read, with these commando-looking operators in full tactical gear. "Whether you are an honest citizen concerned with personal safety or an elite operator whose life depends on being proficient with his weapon, ADE can train you to the highest level you wish to achieve."

Sold. We called immediately.

"Hello?" The voice on the other end sounded like Gary Busey gargling driveway gravel.

"Yeah, hi, I need to learn how to not shoot myself with my new gun."

A pause. "Son, are you drunk?"

"No, I'm Spencer Pratt from *The Hills* and people want to kill me."

Another pause. Then: "All right, I can be there this afternoon. Give me the address."

His name was Bill Beasley, this massive, jolly-looking dude with a white beard who moved like a ghost despite being built like a refrigerator.

"Y'ever shoot before?" he asked when he got to our house, examining our arsenal.

"Uh, I shot a BB gun at camp once," I offered.

He sighed deeply. "Okay. Good thing you called, Mr. Pratt, because when five guys break into your house, you better be ready."

After our first lesson at the gun range, I made him an offer.

"Bill, will you be our bodyguard?"

"Kid, I'm retired."

"From what?"

"SOG. Studies and Observations Group."

"What's that?"

"Covert ops behind enemy lines. The kind of stuff they still won't declassify."

"That's very reassuring. Name your price, Mr. Beasley. We need you."

And that's how Bill became our constant shadow. Our own personal Special Forces Santa. He'd show up to every filming location, every set, this calm presence in cargo pants and Hawaiian shirts.

The producers lost their minds the first time he appeared.

"Who the fuck is that, Spencer?" Sean hissed.

"That's Bill. He's with us now."

"You can't just bring random people to set—"

Bill chose that exact moment to pull out two Spyderco pocket knives, one in each hand, and start flipping them open and closed in perfect synchronization. Not threatening anyone—just casual, like other people fidget with pens.

Click-click. Click-click. Click-click.

"Actually," Sean said, his voice an octave higher, "Bill seems great. Welcome to the team, Bill."

Bill nodded and went back to his knives.

That became our new normal. We'd be filming some dramatic scene about our isolation, about how Speidi had no friends, while Bill sat in the corner practicing his knife work. The sound became oddly comforting—this rhythmic clicking that meant protection was nearby.

Click-click.

Ha ha, Lauren, your dad's construction workers can't hurt us. Click-click.

"So were you really in SOG?" I asked Bill once between takes.

"I protected American interests," he said, never looking up.

Click-click.

Damn, Bill.

Shooting Season 4 of *The Hills* was a surreal, painful experience. We'd been exiled. No more filming with other cast members. We were handed mind-numbing storylines shot in our fake apartment on Curson, the two of us playing house in scene after scene of manufactured domesticity. It was excruciating and carefully crafted to minimize any interaction with the main cast.

Off set, too, we felt like pariahs. Brody, my best friend, wouldn't take on my beef with me and was still acting cool with Lauren despite everything that had gone down. Something had fundamentally shifted. I was watching our brotherhood dissolve, because I'd become too problematic for his "chill Malibu prince" brand.

Eventually, I couldn't take it anymore and had it out with Brody over the phone, a moment that was captured on camera. And yes—the call was real. One of the few authentic moments *The Hills* ever caught. For all the Frankenbiting and staged drama, they somehow managed to record one of the most disappointing moments of my life and beamed it out to millions: the moment Brody and I stopped being friends.

I'd dialed his number, no pleasantries, no small talk. I went straight in—asked him why he seemed to be siding with someone he'd known for six months over his best friend. Brody tried to shrug it off, saying I was being dramatic, overreacting. But I could hear it in his voice—the distance, the impatience. He'd already made his choice.

The call didn't last long. I hung up on him, furious. He called me a "little bitch." And just like that, the friendship was over. Brody and I didn't speak for ten years after that call.

If our positions had been reversed, I know for a fact I would have stood by him. That's why I was so mad. But Brody didn't want any trouble, and our friendship became a casualty of that decision. I've come to accept that maybe I shouldn't have taken it so personally, that maybe he was just protecting himself in the only way he knew how. That my expectations of friendship and loyalty aren't always the same as other peoples'.

Still, it's strange how something so small—one call, one insult—can mark the quiet death of a friendship. There was no funeral, no goodbye. Just silence, and time doing what it does best: moving on without us.

CHAPTER 14

BIRTH OF A SHE-PRATT

When Blood's Not Thicker Than Water

Another thing to come out of Heidi and me being rebranded as reality TV's most hated couple? It gave my sister Stephanie an opportunity to finally make the splash she'd tried years earlier on *Princes*.

She'd seemed to be on an upward trajectory after her heartbreaking suicide attempt in 2005. Unfortunately, with Stephanie, "rock bottom" was a place she seemingly kept returning to. The lowest point—at least, pre–*Hills*—was May 2006, in Oahu. I'll never forget my dad's voice when he called to tell me the news:

"Spencer. Your sister got arrested yesterday in Honolulu."

I'd pressed the phone harder against my ear. "Arrested for what?"

"Shoplifting. From Neiman Marcus. Twenty thousand dollars' worth of merchandise." His voice had that parental tone of fake calm—like if he didn't raise his voice, maybe reality wouldn't be happening.

"Twenty thousand—Dad, that's not shoplifting. That's grand larceny."

"She was wearing it all. Multiple dresses, scarves, sunglasses. Tried to walk out of there, like no one would notice."

She was high on a pharmaceutical cocktail that could've tranquilized a horse—cocaine, Adderall, Xanax, Oxy, and something I didn't even know existed at the time: morphine lollipops.

She woke up cuffed to a hospital bed, then spent three days in an

Oahu jail detoxing—no meds, no mercy, just cold turkey in paradise. My dad tried to spin it: "Three years' probation. She'll be okay."

Stephanie came back to LA fragile, quieter, working toward stability. Heidi met her a few times—coffee, a lunch. Stephanie smiled, played sweet, but her turmoil was always there, gnawing under the surface. One of the first things she said to Heidi was *"Spencer's always been my dad's favorite. He's always had everything."*

That was her wound: the belief that parental love was a limited resource, and I'd taken more than my share. In reality, of course she'd been cherished, just as much as I had been. But somehow it never landed for her the way it was meant to. She always seemed to be searching for evidence that she'd been left out, that her needs were less important than mine.

Then came the incident that got Heidi and me kicked out of my parents' place.

Our parents had gone on vacation, leaving their house in our care. When Stephanie showed up unannounced one night—she didn't live there; she had her own two-bedroom apartment in Brentwood—I couldn't resist messing with her. She put her key in the lock, and I turned the dead bolt from the inside. I heard her confused fumbling as she tried again. *Click*—I threw the dead bolt back the other way.

"What the hell?" Her voice came through the door, already rising.

Third time, I let her in. She stormed past me, filled with rage that seemed wildly disproportionate to the prank.

"You asshole!" She was shaking. "You think that's funny?"

"Jesus, Steph, it was a joke—"

"Everything's a joke to you!" She was already dialing our parents, hands trembling. "Mom? Spencer's here and he—he locked me out and—"

I could hear my mother's voice through the phone, immediately concerned.

Twenty minutes later, my dad called me directly.

"Spencer, you and Heidi need to move out. Your sister is fragile."

"But she doesn't even live here!"

"I know, but we can't have her freaking out every time she comes over."

"Fine, Dad," I said, my heart sinking.

Maybe it was time we left anyway. Heidi and I had been living with my parents for just under a year, and as much as we loved being close to them, it was probably time to have a place of our own.

We found a rental just five minutes away in the Palisades. Ocean views, the kind of place we used to walk past and dream about affording someday. Now, thanks to being the most hated people in the known universe, we could.

Not long after we'd moved out, Stephanie called with the strangest news.

"I just ran up on LC at the club!" she announced, breathless. "Told her not to mess with my brother!"

"You did what?"

"I defended you! At Opera club. Told that bitch to back off."

In my head, I'm thinking: *Since when do you defend me?*

When I was working on this book, I found Stephanie's autobiography. She'd written a passage about defending me that night, an avenging angel protecting her beloved brother. According to her book, the day of that shoot, she'd spent six hours getting camera-ready—hair, makeup, new outfit, the works. Stephanie treated the encounter, which I'm guessing was preplanned between her and the producers, like an audition for her new life. And maybe it was.

When she showed up at Opera that night, Lauren was holding court with Audrina, Justin Bobby, and Frankie Delgado. The cameras were already rolling. Then Stephanie saw Brody. My ex–best friend. Sitting at LC's table like he belonged there.

"Oh my God, that's Spencer's sister," Brody said, noticing her. His face went pale.

Stephanie waved at him, all sweetness and light.

Brody looked terrified. As he should have been.

Stephanie marched through that club like a woman on a mission, parting the Red Sea.

"Brody, what are you doing here?" Her voice cut through the music. "You're on the evil side. Come home with us."

Lauren's face hardened. "I haven't done anything to Heidi. You don't even know me. Do you know me?"

"Heidi's my family now!" Stephanie's voice cracked with what sounded like genuine emotion. "When you hate my brother, it makes me hate you!"

My sister was doing an amazing job, playing the loyal defender on camera. If I'd been there, I might have actually believed she meant it. Maybe she did, in the moment.

"I love your brother," Brody told Stephanie, "but he fucked up. He has to deal with that. Stop getting involved."

"It's just really shitty, Brody."

And it was. Really shitty that my best friend had chosen a side, and it wasn't mine.

The producers loved Stephanie—obviously. Who doesn't love a live wire who might detonate at any moment? I was still naive enough to believe this could work in our favor. Another Pratt in the mix—finally, someone who'd have our backs in the snake pit. Family standing strong against the Lauren Conrad Industrial Complex. Not so much.

MTV planned follow-up encounters between my sister and LC at the fashion school FIDM, where Stephanie was taking classes and where Lauren was also studying. What were the odds? In actual reality—zero. I swear they must have spent days combing through class rosters, manufacturing the perfect overlap, maybe even enrolling Stephanie in school just to tee it up. Or hell, maybe they just plopped her in a random classroom and called it fate.

After class, Lauren approached Stephanie. "Can we talk?"

They got tea at this little place on campus, all casual, just two students working out their differences. Stephanie sat across from LC—the girl she'd just publicly roasted—and apologized for going off on her at Opera.

Then, I'm guessing, LC told my sister her side of the story. And Stephanie—with astonishing speed—completely changed her allegiance. Before long, LC and Stephanie's tea dates became a regular thing, Stephanie begging everyone on the crew not to tell me about her budding friendship with my and Heidi's enemy.

All those bullshit scenes they concocted for Season 4—me crashing on her couch like I was homeless, her playing the concerned sister making me breakfast, me having heart-to-hearts with her about getting my life together. All fictional storylines. The only truth was that my sister was actually Team LC.

Stephanie's smart. I get why she wanted to lean in to the drama—why not? The fans were eating it up, and suddenly she wasn't just Spencer's little sister; she was a character in her own right. She was She-Pratt—a nickname LC lobbed at her like an insult but which instantly became branding. People were stopping her at Coffee Bean, whispering at the gym, pointing at her in Kitson. For the first time in her life, she wasn't just living in my shadow—she was getting her own spotlight.

And the money was real. Not an allowance, not some quiet wire transfer from my parents, but fat MTV checks with her name on them. "I bought these myself," she told Heidi once, flashing a pair of $1,000 Louboutins. That girl always did love to shop. And now she could do it without asking permission, without stealing.

Still, I can't help thinking: If fame and money were her goals—no shade, they'd always been mine, too—she'd have been way better off going full contrarian. She could've been the anti-LC. The defender of House Pratt. That would've made her a legend. Instead, she got folded back into the Lauren Conrad storyline, supporting cast when she could've been a main event.

But I understand. Maybe in the end it wasn't about choosing LC over me, or even fame over family. It was about choosing herself. After years of darker dependencies, she'd found a new, less harmful high: fame. Different addiction, sure—but at least this one came with swag bags, glam squads, and health insurance.

If that's what it took to keep my sister alive, then who am I to judge?

CHAPTER 15

TABLOIDS AND TUNES
Reclaiming Narrative Control

Heidi and I really needed something—anything—that was actually ours. Something untainted by that sex tape rumor scandal. Something the producers couldn't script, chop up, or Frankenbite into oblivion. We decided to double down on Heidi's music career together. It felt like the one thing we could control, now that the villain narrative was no longer in our hands but had taken on a life of its own.

We began talking to Warner Brothers about a real record deal, thanks to David Foster, who'd been given his own imprint there, 143 Records. Before signing, we had Peter Lopez—the lawyer Foster himself had hooked me up with for *Princes*—look over the contract.

"You guys, this is a three-sixty deal," Lopez told us. "They don't just want Heidi's music. They want everything—TV, appearances, endorsements, lemonade stands. Basically, they're buying her life." Lopez looked us dead in the eye. "She's already a TV star. Do. Not. Sign. This."

"Okay, so what do we do instead, Peter?"

"I'll get you a distribution deal. There's this new startup called the Orchard. Nobody's heard of them yet, but trust me—they're gonna be huge."

Back then, the Orchard didn't sound like a music enterprise—it sounded like a juice bar in Silver Lake. "Do you want that album with ginger or turmeric?" But we listened, rolled the dice. Said no to Warner. Decided to self-finance Heidi's record and distribute it through the Orchard when it was ready.

David Foster was cool about us turning down the Warner deal. I saw him at a dinner party right after we said no, and it was all good vibes. He wasn't some corporate assassin trying to strong-arm us. That's not his style. David was about the talent—bringing people in, cultivating stars. He wasn't the one drafting contracts in the back room. And if Peter Lopez was telling us *Don't sign this*, David respected that. No hard feelings.

We'd spend the day filming *The Hills* and then at night we'd roll straight into the recording studio. Glenwood Place in the Valley, the Village in West LA, the Record Plant before it shut down. Rooms where legends like Prince, Fleetwood Mac, and Aerosmith recorded their masterpieces. And now? It was Heidi Montag in the booth, me lurking in the control room. I felt this electric possibility—all the mockery and hatred was just noise, and this was where we'd prove everyone wrong. Music didn't care about our reality show drama. Music was pure. For the first time in months, it felt like we could breathe.

Peter Lopez hooked us up with an independent A&R, Gerardo Mejía; better known simply as Gerardo, the performer behind the early nineties hit "Rico Suave." Fast-forward a few years, he's writing a bunch of Beyoncé's and Usher's hits. We had no clue Heidi was basically workshopping with the guy who'd soundtracked half the R&B make-out sessions of the 2010s.

Through Gerardo, we met Nephew, this low-key genius who'd worked with Dr. Dre. Nephew gave us Heidi's first single, "Higher," which has a weird little cult following now, but at the time it got annihilated online, thanks to the video that I directed on the beach: Heidi frolicking with seagulls, me behind the camera like Scorsese helming "Baywatch After Dark."

I genuinely thought I was making art—this dreamy, romantic visual of my beautiful girlfriend. I was so deep in the Speidi bubble that

I couldn't see how it looked to the outside world: one villain making his villainous girlfriend dance with birds on a beach while he filmed her with a camcorder.

Despite the online cringe, behind the scenes, we still had our eye on the prize. Namely, making the greatest pop record in history with the greatest talents known to humankind. Gerardo put us in touch with Steve Morales—the Miami producer behind hits for Christina Aguilera, Enrique Iglesias, J.Lo, all the heavyweights. He then introduced us to a songwriter named LP. Holy. Shit. *The* LP. Today they're a rock star with a billion streams and stadium tours, but back then they were underground, this chain-smoking genius writing hooks in little LA studios. They took the clichés about Heidi—that she was plastic, superficial, a punch line—and flipped them into her superpower, writing songs that satirized the very way the media had taunted her.

Then came Stacy Barthe—later the secret weapon in Beyoncé's arsenal (and Rihanna's, and Katy Perry's), but back then she was just another hungry writer grinding in LA, waiting for her moment.

And finally, Cathy Dennis, pop goddess incarnate. She wrote Britney's "Toxic." She wrote Kylie Minogue's "Can't Get You Out of My Head." She was a literal hit machine walking the earth, and now here she was writing with Heidi Montag.

Of course, all this cost a LOT of money. But it was okay—being America's Most Wanted meant we had money flowing in nonstop, which enabled us to have past, present, and future GOATs orbiting Heidi. LP, Stacy, Cathy, Gerardo, Steve—like the Avengers assembling in a recording studio.

Ryan Seacrest—already the most powerful man in radio, the man who so smartly took the executive producer job for *Keeping Up with the Kardashians*—had started spinning Heidi's track "Body Language" on KIIS FM, the biggest station in LA. Listeners were calling in. Requesting it. There was real, organic momentum. The kind of thing you can't buy, can't fake, can't manufacture.

So I called Ryan Seacrest and told him to turn it off.

"Don't play it again," I said.

Ryan sounded genuinely baffled. "What? This song's good. Everyone loves it."

"No. Take it off. Forever."

There was a rap verse on the track. A rap verse *I* had recorded. It was supposed to be a placeholder, just until we found an actual rapper. But instead, there I was, rapping like a drunk camp counselor at talent show night, and now it was blasting across Los Angeles airwaves.

Hell no.

I panicked. I was embarrassed. My ego couldn't handle it. Instead of leaning in to the momentum, I stomped it out like a toddler kicking over a sandcastle. If I had a time machine, I'd go back and slap myself—hard. I'd grab myself by the collar and scream: *Shut the hell up and let Seacrest play it until the airwaves collapse.* Then I'd march into Peter Lopez's office and say, "Look—it's already a radio hit. Get us a better Warner deal."

But no. Instead, I murdered "Body Language" because I couldn't handle the sound of my own Dollar Tree Eminem flow. Still, though, maybe I did everyone a small favor. Because did the world really need to hear me rap: "Yeah, I be chillin' in the back of the club tonight . . . / From Paris to Beverly Hills / We that ill?"

Probably not, right?

By this point, Peter Grossman, photo editor of *Us Weekly*, and I were basically on speed dial. He was our gossip godfather—always ready with advice, coaching us through media crises out of the sheer goodness of his rumor-obsessed heart. One time I even dragged him to Cloverfield so he could sit in on an ADR session. Totally off the record. I just wanted him to see how fake the whole reality TV machine really was. People blamed tabloids for making up storylines, but trust me—compared to *The Hills*, the tabloids were Pulitzer-level journalism.

"I can't believe it," Peter said afterward, looking shell-shocked. It was like I'd told a little kid Santa wasn't real.

By this point, our power attorney, Dan Black, had negotiated us a fat raise on *The Hills*—$120,000 an episode. Add to that the money we were beginning to make from our paparazzi empire, where Heidi and I had turned staged photos into a science. Speidi at the pumpkin patch, Speidi shopping on Robertson, Speidi having a "private" moment working out at the beach, in full hair and makeup. *Ka-ching*.

Everyone else was out there acting surprised or hostile to the paparazzi—Paris doing her fake "ugh, not again" face, the Kardashians pretending they "just happened" to be mobbed at Starbucks. Meanwhile, I was texting photographers like I was ordering pizza:

"Pumpkin patch at 2? Matching flannels secured. Bring a wide lens."

We weren't just performing for cameras anymore—we were living for them. Every moment became content, every private experience became a potential payday. The line between our relationship and our business had dissolved so completely that I wasn't sure we knew how to exist without an audience. A sunset dinner wasn't romantic unless there was a photographer to capture it. A shopping trip wasn't fun unless it generated coverage. We'd turned "villain lifestyle" into a content factory.

Was it weird? Absolutely. Was it sustainable? Probably not. But did we bank half a mil in six months just from being photographed buying groceries? You bet your ass we did.

If people are going to watch your every move anyway, why not choreograph the show?

CHAPTER 16

THE WEDDING NO ONE EXPECTED, INCLUDING US

Elope Now, Explain Later: Our Nuclear Option

"Lauren said if you and Heidi aren't kicked off the show, she's walking," an MTV executive told us. I won't name names, but let's just say this person had serious pull at the network. We got this news during the height of Season 4 filming, just as we were deep in Season 5 negotiations.

"What did you tell her?" I asked.

"I told her we're not letting you and Heidi go."

I smiled, satisfied.

"Good. Tell her 'bye.' Don't let the door hit her on the way out."

MTV wasn't about to kill its golden goose—not when we'd become America's most bankable villains since Bonnie and Clyde.

Still, we were rattled by the thought of being booted off the show. Without *The Hills*, who were we? Just two twentysomethings with a pop record no one had heard, and no other backup plan. Meanwhile, our rent was real. The credit card bills from trying to keep up appearances were real. It costs a lot of money, being famous. And every time Heidi hit the studio, the meter was running. The cost of her album was ballooning like the national debt—we'd already sunk a million of our own money into it.

The Hills was our oxygen, and we couldn't lose that income. We needed a strategy, some form of protection from the ballooning wrath of Lauren.

I called Peter Grossman at *Us Weekly*—our confessor, our guide through the inferno.

"You're asking what would protect you?" Peter mused. "What story would make you unfireable?"

"Exactly."

"That's easy. You and Heidi should get married."

The words just hung there. I blinked, trying to figure out if he was serious or just testing out a new punch line.

"Okay . . . ?" I said finally.

"Listen to me." Peter's voice shifted into strategist mode. "You have two nuclear options. Either you and Heidi tie the knot or you break up. Both are massive stories. Both dominate the news cycle for weeks. MTV can't fire the couple having a secret wedding *or* the couple having a devastating breakup. Either way, you become the story. Whatever leverage LC may think she has, poof—gone."

I looked at Heidi across our kitchen table, Peter's voice still echoing on speakerphone. We'd been dragged through the mud, turned into villains, clowned by strangers, and somehow we were still sitting here, still together. Honestly, marriage seemed like the easiest decision we'd ever make. A no-brainer.

Heidi smiled at me, nodding—already reading my mind. As always, we were in sync.

I mouthed, *I love you.*

She blew me a kiss back.

"You need to do it somewhere exclusive," Peter continued. "Remote. Romantic. This has to be a STORY."

"We love the Palmilla in Cabo," I said. "That's our spot."

"Perfect," Peter said. "Luxurious, photogenic. *Us Weekly* will pick up the tab, of course. We'll pay you well for the exclusive."

Three days later, we were boarding an Alaska Airlines flight to Cabo—me, Heidi, and Peter Grossman—the world's strangest throuple headed off to plan a destination wedding slash magazine cover. We weren't worried about upsetting our families with an elopement because, honestly, it felt like just another performance. After two years of staged storylines and manufactured drama, this was one more scene for the cameras.

We told ourselves we'd do a real wedding later—something genuine with our families there—when all this madness was over. We'd make it up to them then. Until then, we'd keep all this a secret.

The next morning—November 20, 2008—Speidi put a ring on it.

Heidi wore a simple white dress by Elyse Walker. Our rings were straight from the resort gift shop—pleather bands that cost less than our breakfast buffet. Peter stood off to the side with the photographer, both trying to be invisible.

When the officiant, José, asked if I took Heidi to be my wife, my face cracked open with joy.

"I do!" I beamed.

"There," I heard Peter whisper to the photographer. "Get that angle."

"Do you, Heidi, take this man—"

"I do," she cut him off, grinning.

Later that night, sitting on our balcony overlooking the ocean, Heidi took my hand. The waves crashed below us in the dark. Our new life stretching out before us.

"So," I asked, trying to keep my voice light, "any regrets?"

"None."

"Not even one?"

"Nope." She squeezed my hand. "I made peace with losing everything the day I chose you."

"You would have given up *everything* for me?"

"I gave up everything that didn't matter," she said quietly.

She turned to face me, and in the dim light from inside, I could see her expression—calm, certain, almost serene.

"When I moved out of Lauren's apartment, I already knew I might never be on the show again. I was ready for that. I knew what I was choosing, and I was fine with those consequences. Because I knew I'd already won."

"Heidi—"

"Spencer, stop." She knew what I was about to say. "I need you to understand something: I'm happy. We have each other. That's what matters to me."

"I love you," I said, because I didn't know what else to say.

"I know you do." She leaned her head on my shoulder. "That's why I'm still here."

In that moment, the strategic part of my brain went quiet. All the noise—the ratings calculations, the publicity angles, the revenge fantasies, the constant mental chess game of how to stay relevant—just stopped.

This wasn't about proving something to Lauren or anyone else watching. This was about me, next to the one person who'd looked at everything I was—the chaos, the ego, the impulsiveness, all of it—and decided I was still worth choosing.

In that moment, I felt something even deeper than gratitude. Deeper than love, even, though I loved her more than I knew how to say.

I felt saved.

Whatever happened next—whatever the tabloids said, whatever MTV aired, whatever hate came our way—we'd face it together.

It felt like the only thing that was real.

The next morning, Peter knocked on our door.

"Congratulations to the happy couple! Oh, and by the way, you made the cover of *Us Weekly*."

Peter slipped proofs under the door.

"HEIDI AND SPENCER ELOPE!" screamed the headline, our exclusive photos splashed across the cover. The prophecy I'd made when I was sixteen had finally come true. I was on the cover of *Us Weekly*. But even better than my teenage fantasy, I wasn't alone. I was on the cover with my beautiful bride.

Us Weekly paid us $100,000 for that cover, part of a four-cover deal worth $400,000. We'd managed to turn romance into revenue, love into leverage. Call it what you want, but in that moment, it felt like we were winning.

Peter wasn't exaggerating about the impact—the wedding made us omnipresent. *People, OK!, Star, InTouch*, Perez, *E! News*. For three nights straight, we were the lead story. America might've hated us, but dammit if they couldn't look away.

My phone exploded with missed calls. MTV, producers, my parents, Heidi's family. The voicemails ranged from confused to furious. We turned our phones off, retreated to our hotel room, cuddled on the bed, and watched the media storm we'd created from afar.

Adam DiVello's voicemail was my favorite. I played it for Heidi three times:

"You can't just elope without telling production!"

"An elopement that 'just happened' . . . with *Us Weekly* there? Really?"

"You need to go back to the chapel RIGHT NOW and redo it for the show! I'm sending a crew."

That's how fake reality TV is—that same week, they flew a crew out and filmed our "spontaneous" elopement. The crew had to skip Thanksgiving, and they sure were pissed.

The way the edit turned out, Heidi looks drunk and it seems as though I got her wasted and tricked her into marrying me. Yup. They made me look like I'm an emotional lunatic who dragged my girlfriend to Mexico and manipulated her into marriage.

Jeez. FINE. Just pay me.

Either way, our plan had worked. The elopement made us unfireable, for now at least. MTV couldn't lose us without losing their main storyline. Speidi was everywhere. *USA Today* named us the third most popular couple in the country, just behind Brad Pitt and Angelina Jolie, and the Obamas.

It was nonstop paychecks—video game launches, nightclub appearances, random product placements. Fifty grand here, a hundred grand there. Every Monday night, MTV painted us as villains. And by Tuesday morning, the world was still hungry for more.

Heidi and I met my parents at Giorgio Baldi in Santa Monica for dinner one night. It was *our* place—family birthdays, graduations, milestones, all anchored at that corner table overlooking the Pacific. The owner knew our drink orders before we sat down. This was Pratt home turf. Which is why my mom waited until after we'd ordered—when I was trapped between the bread basket and the ocean view—to drop the bomb.

"Your father is having . . . issues," she said, studying her menu. "With patients."

"What kind of issues?"

"They're talking about you. About the show. About . . . everything."

I set down my water glass. "And?"

"They don't like you, Spencer. So we were thinking, maybe you should change your name."

Around us, other families clinked glasses, laughed, celebrated. And there was my mother, in the restaurant where she once told me she was proud after a soccer championship, telling me I was now such a disgrace that I needed to stop being a Pratt?

"The business is suffering," she continued. "Patients are leaving. This is our livelihood, honey."

I looked at my dad, who was inspecting his fork. For thirty years, his job had been simple: keep patients happy, avoid drama, polish teeth. Now his son was the villain on MTV, and it was messing with his molar margins.

"Dad?" I asked. "You want me to change my name too?"

He shifted, miserable. "Your mother and I just think . . . maybe some distance would help. From the show. From all of it."

"You want me to change my name because your patients don't

like what they see on MTV?" My voice was louder than I meant it to be.

"Spencer, please," my mother whispered. "You're making a scene."

I laughed. "Mom. My whole life is a scene. Relax. This one's free. Usually I charge a hundred grand an episode."

My parents stared at me like I was a stranger.

"Look, I'm not changing my name," I said quietly. "This is who I am now. We just have to get used to it."

My mother reached across the table, and I took her hand. I wanted to tell her that that underneath all the headlines and manufactured drama, I was still her son, the same Spencer I'd always been. But the truth was more complicated. The old Spencer still existed, but he was sharing space with someone else now—someone who turned weddings into magazine exclusives. Someone whose day job was being a villain for hire. Someone so good at his day job, he wasn't sure if he could even clock out.

CHAPTER 17

WEDDING REBOOT

'Til Fake Do Us Part

April 25, 2009

Six months after our *actual* wedding in Cabo—the one where we meant it—we were back at the altar like some cursed Broadway revival. Crowds of *Hills* fans had gathered outside Westminster Presbyterian Church in Pasadena, waving and calling our names as we performed the sacred ritual of Holy Ratings for America's viewing pleasure.

The church was gorgeous, I'll give them that. Stained-glass windows, vaulted ceilings.

But this wasn't holy matrimony. This was *The Hills* Season 5, Episode 10: "Something Old, Something New." MTV taking our actual marriage and giving it the full Hollywood treatment—better lighting, and more extras.

Adam DiVello came up beside me, his producer hand landing on my shoulder.

"Spencer," he whispered, "if you're having second thoughts, we can postpone this whole thing."

I turned and laughed. "Dude, I'm not going anywhere."

He blinked, and I could tell he was disappointed—I felt like he was *praying* I'd bolt. *Runaway Groom: The Spencer Pratt Story*. Think of the ratings! Even at our wedding—*especially* at our wedding—it seemed like some people were still plotting our demise. Trying to get me to abandon Heidi at the altar or, better yet, convince Heidi to make a run for it in her $30,000 dress.

She and I had actually talked about it that morning: If they offered us a million to call it off right there, would we? I probably would've considered it. Heidi? She said no.

"Not even for a million?"

"Not for any amount."

I looked at her. "Come on."

"My whole family is here, Spencer." Her voice was quiet but firm. "My parents. My grandparents. People who've known me my entire life. They're all sitting in those seats because I asked them to witness this."

"So?"

"We already had one wedding without them. I owe them this one."

Two hundred guests packed the pews like it was the Super Bowl of fake weddings—real family and real friends interspersed with fake family and frenemies. Heidi floated down the aisle in her Monique Lhuillier masterpiece, dripping in a million dollars' worth of borrowed Neil Lane diamonds, and for exactly three seconds, watching her walk toward me, I completely forgot about the cameras crawling around us. Heidi looked *happy*. Not fake-happy, not TV-happy—actually, genuinely, stupidly happy. That's Heidi's superpower and her kryptonite rolled into one: She can always find the joy, even in a hurricane.

"Love you," I whispered when she got to the altar.

"Love you, too, babe," she whispered back.

Then I saw *her*.

Lauren Conrad. Sitting there in a pew. My stomach dropped.

Heidi hadn't invited her. I sure as hell hadn't invited her. But there she was, positioned perfectly in the camera's sight line, impossible to miss.

Of course.

MTV was paying for this wedding. They wanted their money's worth. And their money's worth meant drama. Meant conflict. Meant the villain's wedding day interrupted by the hero he'd wronged.

I should have known. The second we'd agreed to let them film it, we'd handed over creative control. This wasn't our wedding anymore. It was an episode. And every episode needs a climax.

I felt Heidi's hand tighten on my arm. She'd seen Lauren, too.

"Did you know?" she whispered.

"No."

What could we do? Storm out of our own wedding? Demand they remove her? The cameras were already rolling. We'd sold them our wedding day. Now they were getting their return on investment.

I made the executive decision there and then to pretend Lauren Conrad didn't exist. If they wanted us to share a scene, they'd need to call our lawyer and pay extra.

Then I noticed LC's nemesis, Kristin Cavallari, sitting behind her. What on earth did this mean? What drama had these producers cooked up?

After the ceremony, Heidi hurled her bouquet into the crowd. It sailed through the air in a perfect arc—too perfect, obviously, as instructed—and landed directly in Kristin Cavallari's waiting hands.

Scripted, of course. Staged to the second. The passing of the torch, they later told us. Lauren was leaving the show, and Kristin would be stepping in as the new narrator, the new voice guiding viewers through the drama. MTV had squeezed two storylines out of our wedding: the Lauren confrontation and the Kristin coronation.

I should have felt victorious. We'd won, hadn't we? Lauren was leaving. Moving on to build her fashion empire, her lifestyle brand, her persona outside of *The Hills*. She'd gotten out. Meanwhile, we were stuck. Still here. Still playing our parts. Still being Spencer and Heidi, the villains everyone loved to hate, because that's all we knew how to be. That's all anyone would pay us to be.

Mr. and Mrs. Pratt. Just two ordinary kids in love, trapped in the same well-paid disaster, with no visible end in sight. Married to each other, but still married to the beast.

CHAPTER 18

MAYDAY IN THE JUNGLE— PART ONE

When Our Dry Shampoo Commercial Turned into Tropic Thunder

DATE: May 2009
LOCATION: Costa Rica
TIME: 3:47 a.m. Pacific
TRANSCRIPT: voicemail to Dan Black, lawyer

Dan, it's Spencer. I'm freaking out. Snakes. Rats. Ants. Spiders the size of my face. NBC won't let us leave the jungle. This isn't television—this is *a hostage situation*. Please, I'm begging you, call the State Department or the UN or whoever handles celebrity kidnapping. You have to get us out of here!

FLASHBACK:

One month earlier

By the spring of 2009, *The Hills* Season 5 was in full swing, and MTV had split it into two parts—ten episodes in the spring, another ten scheduled for fall. Part One had wrapped in April with our televised wedding spectacular, but just as Part Two was gearing up for production, NBC came calling with what seemed like the opportunity of a lifetime.

Ben Silverman, co-chairman of NBC Universal, made his pitch over dinner at Giorgio's. He leaned across the white tablecloth and said: "So guys, we're bringing over a British phenomenon—*I'm a Celebrity . . . Get Me Out of Here*. Five nights a week, prime time, for an entire month. NBC is betting the farm on this thing, and Spencer, Heidi—I want you two beautiful people to be our headliners."

"Ah, Ben, I wish we could," I said. "But we're locked into an exclusive deal with MTV. They already blocked us from doing *Dancing with the Stars*."

Ben just smiled.

"Don't worry, I've already talked to Tony DiSanto. We can make it happen. We'll air the episodes on MTV as well as NBC. It's all good."

"So what's the show about?" I asked.

"It's so fun, you're gonna love it," he said, grinning. "We'll fly you to Costa Rica. You hang out, do challenges in the jungle with other celebrities. Cool, right?"

"Wait—we're not *sleeping* in the jungle?" I said, my germophobe alarm bells already going off. "Ben, I don't use towels twice. I shower multiple times a day. The jungle and I are not compatible."

He chuckled like I was being adorable. "Spencer, Spencer, Spencer. Don't worry, I'm pretty sure after the cameras stop rolling each day, you get taken back to a resort with room service. That's how it usually is."

"You're absolutely sure about this?"

"Well, here's what I know," he said. "This is career-changing entertainment on network TV, not some survival documentary."

"Okay, then. How much money are we talking?"

"Well . . . everyone gets the same. Fifteen thousand."

I nearly choked on my breadstick. "Fifteen grand? For three weeks in the jungle? For the *whole thing*? I get paid more than that to hold a can of Coke!"

"Wait," Heidi said, her eyes suddenly lighting up. "Maybe we could plug Montag Dry Shampoo on the show? I'm about to launch on QVC next month, and dry shampoo in the jungle humidity? It's like the ultimate product demonstration!" Heidi grabbed my arm, excited. "Spencer, this could be huge for the launch."

"Okay. But, Ben," I said, needing one final confirmation. "You're absolutely, one hundred percent sure we don't have to actually sleep in the jungle, right?"

"Listen, if you're not happy out there, Spencer, if you wanna leave, all you have to do is look in a camera and say: *I'm a celebrity, get me out of here.* They'll chopper you straight outta there."

"That's it? Just say those words and we're out?"

He nodded. "Just say the magic words."

Baby I get paid
I don't volunteer
I'm a celebrity, get me out of here

As part of the deal, Ben Silverman asked me to rap the theme song to the show, resulting in the transcendent hip-hop masterpiece "I'm a Celebrity," which somehow caught the attention of Todd Moscowitz, the executive vice president of Warner Bros. Records. He said that after we got back from the jungle, he wanted to fly me to Atlanta to work with Gucci Mane, with OJ Da Juiceman personally handling my lyrics. Two legitimate trap gods were ready to collaborate with me.

"No way, you're not going to Atlanta," Heidi said flatly.

"Why not?"

"BECAUSE GUCCI MANE MURDERED SOMEONE!"

"Only in self-defense! The charges got dropped!"

"I DON'T CARE!"

Alas, Heidi put her foot down, and there was to be no trap era for Spencer Pratt.

A few weeks after our dinner with Ben Silverman, we did a promo photo shoot with the other celebrities who would be joining us in the jungle—and what a lineup it was.

Janice Dickinson, the original supermodel.

Stephen Baldwin, the youngest of the Baldwin brothers and my personal favorite, thanks to *The Usual Suspects.*

John Salley, former NBA champion who'd won rings with three different teams.

Lou Diamond Phillips, movie star from *La Bamba*.

Sanjaya Malakar, the *American Idol* phenomenon.

Rod Blagojevich, former governor of Illinois, who'd gotten caught up in a massive corruption scandal for trying to essentially "sell" Barack Obama's vacant Senate seat.

At the party, I walked up to Rod and said, "Oh cool, you're a governor! That's awesome, dude." He looked at me with these exhausted, haunted eyes—the kind you get when the FBI is tapping your phones—and said, "Kid, stay out of politics. It's dangerous." (He ended up going to federal prison the week before we left and was replaced by his wife, Patti Blagojevich. He was eventually pardoned.)

At the promo shoot, it struck me that these celebrities fell into two broad camps. You had the legends in the second act of their careers, here to remind America why they mattered. Then you had the lesser-known talents, people I'd never heard of, like Torrie Wilson, some WWE superstar; and Frangela—Frances Callier and Angela V. Shelton, a comedy duo. For them, fifteen grand and prime-time exposure was probably the opportunity of a lifetime. A chance to break through to a huge mainstream audience.

I couldn't help but ask myself: What the hell were *we* doing here? We were at the absolute peak of Speidi, pulling in millions per year, constantly splashed across tabloid covers. We didn't need the press. We certainly didn't need NBC's $15,000.

The only reason we were here? The dry shampoo. Heidi's QVC launch. The ultimate product demonstration. If we could just keep that bottle in frame, spray the hell out of it every chance we got, make sure that beautiful MONTAG DRY SHAMPOO label was visible to America's prime-time audience—then maybe this whole jungle excursion would be worth it.

A few days later, we were Costa Rica–bound. We were allowed to bring exactly one item from home into the jungle—Montag Dry

Shampoo, of course. They put us up for a few nights at the Marriott in San José. Then came the helicopter ride to the deep jungle.

We pulled up to this tiny local airstrip that looked like it hadn't been inspected since the Reagan administration, and waiting for us was our "luxury helicopter"—and I use that term very, very loosely. This thing looked like something they'd found in a junkyard. The rotors wobbled, the paint was peeling off in chunks, and I'm pretty sure that wasn't decorative duct tape holding the passenger door together.

Heidi and I climbed into the back, death-gripping each other's hands like we had just boarded the world's most terrifying carnival ride. Meanwhile, up front in the copilot's seat, Janice Dickinson, supermodel, kept reaching over to grab the pilot's controls, cackling like she thought this was all some hilarious game.

That's when the contract we'd signed—the one with the fine print saying we could legally die on set—stopped feeling like boilerplate and more like a warning about our immediate future.

They dropped us off in the middle of nowhere. The kind of place where GPS just shrugs and gives up. We're hiking into the jungle for the first time, cameras rolling, everyone trying to look like intrepid explorers instead of terrified celebrities who'd rather be getting pedicures, when Patti Blagojevich, the governor's wife, trips over a root and goes flying straight into a river.

This wasn't in the script. This wasn't some producer in a headset going "More drama! Make it look dangerous!" This was the actual wife of an actual politician getting swept away while we all stood there, watching her tumble toward what looked suspiciously like a waterfall that could turn this moment into a very tragic footnote in Illinois political history.

Out of nowhere, commando-looking production guys materialized from the canopy, diving into the rapids like they were auditioning for a Jason Bourne movie. In the end, it was mainly us intrepid celebrities who actually saved her, instinctively forming a human chain, grabbing onto one another and hauling Patti back to shore. Standing there, soaking wet, watching the governor's wife cough up river water, that's when it really hit me: This was a genuine survival situation where real people could actually die.

Welcome to the jungle, I guess.

We got to the camp. The humidity was thick. Our clothes stuck to our bodies like plastic wrap. Good Lord, the mosquitoes. But also, *bullet ants*. These weren't your backyard picnic ants. These psychotic insects, a full inch long, deliver a sting that's literally compared to getting shot—hence the name—and they were already eating poor Sanjaya from *American Idol* alive.

At least we're not sleeping here, I thought.

I kept waiting for someone to hand us a room key, maybe a welcome cocktail with one of those little umbrellas. Instead, slowly, like a horror movie reveal, the truth began to dawn on us.

There was no hotel. There was no resort. This was it. Our "luxury accommodations" were a few hammocks strung between trees. Our "toilet" was literally just a hole in the ground—squat, pray, and hope the local wildlife didn't decide your ass looked like dinner.

"Spencer," Heidi asked, "where are we supposed to shower? Where are we supposed to sleep? They promised—"

"We *thought* they promised," I said, slapping a mosquito that was drilling into my neck.

Around us, everyone was getting organized about camp life. And by organized, I mean scheduling who was going to be in charge of the communal poop bucket. Yes, we were supposed to take turns dumping a bucket of human feces into the bushes. A bucket that *everyone* was using. This, my friends, is where Spencer Pratt drew the line in the sand.

I marched up to a tree and yelled, "YO! I'M A CELEBRITY . . . GET ME OUT OF HERE!"

I was still fairly chill at this point, assuming as soon as I said the magic words, the next helicopter would start warming up for me.

No response. Just howler monkeys, shrieking.

"HEY, YOU GUYS! I'M A CELEBRITY . . . GET ME OUT OF HERE!" I bellowed again, louder this time, really putting some authority behind it.

Finally, a tinny voice crackled out of some hidden speaker in the tree: "Sorry, mate, that's just for elimination. You can't actually leave just yet."

Excuse me? That was the *entire reason* we agreed to come here. The escape hatch. Say the words, you're out. Instead, here I was yelling at a tree while the monkeys mocked me. This no longer felt consensual, so I began to climb the tree, trying to cover the cameras with our jungle prison outfits, to which some producers came creeping out of the jungle, whispering: "Spencer, mate, calm down."

"I NEED TO TALK TO BEN SILVERMAN—*RIGHT NOW*!"

Someone eventually handed me a satellite phone, with Ben on the other end.

"Where's our hotel, Ben? They've got us sleeping in hammocks. There's a community shit bucket. This is not what we signed up for! I'm too rich and too famous to be sitting with these people . . . this cast is devaluing my fame!"

Ben sighed. "I'm so sorry, Spencer—there must have been some misunderstanding. I had no idea. Just hang in there, buddy, I'll see what I can do."

Then the producer took the phone and melted back into the jungle, like he'd never existed.

Heidi and I looked at each other and just collapsed into a hammock, holding hands. Challenges were coming up—gross food, bug stunts, whatever sadistic circus they had planned—but we'd already made our decision. We were OUT.

When it became clear that we were refusing to play ball, the producers shuttled us to this production hut by a river. There, a kind British lady took pity on us and made toasties—British-style ham-and-cheese sandwiches. I inhaled three like a starving raccoon. Apparently, Paul Telegdy himself, head of alternative programming from NBC, was on his way, flying in personally from LA to talk to us and renegotiate our deal.

"Great," I said. "I'll tell him what I told Ben Silverman—we're not going back out there without a king-sized bed, a roof, and a fucking minibar."

Hours later, Paul Telegdy finally touched down in the jungle by helicopter. I thought he'd arrive like a diplomat—shake our hands, apologize for the misunderstanding, maybe thank us for our patience. Instead, he stormed off that chopper, red-faced and absolutely furious. "YOU CUNT!" he bellowed in my face, before shoving me so hard I stumbled back. "What the hell do you think you're doing, ruining *my* show, you cheesy bastard?!"

This wasn't some field producer losing his cool. This was Paul Telegdy, kingmaker of prime time. The producer who brought *The Apprentice* to America, and now here he was, screaming in my face in the middle of the jungle, starting some shoving contest like it's me and Brody back on that school bus. I just looked at him and laughed. No way in hell was I going back into that damn jungle, not after being talked to like that.

I called Dan Black, our attorney, and told him exactly what was going down. How we felt that we'd been lied to, hustled. How I was getting yelled at by studio execs while they held our passports hostage like we were political prisoners.

I expected fire and brimstone from Dan, some knight-in-shining-armor shit, a cease and desist, threats of international incident charges. Instead, I got the Hollywood equivalent of "thoughts and prayers." "Spencer, it's obvious that everyone's getting very upset," Dan said, his voice carrying that diplomatic tone lawyers use. "It's in your best interests to adopt a calm and pragmatic approach."

"Dan, this feels like kidnapping disguised as reality television."

"*Kidnapping* is a very strong word."

"It's also the CORRECT word, Dan!"

(All our accusations of kidnapping, false imprisonment, and Paul

Telegdy's assault were denied by ITV Studios, producers of the series, and Paul.)

It felt to me like Dan wasn't listening. It felt as though the Hollywood suits were closing ranks, and we were on the wrong side of the velvet rope.

Thankfully, the production nurse—God bless this enabler—kept slipping me Xanax. They were obviously trying to sedate me, calm me down, and I wasn't against the idea, even though I hadn't touched benzos since USC. On an empty stomach in 100-degree heat with 90 percent humidity, those things hit like a freight train. One pill and I was floating.

My phone lit up with a single bar of service. Caller ID: Harvey Levin, TMZ.

"Spencer, this is AMAZING! You need to get back on that fucking show, ASAP!"

I blinked. "Huh?"

"Speidi having a meltdown in the jungle is bigger than the moon landing," Harvey said.

"It is?"

"YES! You're trending worldwide! This is massive!"

"But we have to poop in a hole."

"Who cares? GET BACK IN THE JUNGLE!" Harvey barked. "Do you hear me? Go back in there and lose your goddamn minds."

And that, my friends, is the ONLY reason we went back into that bug-infested torture chamber. Because TMZ told us to. Not because it felt like Paul Telegdy bullied us, or because our lawyers and agents coaxed us into submission. It was Harvey Levin, reminding us of one simple truth: America was living for this drama, and drama was our job.

As Heidi and I psyched ourselves up to go back into camp, a Daniel Craig–looking security guard at the safe house slipped me a bag of weed. "Here you go, mate," he said. "You need to chill out, yeah? This whole situation's gone a bit mental."

"Sure, thanks," I said.

I parked myself by the river and rolled my very first spliff—weed, tobacco. I sparked it up, took what I thought was a casual, experienced inhale, and immediately realized I'd made a catastrophic miscalculation. Introducing marijuana to my existing cocktail of Xanax, severe dehydration, sleep deprivation, and full-blown existential crisis was like adding rocket fuel to a garbage fire.

"Spencer, what are you doing?" Heidi appeared through the trees, looking concerned and slightly horrified.

"Relaxing," I squeaked. "The nice man said I needed to chill out."

Within minutes, I was stumbling through the jungle, with Heidi trailing behind me like a worried camp counselor.

"Spencer, sit down before you walk into a tree!"

I made it maybe fifty feet before completely surrendering to gravity and collapsing by the riverbank. That's when I proceeded to projectile vomit every single ham-and-cheese toastie I'd stress-eaten earlier, launching those poor sandwiches into the Costa Rican ecosystem in a full-on *Exorcist*-level evacuation.

I saw angels perched in the treetops, the river glowing like holy water, and birds literally walking on the surface like tiny Jesuses performing miracles for an audience of one very stoned reality TV star. (Those were real, by the way—google it. They're called "Jesus birds," which felt like way too much religious symbolism for my brain to process.)

As I knelt there, retching into the jungle like a lawn sprinkler, I couldn't help thinking: *The things I do in the name of Montag Dry Shampoo.*

Once my nausea finally passed—back in we went. Skulking, defeated, but ready to see this nightmare through. Production had promised us one concession: a mattress. A single, glorious mattress in the jungle. Our reward for agreeing to reenter hell.

We walked back into camp, and immediately Sanjaya delivered us some bad news with a sheepish smile: "Sorry, you were gone too long, I've taken your bed."

I stared at him in disbelief. "You trying to be funny?"

"No."

"Good news, guys, we're having Sanjaya for dinner," I announced to the camp. "I'm gonna cook him alive."

Adding insult to injury, the "comedy" duo Frangela had gone through our bags like scavengers and distributed our belongings among the other celebrities. HA HA. SO FUNNY.

I was already pissed as hell about being dragged back to this insect-infested nightmare, but what really sent me into orbit was discovering that Torrie Wilson had deliberately ripped the labels off Heidi's dry shampoo while we were gone.

Our one shot at product placement.

The entire goddamn reason we'd agreed to this psychological torture experiment in the first place.

Gone.

Destroyed by someone who apparently had nothing better to do than vandalize hair products.

SHE KNOWS WHAT SHE DID.

When Heidi saw what had happened, she just broke down. As for me, I hadn't been this furious since the Lauren Conrad team fiasco. The rage was so pure, so white-hot, that for a moment I forgot about the cameras, the show, the fact that we were being filmed. All I could see was my wife, crying over her dry shampoo.

Today, if you look up "Spencer loses it in the jungle" on YouTube, you can see for yourself how I reacted. I started with Angela, and knocked her water bottle right out of her hand. Cool. You mess with my stuff, I'll mess with yours.

"DON'T HIT ME!" she yelped like I'd punched her in the face.

"Uh, I was standing right here," Janice said. "Spencer did NOT hit Angela's hand, he just whacked her bottle. He was trying to make a point."

But Angela wasn't backing down.

"Chill out," she said.

"No, I'm not gonna chill out," I fumed, looking at the remains of our dry shampoo branding. "I actually made this label and it took me all day! ARTS AND CRAFTS!"

John Salley, seven feet tall, was pulling me away as Angela continued to say I hit her, and I continued to point out that, actually, I hit the water bottle, and there's a difference.

"You don't know who you're talking to," Angela said, and I started hooting and howling like a damn hyena. *Aooooo!* Like, hell yeah, I didn't know who I was talking to because these people were nobodies.

Even Stephen Baldwin was enjoying the madness.

"I've heard of jungle fever, but this is ridiculous!" he said, grinning.

"WHERE'S YOUR STUFF? LET'S PLAY!" I shouted, lunging for Frangela's bags.

"Spencer, calm down!" Angela pleaded.

"I can't," I said truthfully.

In the middle of this volcanic meltdown—heart pounding, eyes bugging—I just stopped, pulled out the dry shampoo, and started spraying my hair. Puff. Puff. Puff. Stephen Baldwin sidled up, lifted his hat.

"Give me some," he said, so I sprayed his scalp.

"Hallelujah," he declared.

I was calm for about thirty seconds. Then I remembered: Torrie was the real person I was after. She was just sitting there all quiet, like it wasn't HER who'd started the whole thing, peeling the labels off the dry shampoo, letting Angela take the fall. Nice move.

"I can understand playing with my stuff," I sneered, "but ripping off the label, going 'Torrie's shampoo, Torrie's shampoo'? Nah. TORRIE CAN ONLY SELL STEROIDS!"

John Salley and Janice Dickinson were losing it, cackling like hyenas. They knew a good showdown when they saw one.

"I DID NOT TAKE STEROIDS!" Torrie clapped back, pathetically.

"Eh, you can't be that buff without steroids," I shot back.

"Have you ever worked out in your life?" she demanded.

"No," I said. "I'm too busy making money while you're lifting weights."

"Me, too! I have lots of businesses!" she countered.

"Yeah, I heard about them," I smirked. "That's why I had to google you to figure out who you even were."

The silence that followed was beautiful. Even the jungle seemed to pause to appreciate the carnage.

Game, set, match. Spencer Pratt.

CHAPTER 19

MAYDAY IN THE JUNGLE— PART TWO

Inside the Lost Chamber

Now that we were back in the jungle prison, we had to participate in our first challenge. The "Lost Chamber" sounded like something straight out of an *Indiana Jones* movie, except instead of treasure, we were competing for the privilege of eating actual food instead of the slop they'd been serving us.

The setup was simple but sadistic: Inside this pitch-black chamber of horrors, twenty star ornaments were hidden in the darkness. Heidi and I each had three minutes to find as many as possible, going in separately. If she collected more stars than me, the women would get to feast on grilled fish that night. If I won, the men would get the decent meal while the women got stuck with another serving of mystery rice and beans.

"No surrender, no retreat," I muttered to myself, psyching up like I was about to storm the beaches of Normandy instead of crawling around in a dark box looking for Christmas ornaments.

Then they opened the door to the Lost Chamber, and I got my first glimpse of what NBC considered "entertainment."

Immediately—rats. Not one or two rats. A *colony* of rats, like they'd been holding a town hall meeting in there. Scampering over my shoes, around my ankles, squeaking.

Then honest-to-God snakes, hissing in the darkness, slithering past my legs.

I felt something wet and slimy dripping from the ceiling. EEL SLIME. And then—because apparently NBC's torture budget has no limits—they started dropping cockroaches from the ceiling. Not a few cockroaches. Hundreds of them. A cockroach avalanche. A roach piñata, exploding above my head.

Every few seconds, a little flicker of light would flash on, just long enough for me to see the full scope of my nightmare. I remembered what someone told me once, how you're supposed to suffer in the name of art, except this wasn't art. This was a reality show, and my suffering wasn't going to win any Palme d'Ors or change the course of history. At best, maybe it would win a Teen Choice Award for "Most Disgusting Moment."

When I finally stumbled out of that chamber, covered in eel goo and the remnants of my shattered dignity, I could barely form words. To this day, nothing has topped it. That Lost Chamber was NBC's masterpiece of human suffering.

Then it was Heidi's turn. She walked in with the confidence of a woman entering Bloomingdale's. "Just pretend I'm shopping," she told herself. My brave, beautiful wife emerged three minutes later, with the thousand-yard stare of someone who'd seen things that couldn't be unseen. Zero stars in her bag. At this point, she, too, was probably wondering if some TMZ headlines were really worth all this suffering.

Back at camp, Stephen Baldwin materialized beside me. He'd had a full-blown spiritual awakening, reinventing himself as a born-again Christian, writing books about Jesus, starring in straight-to-DVD evangelist films. (Clearly, the man's prayers worked—his daughter grew up to marry Justin Bieber and launch a billion-dollar makeup line. The man basically prayed Hailey into billionaire status.)

Maybe he sensed my spiritual crisis. He sat down next to me without a word at first, just this quiet presence, like he wasn't there to film a show. Like he was there on assignment from God.

"Spencer," he said finally, his voice low and steady, "I can see you're hurting. But brother, there's another way. There's peace."

I laughed, sharp and bitter. "Peace? Out here?"

He didn't flinch. "Spencer, do you believe in Jesus Christ? Do you accept Him as your Lord and Savior?"

"Obviously, but I also believe in a hotel. A bed. In getting out of here."

Stephen leaned closer, his eyes fierce but not unkind. "Let me baptize you in this river, Spencer. Wash away the chaos. Start fresh."

I stared at the water.

"You're serious?" I muttered to Stephen.

He nodded, smiling. "Yes. Let Jesus meet you here. Let Him carry the weight you're trying to drag on your own."

By the river, with cameras rolling, Stephen Baldwin dunked me under brown water, baptizing me. "You're saved now, brother!" he cried as I came up gasping.

John Salley sat there, watching, shaking his head.

Later, he pulled me aside.

"You should be a Mason, Spencer."

"Like, a Freemason?" I croaked, still wet from my baptism.

"Yeah. You could reach the thirty-third degree. Because you were married before twenty-five, it's the most powerful way."

"Huh?"

"And why are you wearing a cross?" He pointed at my Jason of Beverly Hills black diamond piece—thirty grand of Jesus bling around my neck. "If Jesus was killed with a Glock, would you want people wearing pistols around their necks?"

My brain was fried—dehydrated, benzo'd, halfway to delirium—and suddenly I was in the middle of some holy war I hadn't even realized I'd enlisted in. And in that moment of weakness, of cosmic confusion, I took off my diamond cross.

Lord, forgive me.

No longer protected by Christ's bling around my neck, I was informed that Heidi and I would be facing special punishment for our earlier rebellion. They were making us spend an entire night in the Lost Chamber—a whole night in that pitch-black box of evolutionary nightmares.

I've honestly blacked out most of this experience. All I remember is a sense of pure, distilled horror. Every hour, like the world's most sadistic room service, they'd add a new category of creature to our darkness. First more rats, scratching and squealing in the corners. Then additional snakes, slithering around our feet. More jungle roaches the size of smartphones. Fresh eel slime raining from the ceiling like Satan's tears.

All night, Heidi clutched my arm so tight I thought she might actually snap bone, while I whispered every prayer I could half remember through my drug-and-terror haze: "Please God, please Jesus, please Stephen Baldwin, get us out of here."

By dawn, I was genuinely convinced this wasn't television at all—it was actually some kind of live psychological experiment designed to measure the exact moment when human beings lose their sanity on camera.

Day three. We emerged from the Lost Chamber like two shell-shocked veterans stumbling out of a foxhole, fully traumatized but somehow still breathing. At this point, we'd been so systematically gaslit by the producers that we'd actually started accepting medieval torture as a reasonable price to pay for prime-time television exposure.

The psychological manipulation was masterful, really. They'd broken us down so completely that when they announced the next challenge—a bug-eating contest—Heidi didn't even flinch. Consuming actual vermin was just part of our job description now.

"I can do this," she said, psyching herself up as they laid out the spread. Scorpions. Rat tails—actual rat tails, some still sporting tufts of fur like grotesque little feather dusters. Here's the thing about Heidi—she's pathologically competitive. Always has been. So when they lined up all the contestants and explained that the winner would get actual food that night instead of rice and sadness, something primal activated in her already-delirious brain.

"I'm not losing," she muttered.

My wife—who won't eat sushi that's been sitting out for more than ten minutes—grabbed those scorpions and started crunching through them like they were appetizers at a cocktail party. The rat tail with actual hair still attached? She treated it like a breadstick, chewing methodically, systematically demolishing every disgusting thing they put in front of her while John Salley—a man who'd probably eaten everything from Detroit to Los Angeles—started gagging and tapped out.

She won. Decisively. And for about thirty seconds, watching her victory dance, I actually forgot we were in hell.

Until she collapsed, and started vomiting. It wouldn't stop, so eventually they brought over the medic—he took one glance at Heidi's pale, sweaty face and immediately started looking like he wished he'd chosen a different career path. "I'm not sure what's happening, but it could be stress ulcers, a parasite, severe dehydration, complete exhaustion," he rattled off like he was reading from WebMD. "She needs a hospital. A real one."

They loaded us into some kind of medical transport and drove us to a small local clinic, stationing the guard outside like we were flight risks instead of people seeking medical attention for my potentially poisoned wife.

A few hours later, my phone rang. It was Dan Black, our attorney.

"How's Heidi doing?" he asked.

"They think it's a gastric ulcer or gastritis," I told him. Then he got to the point: NBC was offering $845,000 if I went back into the jungle. I told him I didn't care about the money. Heidi had eaten rats and scorpions, landed in a hospital, and this nightmare had to end. I was done.

"Life's short," Dan said, slipping into that fatherly tone. Nearly a million dollars on the table. Maybe I should consider going back in alone, while Heidi recovered under medical supervision? I said no, because back then, I was convinced the money would never stop flowing. A million dollars? Who cares. Not for ten million would I go back in there and leave my wife alone.

Looking back now, I know Dan was only trying to protect my interests, the way he always had. And sometimes, I do wish I'd taken that money. Sure would have made the years that followed a little easier.

Later that day, when I vented to Harvey Levin and TMZ about everything, I was so pissed I must've said something that sounded like I'd fired my attorney. Word travels fast, and Dan Black was apparently out at drinks when someone leaned over and said, "Hey, saw in the *Hollywood Reporter* you got fired by that douche nozzle, Spencer Pratt."

The man who helped me negotiate some of the most important contracts in my life felt, understandably, insulted to hear the news. The kind man who once sent us Hermès scarves every Christmas would no longer send us scarves. And even though his firm technically still reps us, Dan himself would never speak to me again.

I'm very sorry, Dan Black. Consider this my formal apology.

In the hospital room, Heidi stirred, her eyelids fluttering. "Spencer?"

"Right here, baby." I took her hand.

"Why . . ." A cough, weak and wet. "Why is this happening?"

I swallowed hard, tasting regret. "Remember what you always say? That God uses everything for good? Maybe this is just . . . part of His plan, you know?"

Her fingers tightened around mine, a ghost of her usual strength. "God's plan sucks."

Even in that moment, Heidi could still make me laugh.

"Hey, Spencer?" Heidi's eyes were closed, her voice a whisper.

"Yeah, baby?"

"Next time someone offers us a reality show, can we just say no?"

I pressed my lips to her forehead.

"Absolutely, angel," I said. Neither of us believed it, of course. But it sounded comforting in the moment.

After being pumped full of fluids and antibiotics, Heidi finally started to improve. They moved us to the Marriott in San José—full circle, right back where this nightmare began. After twenty-four hours of stalling, someone finally handed over our passports. The second those little booklets hit our hands, we were gone. Bolted. We threw $1,000 in cash at a taxi driver and told him to floor it—eight hours across Costa Rica, straight to the Four Seasons in Papagayo.

Finally, it was over.

At the Four Seasons—Heidi trembling in a hotel robe, me sipping a mai tai by the pool—we called NBC to tell them we were officially finished.

Oh, and they'd be hearing from our lawyers. (Not Dan Black—he was no longer taking our calls—but someone else at the firm.) Because that's what happens when you take Heidi Montag's innocent dry shampoo commercial and turn it into *The Hunger Games* with rat tails and river baptisms.

And people wonder why we trust no one.

The press went crazy. There were front-page stories about whether NBC had literally tortured us. TMZ called what happened to us "abuse." Heidi's dad went on national TV, furious at the network. For once, it wasn't just *our* reputations on the line—it was NBC's. Telegdy had gone on the record, bragging about how he'd wanted to break us; he used the phrase "deconstructing our value system." Now NBC was backtracking, scrambling to issue statements about how there were medics on hand, how we were never in danger, how we'd had food and water that night in the Lost Chamber, as though that would have made the experience any less horrific.

But the truth is, the damage was already done. This wasn't just a bad look for NBC—it was a bad look for the entire reality TV machine.

People started questioning the ethics of these shows, wondering if the networks had crossed the line from "competitive fun" into psychological warfare. The executives, too, started asking themselves questions. About *us*.

For years, Heidi and I had been their perfect villains, the safe, bankable bet—the couple you could count on for ratings because no one cared if we got hurt. But when Heidi landed in that hospital, the narrative shifted. Suddenly, this didn't look like entertainment anymore. It seemed like exploitation.

Suddenly, Speidi was radioactive—the talent that wouldn't do as it was told, the cash cow that had become a liability. If we couldn't be controlled, if our suffering didn't make people laugh anymore, then what good were we?

And that, my friend, was the beginning of the end of our villain era. From that moment on, networks looked at us not as a ratings guarantee, but as a risk. And once you're not profitable anymore, once you're not safe to exploit, Hollywood moves on.

Fast.

CHAPTER 20

SHELTER FROM THE STORM

*Crystals, Plastic Surgery, and
Other Safe Spaces*

The morning we landed on *Today* to talk about our jungle escapade, I was actually looking forward to it. Al Roker—America's beloved weatherman—would be interviewing us, and I figured we'd probably have a friendly chat about surviving Costa Rica, maybe even a bitter laugh or two about the Lost Chamber and that one time Torrie and Frangela stole our dry shampoo.

Instead, we walked into an execution.

"There are some who say you two are everything that's wrong with celebrity in this country," Roker opened, after screening a highlight reel from our wildest moments on the show.

I could feel my face getting hot, that familiar surge of adrenaline that comes when you realize you're under attack and there's nowhere to run.

I tried to laugh it off, making some joke about the highlight reel, desperately hoping to steer this ship away from the rocks. But Al wasn't interested in changing course. He was locked and loaded.

"When you look at this stuff, that you have on this tape, do you have any regrets about doing what you do?" he pressed, his voice carrying this sanctimonious tone.

Something stubborn and defensive rose up in me. I wasn't going to grovel for his approval.

"I was actually going to ask your producers to get a copy of that highlight reel—because that was one of my favorite things I've ever watched," I said.

The theatrical sigh he let out. "Is it really?"

"Absolutely," I doubled down.

He asked me if I want to be the villain, and I reminded him I only wanted to be a villain on TV, not in life. I want to be the hero in real life.

"When you act like that, how do you expect people to think of you as a hero?" he asked.

It was like being slapped by your grandfather in front of the whole family at Thanksgiving.

As I watched him turn to Heidi, my protective instincts kicked in. She was trying to explain, to give context, but he steamrolled right over her, asking her if she was proud of the way we "behaved." I could feel her confusion and hurt radiating across the set. She managed a weak, "I'm not ashamed," but even that wasn't enough for him.

"But are you proud of it?" The disgust in his voice was unmistakable.

When Heidi just shrugged and said "Sure," I knew we were done for. But Al wasn't finished with me yet.

"You say 'villain'; some people say 'jerk.'"

The blood was rushing in my ears now.

"Tomato, tomahto," I managed, trying to sound casual. If only this guy knew what we'd actually been through out there—how my wife had nearly died in that jungle, how I'd watched her collapse, how terrified I'd been that I might lose her . . . But wait. He did know. He knew all of that, and he *still* came for us. And he's calling *us* the jerks?

Interesting.

We walked off that set, Heidi in tears—real, raw sobs of someone who'd been genuinely hurt. She kept saying how shocked she was, how mean Al had been. Seeing her like that, seeing what he had done to her . . . well, by now you know what it does to me, when people come at my wife. The Hulk comes out.

In an interview with Ryan Seacrest a few days later, I said it was a good thing I'd been saved by Jesus; otherwise, I would have ripped Roker's head off. By the time we got to *Larry King Live* a few nights later, I'd had time to calm down a bit, and strategize. Peter Grossman from *Us Weekly* had given me the perfect angle: "Just turn it around on the weatherman," he'd said. "Make him look ridiculous."

So I did. (Although, let's be honest, making Al Roker look dumb isn't exaaaactly a heavy lift.)

"Obviously, any male, especially an elderly male, who thinks he can berate my twenty-two-year-old wife on television . . . it was a very difficult situation," I told Larry King. "But we forgive him. It was early in the morning. Maybe he was upset he had to report some bad weather coming up later this week."

In that moment, I thought I was winning. I thought I was getting the last word. Looking back now, though, I realize nothing I could have said would have made any difference. Our ship was already sinking. Hollywood had had enough of Speidi.

We were still up to our tricks trying to get attention, to get us back in the good graces of the public. But we often missed the mark and wound up doing more harm than good. After Heidi did a spread for *Playboy*, for example—no nudity—we crashed the *G.I. Joe: The Rise of Cobra* premiere uninvited, with me waving her *Playboy* cover above my head like a championship belt. Who cared about Channing Tatum in fatigues when Heidi Montag was on the newsstand?

I waded straight into the middle of the red carpet, grinning as flashbulbs went off and heads turned. For a second, I felt like I'd hacked the system. I guess I thought I was doing the magazine a solid, but we managed to piss off the entire *G.I. Joe* production instead. In the industry's eyes, this twenty-five-year-old kid was just proving what they already suspected—that I was out of control, a liability with no respect for the rules.

By this point it was obvious that the whole narrative had shifted against us. And it definitely showed in the way we were portrayed on-screen on *The Hills*, too. By the time Part Two of Season 5 aired that fall, what people saw wasn't the fun Spencer-and-Heidi villain show anymore. Instead, it was two whack jobs seemingly losing their minds on camera. We looked paranoid, isolated, out of touch, completely cut off from everyone who used to matter.

Which, honestly, wasn't that far from the truth.

We'd become *those people*—the ones who trusted no one, who'd rather barricade themselves in their house with guns, dogs, and the few humans we still believed wouldn't sell us out. Our circle had shrunk down to almost nothing: our families, Peter Grossman, our doctor; our security guys; a couple old Palisades surfer and jiujitsu friends; and "King" Kevin Casey, the MMA fighter from South Central I was managing at the time, investing in his fighting career.

Kevin had earned a brown belt under Rickson Gracie, which is how I knew him—the most intense human being I've ever encountered. I was doing my full Don King promoter thing, going to the press and talking him up like he was the second coming. I'd say shit like: "King Kevin is on the warpath like an Apache working for Geronimo. God put me in his life to warn people." I'd get completely carried away: "I see him being the most successful athlete of all time. Bigger than Tiger Woods, bigger than Michael Jordan."

Kevin's crew rolled through all the time—a couple of them were guys with reputations, with ties to the Rollin' 60s Neighborhood Crips, one of the largest and most well-known street gangs in Los Angeles. On paper, they were trouble. But in practice? They were good guys, to us. More real, more honest than most of the people I used to call friends. Heidi and I truly felt safe when these guys were around. Unlike how we felt the other twenty-three hours of the day.

Yeah. Safety. That's what it all boiled down to in the end. Every word out of our mouths, every stunt we pulled, seemed to get us in deeper trouble with the outside world; so, subconsciously, Heidi and

I were clawing for something—anything—that made us feel protected inside our own little sphere.

Believing in God helped—when the whole world hates you, it's comforting to think at least the big guy upstairs has your back, so long as you repent. And repent I did. Every week. Heidi and I started going to church every Sunday, and I'd march down the aisle each time to get "saved" over and over again. After the third altar call, the pastor finally pulled me aside and said, "*Son, salvation is a one-time deal. You don't need to keep coming up—you're already saved.*"

But I couldn't stop myself. I needed the receipt stamped weekly, like a parking validation, just to make sure it stuck.

When we weren't in church, we chased safety the only other way we knew: by spending, by proving just how much money we had. Five hundred thousand dollars' worth of Birkin bags for Heidi. About the same on designer suits for me. Three hundred thousand dollars' worth of ammo—endless ammo. Tens of thousands of rounds stacked in the closet right next to my Armani. Faith in God, faith in consumerism, faith in firepower. Our holy trinity of survival. Nothing could've been more American.

I also started investing heavily in cybersecurity—not just for protection, but because I saw it as the ultimate power play in a digital world where everyone was vulnerable. I had heard that, within the next five years, the US government was going to be spending almost fifteen billion dollars on private cybersecurity contracts, and I wanted in on that action. I was hiring guys straight out of MIT to build digital fortresses around our systems.

Fast-forward to today—massive data breaches, infrastructure attacks, social media manipulation campaigns, entire power grids getting shut down by hackers.

TELL ME I wasn't ahead of the curve on this one.

TELL ME I was just being paranoid when I said our entire civilization was one cyberattack away from collapse.

Pratt Daddy knows, okay? Remember my ancestry? I come from a looong line of so-called "conspiracy theorists" who turned out to be dead-on accurate, because it's only a conspiracy theory until it becomes breaking news. Then, suddenly, everyone's acting like they saw it coming all along . . .

Around this time, I developed what you might call an expensive hobby—though hobby doesn't quite capture it. This *obsession* would fill our house with ancient energy and ultimately burn to nothing along with everything else we thought was permanent.

Crystals.

The journey began on what should have been an ordinary day. I was heading to Bay Cities Deli in Santa Monica to grab a sandwich, and there, in the window of a store called Wonders of the World Museum & Gallery, was this thing that looked like it had fallen from another planet. A two-thousand-pound quartz crystal. Calling to me.

A sign on the window said "Call or text for an afternoon or evening appointment as we have no schedule." Luckily, they were open, so I stepped inside and marveled at the gems and oddities everywhere. Meteorites that belonged in the Smithsonian, crystals that seemed to have been hand-carved by angels.

I met Henry, the proprietor, to discuss purchasing the giant crystal. What a character. He told me he was an alien. Not an "I'm quirky and spiritual" alien. Like, "I'm literally from another planet and crash-landed here" alien. Welcome to Los Angeles.

Anyway, Henry the Alien was the best damn salesman I've ever encountered, and I've met a few. "You'll be the most famous celebrity that ever lived if you become 'the crystal guy,'" he told me with complete conviction. "These stones are millions of years old. You'll be more famous than Elvis and Marilyn combined." SOLD.

That massive quartz was my gateway drug—I bought it for $75,000, which was spare change at that point, peak Speidi money. I hauled it home, and before long, our entire house became a crystal sanctuary, as though that first crystal created some form of magnetic energy that made me want to buy every mystical crystal I could find.

"Bro, just sell me a rock," I'd beg Henry during my weekly visits.

"Nah," he'd say, not even looking up from whatever ancient text he was studying. Henry was notorious for NOT always selling—which, of course, only made me want his stuff more.

Before long, we had upward of a million dollars' worth of crystals and counting. Every room filled with amethyst geodes, massive quartz points, rare specimens that museums would kill for. I'd walk through our home and feel like I was living inside a gemstone cathedral, surrounded by millions of years of Earth's most beautiful creations.

Zero regrets.

Of course, they're all gone now, pretty much. Every single stone, every rare specimen, every piece of ancient Earth energy—turned to ash and dust in the fires. When I think about those flames consuming millions of years of crystalline perfection in a matter of hours, it still breaks my heart. All that beauty, all that history, all that power—reduced to nothing.

But I'll always be grateful for what they provided me with during that time—a focus that I desperately needed during the darkest period of my life. When everything else felt chaotic and unstable, there was something so grounding about holding a piece of Earth that had been forming for millions of years.

Heidi was also on a path to self-empowerment. She collected crystals alongside me, but for her, self-care also meant sculpting herself into the version she saw in her head—the one that couldn't be broken by jungle torture or network executives or public humiliation. If the world was going to turn her into a character, she'd take control of that narrative and write that character herself. Rebuild herself from the outside in. Both of us were searching for the same thing, I guess—a sense of control, a way to feel powerful in a world that had made us feel powerless. We just chose very different methods.

Heidi had already gotten a boob job and a nose job in 2007, thanks to Beverly Hills plastic surgeon Dr. Frank Ryan. He was a go-to guy in Hollywood, secretly working on all the A-listers. Ryan agreed to do Heidi's surgeries for free once *Us Weekly* promised to run a feature about it.

She'd healed beautifully and was completely transparent about the work she'd had done, which was revolutionary at the time—other women in Hollywood were getting the same procedures and then gaslighting the entire world, claiming they'd just "grown into their faces" or discovered some magical makeup technique.

But Heidi? She owned every single procedure like a badge of honor. She'd pose for *Us Weekly*'s before-and-after spreads, walk red carpets talking openly about her surgeon, even give detailed breakdowns of her recovery process.

It was refreshingly honest in an industry built on carefully crafted illusions. While everyone else was pretending their transformations were natural miracles, Heidi was saying, "Yeah, I paid for this face, and I love it." She turned plastic surgery from Hollywood's dirty little secret into a form of self-expression.

Which is why what happened next was so devastating.

Heidi got injured when she was filming the music video for her song "Overdosin'"—a backup dancer's elbow connected with her nose, dented it in. We're talking visible dent. She'd dealt with it for two years before deciding to go back to Dr. Ryan to get it fixed.

The morning of the surgery, on November 20, 2009, I drove her to the surgical center at dawn. Dr. Ryan met us in pre-op with a blue surgical marker.

"While you're under," he said, uncapping the pen, "we could just . . ."

And then came the word that haunts me: "Minor."

"Minor adjustment here." Blue mark on her chin.

"Minor refinement here." Blue line down her back.

"Minor, minor, minor." Blue marks multiplying across her body like a road map to someone else.

This doctor was playing Picasso with a blue pen, turning my wife into a connect-the-dots puzzle.

"How much are we talking?" Heidi asked.

Dr. Ryan started rattling off numbers like an auctioneer. "Chin reduction, twenty-five thousand. Back scoop, fifteen thousand. Ear pinning, ten thousand . . ."

By the time he finished, we were looking at a quarter million in procedures.

"But for you? Free. All of it. My gift."

I saw Heidi's eyes light up. In her mind, she'd just won the lottery. A quarter million in free improvements? That's just good business.

"Okay," Heidi said. "If it's minor. I'll do it!"

I kissed her forehead. "Love you, baby. I'll be back this afternoon. Good luck."

I got home to the Palisades and was about to feed our two Pomeranians and two Maltipoos when Bill Beasley, our head of security, called. I'd hired him and his team—a security detail of six guys—to keep an eye on Heidi while she was in the aftercare clinic.

"Spencer, you need to get here. Something's wrong with your wife."

He sounded shook.

"What do you mean?"

"She's not breathing right. Just get over here."

I don't remember getting in my car. Don't remember the drive. Just remember speeding down Wilshire, blowing through red lights like they were suggestions, my hands white-knuckling the steering wheel.

By the time I screeched into the hospital parking lot and sprinted through those doors, my twenty-three-year-old wife, the love of my life, was unconscious on a recovery table, barely breathing.

Thank God we'd had our own security in that recovery room. If we hadn't, Heidi would be dead. It was one of our guys—an ex-

Marine named Torres—who had noticed something was wrong. "Her O_2 levels are crashing," Torres had said, watching the monitors. They called in the actual medical staff, by which point Heidi was turning blue.

Later, when she was revived, Heidi would describe what had happened during those moments when she'd hovered between life and death. This incredible sensation of flying through galaxies, soaring past stars and nebulas, traveling faster than the speed of light through cosmic landscapes. She said it was the most beautiful, peaceful experience of her life—this weightless journey through infinite space while her body fought to stay alive on Earth. Meanwhile, the rest of us were sitting in that waiting room, praying she'd choose to come back to us.

Did I mention it was our wedding anniversary? Yeah. Exactly a year since we'd gotten married in Cabo.

What a way to celebrate.

The cause of Heidi's near-death experience was Demerol overdose, administered post-surgery at an aftercare facility that has since closed. Demerol is one of those old-school narcotics that can go sideways fast. Too much, and your body just . . . shuts down. Breathing slows, blood pressure tanks, lights out. I was furious. My mind was racing with thoughts and theories. What if someone had done this on purpose? What if someone had "accidentally" upped Heidi's dosage? Far-fetched as it sounds . . .

Back then, Randy Quaid—the "shitter's full" guy from *Christmas Vacation*—was going off about his "Star Whackers" conspiracy. He claimed Hollywood had secret assassins taking out celebrities so studios and handlers could cash in on their deaths.

Heath Ledger dies and instantly his movies are rereleased, his face everywhere, old work suddenly "valuable" again. Same with David Carradine, Chris Penn—tragedy flipped into business plans overnight. The corporations, the labels, the lawyers—they're the ones who profit.

Because a dead star in Hollywood isn't just a tragedy; it's an opportunity. *Maybe Quaid is on to something*, I thought.

Heidi had undergone ten surgeries in one day. Afterward, understandably, she looked like she'd been hit by a train. And honestly? That's what it felt like for both of us.

People don't understand what "ten procedures in one day" actually means. It means your wife can't stand up without screaming. It means she's taking so many pain medications she can barely form sentences. It means watching someone you love shuffle to the bathroom like they're ninety years old, and you can't do a damn thing to help.

"I'm going to die," she whispered one night, about a week post-op. She wasn't being dramatic. She genuinely believed it.

"You're not going to die," I told her, but honestly, I was scared, too.

She couldn't think clearly. Couldn't focus on anything beyond just surviving the next hour. It was like watching someone in a prison of their own body—trapped, terrified, and completely alone in the pain no matter how much I tried to be there for her.

The only way she got through it was by going somewhere else mentally. She'd lie there with her eyes closed, and I knew she wasn't sleeping—she was in some kind of meditative, spiritual space. Retreating inward because that was the only escape available to her.

Her recovery was brutal. The swelling was intense. Her face was puffy and distorted. Her body was bruised and swollen. I kept thinking, *What have we done? What did we let happen?*

But slowly—so slowly—the swelling went down. Her body started to heal. And once it did, once she could finally see the results she'd been hoping for, something shifted.

"I love it," she whispered one morning, looking at herself in the mirror. Relief in her voice. The pain was still there—dull and persistent—but the regret she'd braced herself for never arrived. This was who she'd always been. She was just meeting herself for the first time.

Less than a month after her surgeries, Heidi had to return to work. There was no luxury of recovery time, no gradual reentry into public life, and she was still incredibly fragile from her surgeries when we started filming Season 6 of *The Hills* in 2010.

She didn't have bandages on her face anymore, but she was nowhere near recovered, and looking back, she shouldn't have been in front of a single camera, filming a single scene. The smart move would've been to take six months off, let her body recover, and come back when she was actually ready.

But that's not how reality TV works.

MTV was insisting she fly to Colorado to film a big "surgery reveal" scene with her family.

They wanted to capture her parents' reactions to their daughter's transformation. Heidi really didn't want to do it. She even offered her mom the same amount MTV wanted to pay. But her mom assured Heidi that she would be nice, supportive, and comforting. They knew everything she'd been through—that she had nearly died and been revived, how fragile she was physically and mentally, how she could barely move without wincing. Only upon her mother actively lobbying for Heidi to go did Heidi finally agree.

Every instinct in my body was screaming *"Danger!"* as she got ready to head to her parents'. I knew she wasn't ready for any kind of emotional confrontation—she could barely handle me helping her change her bandages without breaking down in tears. The whole experience had been way more extreme than either of us could have imagined. The recovery, the pain, the psychological toll of having your entire face and body reconstructed—it was outrageous.

And the producers were insistent. They even chartered a private jet to fly her out in maximum luxury, knowing exactly how to play to Heidi's weaknesses—she's never met a deal or a private jet she didn't love.

Before she left, she called her mom.

"Mom, seriously, if you can't control yourself, I'm not coming," Heidi said, her voice shaky but firm. "Please don't say anything negative. I can't handle it right now."

"No, I promise I won't," her mom replied.

The producers had banned me from going—they wanted her isolated, vulnerable, alone with her family's reactions. I was too young and naive to know that they had no authority to tell me not to go. I should have known better. She arrived in Colorado, wrapped in layers like a mummy, sunglasses on even though it was cloudy, moving slowly, careful not to strain her stitches.

When she pulled up to her house, her mother, Darlene, was standing in the doorway.

Heidi took a shaky breath and walked up those steps.

Darlene hugged her, but it was one of those hugs where your hands barely touch the person's back, like you're afraid you'll hurt them. They went inside, the cameras tracking them like predators, and, as broadcast on the premiere of the final season of *The Hills*, what followed was a conversation that would destroy a mother-daughter relationship for years to come.

"You act like I have a new face or something," Heidi said when she settled in for what she had assumed would be a gentle chat.

"Well, that's pretty much what it is," said Darlene. "It takes a little getting used to. It's very weird and very awkward. I'm sorry."

Speaking in the low, careful tones of someone whose face could barely move, Heidi began explaining to her mom and sister, Holly, all the work she'd had done. As the list grew longer, her mother's horror became more apparent.

"It sounds to me like you want to look like Barbie," Darlene said, her voice thick with disapproval.

"I do want to look like Barbie," Heidi replied honestly.

"Why would you want to look like Barbie? To everybody else that saw you, you were Heidi. Nobody in the world could have looked like Heidi Montag."

Heidi, hoping for some validation—any sign that maybe this hadn't all been a mistake—pressed for the answer she needed to hear.

"Are you telling me you don't think I look good?"

Her mother tried to dodge. "Maybe you should rephrase the question."

But Heidi wouldn't let it go. "No. Do I look good?"

The silence stretched between them before Darlene delivered her response. "How do I go and say that of course I thought you were more beautiful before? I thought you were younger, I thought you were fresher-looking, I thought you were healthier. What's done is done, so that's a terrible thing for me to say, but, yes, that's how I feel. I felt that you were much more beautiful before, and I hope that some of this will fade away."

By the way, and I know I'm biased, but Heidi, if you're reading this, you looked beautiful. You always have, and you always will.

Through tears and a voice cracking with hurt, Heidi said: "You don't have to support it or think it looks good, but you have to realize what I've been through. You have to realize that I've been through so much pain, and coming here and having you attack me is just really hard . . . Mom, this is what I chose, and there's nothing that I can take back."

This conversation marked the beginning of a two-year estrangement between mother and daughter, captured in excruciating detail for the world to see.

Hearing about what happened, I wished I'd fought harder to be there. I would have walked us straight out of that house the second her family started to criticize her. Her family kept up the criticism after the cameras stopped rolling, too. As if the public humiliation wasn't enough.

Bottom line, we were two kids who'd gotten famous too fast, rich too quick, and hated by the world too completely, scrambling to build some kind of fortress around what was left of ourselves. The crystals, the guns, the church, the surgeries, the isolation—they were all just different versions of the same prayer: *Please let us make it through this alive.*

CHAPTER 21

VISION QUESTS IN A WORLD OF ILLUSION

Gurus, Psychic Protection, and the Search for Something Real

Weeks after returning from Colorado, Heidi was still in excruciating pain. The painkillers—these supposedly top-tier post-surgery pharmaceuticals—were like Tic Tacs against what she was going through. A week straight, no sleep. Just her in our bed, sobbing while I sat there feeling useless.

At a loss, I googled "alternative healing methods for pain" at, like, 3 a.m.

That's when the universe served me up sugilite—this purple crystal that's supposedly the ultimate pain stone. The website said it worked on a "cellular level," which honestly sounded more legit than whatever Big Pharma was pushing.

Mind you, we already had a million dollars' worth of crystals at this point—our house looked like the Natural History Museum—but no sugilite. So the next morning, I rolled up to our crystal shop in Santa Monica, where Henry the Alien led me to a locked case in the back. Inside was a massive chunk of sugilite. Price tag? Fifteen thousand dollars.

"Can do," I said, pulling out my credit card.

I brought it home, put it in Heidi's hands, and said, "Just hold it where it hurts, honey."

She just clutched it to her chest and closed her eyes. Then—and I swear on my entire lost crystal collection this is true—she slept. For the first time in over a week. No pain. No crying. Just deep, peaceful, $15,000 sleep.

I'd always wanted to believe in the power of crystals. And watching that purple rock do what a pharmacy couldn't? That's when I became a Crystal Daddy for real.

First, I bought a copy of *Love Is in the Earth*, an iconic book written by a person called simply "Melody" that is THE crystal book. The rock Bible. Seven-hundred-something pages of pure rock intel. The book had three pages just on sugilite—calling it "the premier love stone," explaining how it works on cellular memory, how it removes pain from all bodies (physical, emotional, etheric).

Ahhh.

I guess that's why it had worked so well for Heidi.

I kept reading, educating myself.

The high priestesses in ancient times? Covered themselves in lapis.

King Tut? Made sure he was buried with tektite.

Our iPhones have quartz in them.

When I read that the F-22 Raptor targeting system used kunzite, that's when I was fully sold. If it's allegedly good enough for America's most advanced fighter jet, it's good enough for Spencer Pratt, and I've been collecting kunzite extensively ever since. (Some of my pieces even made it out in my go bag during the fires, thankfully.)

I noticed how certain stones would make my teeth tingle or create heat in my palms. I'd be reading *Us Weekly* and Perez but also learning how to create interdimensional communication grids with Herkimer diamonds and selenite. If I knew that there were haters around, which was often, I'd carry quartz and black tourmaline together—I'd read that Native Americans believe that if someone tries to send you bad vibes, that combo bounces it back to them. *See how you like that negative energy back atcha!*

After Heidi's sugilite miracle, we told Heidi's plastic surgeon, Frank Ryan, that we were getting into alternative healing. He recommended his personal healer to us, a woman who worked in his office. She showed up with hot jade stones and essential oils and started working on Heidi. "She needs Kundalini yoga," she told us. "It works with the same energy systems as crystals."

Enter the Kundalini teacher. This woman was DEDICATED, and so were we. We're talking 4 a.m. sessions. She'd show up in all white, carrying a sheepskin rug.

"The veil between worlds is thinnest at dawn," she'd say.

We thought Kundalini was just fancy stretching. Turns out we were practicing an ancient technology—using breathing techniques that moved energy through your chakras, poses that opened portals. After a month of this spiritual boot camp, our yoga teacher said, "You should meet my healer friend. Third generation. His grandfather healed people in Europe."

Okay.

Enter: Hugo.

He started doing healing sessions on Heidi. Waving his hands over her body, never touching, just . . . sensing. He'd frown and go, "There's an entity here. We need to cut this cord." Using his selenite knife, he'd cut the cord connected to the entity. Cost? Five hundred dollars a session. But it didn't matter to us. Heidi was clearly getting better, now that her entities were being invisibly severed from her being.

Even though I was seeing results, I was still skeptical, deep down. Like, *Who is this guy? What's really happening here?* I needed to run some tests of my own, so I started buying healings for my friends as litmus tests—not to validate my sanity but to see if this was actually legitimate. And I'm not talking about my yes-man friends who agreed with everything I said. I specifically chose my asshole friends, the ones who called me an idiot to my face and wouldn't hesitate to tell me I'd completely lost my mind.

"Here's five hundred dollars," I'd say. "Let this wizard touch your aura and then tell me I'm crazy."

Every single one came out looking like they'd seen God.

One day, Hugo dropped this on me: "Spencer, you're psychic. You just don't know how to use it." When I'd question his prices or methods, he'd grab his temples and go, "You're targeting my brain with your untrained psychic abilities! You need to learn control!"

Working on it, Hugo. Still am.

He told me that the Illuminati all have their own Hugos—spiritual bodyguards creating psychic shields around them 24/7. He even claimed President Obama had one, pointing out certain Secret Service agents in photos who were supposedly doing his "protection field" work alongside the regular security detail. According to Hugo, that's exactly why the CIA's remote viewing program can't touch the real power players—they're all spiritually protected by people like him. My brain exploded. If the elites have psychic armor, then I NEED THIS SHIT.

Next thing I know, we're driving around LA with Hugo in the back seat opening portals to manipulate the time-space continuum so we can find parking and avoid traffic. "Focus on where you want to be," Hugo would say. "Visualize the parking space. Now OPEN THE PORTAL." And I shit you not—we'd ALWAYS find parking. Every light would turn green. Traffic would open up like magic. When you're operating on those frequencies, reality becomes negotiable, my friends.

Heidi got a $3,000 crystal wand from some ancient Tibetan collection and began doing protection spells at every doorway like she was warding off vampires. Hugo had taught us that every doorway is a portal and you need to set an intention before crossing through it. We'd be pulling up to Giorgio Baldi and Heidi would whip out the crystal wand before we got our sweet corn agnolotti, waving it around the restaurant entrance like we were about to perform an exorcism instead of ordering dinner.

In Seasons 5 and 6 of *The Hills*, you'll see I'm wearing crystals a LOT—still designer quality because I never bought cheap crystals, only genuine gemstones. People on set thought we were complete lunatics, but they probably assumed it was another one of our staged bits since we'd manufactured so much drama already. I got this weird call from Viacom business affairs asking for the names of all the crystals I was wearing on the show. It was such a bizarre request that it sent my already heightened paranoia into overdrive. *Why does the legal department at Viacom care what crystals I'm wearing? Were they worried about some kind of liability? Was my spiritual protection being monitored and cataloged by the machine?*

Hugo introduced us to this incredible metaphysical bookstore in West Hollywood called the Bodhi Tree. When I learned they were closing down, I marched in there and made them an offer they couldn't refuse. I bought their entire remaining inventory, dropping maybe $50,000 on ancient texts and rare manuscripts. Original Aleister Crowley works (hey, I didn't realize at the time he was into dark magic), first edition books about Atlantis that traced connections to Egypt, to aliens, to Jesus.

Some of these books were so old they'd crack when you opened them—literally sealed since the 1800s. I organized my collection by category: astral projection, crystal healing, ancient civilizations, secret societies, dimensional travel. I had built myself a complete library of spiritual knowledge spanning galaxies and the multiverse. All of it—every single book, every rare manuscript, every piece of ancient wisdom—went up in flames. Still breaks my heart thinking about it.

The Nag Hammadi texts became my total obsession. The Gnostic Gospels—ancient Christian manuscrips that the early Church had tried to destroy because apparently they revealed too much about the true nature of reality, about Jesus's real teachings, about the divine spark within every human being. These texts had survived, buried in Egyptian caves for over a thousand years, and I developed this ritual around them where I'd sit in silence, close my eyes, and pray with complete sincerity.

"God, infinite creator of all realms, all dimensions—show me what I need to know," I'd say.

Then I'd randomly open the book and let my finger land wherever it wanted.

Every. Single. Time. It would hit exactly what I needed to read in that moment. The synchronicity was undeniable.

Some passages, at least the way I interpreted them, were meant to be recited underwater—something about the symbolic rebirth, the cleansing, the connection to primordial consciousness. So me being me, I'd often find myself at the bottom of our bathtub, holding the ancient text above my head to keep it dry, chanting in broken Coptic like I was trying to unlock the cheat codes to reality.

One particular night, I'd been in that tub for what felt like hours, completely absorbed in these ancient words. The next thing I knew, I was in our bed, and Heidi was shaking me awake.

"Spencer! What are you doing!" she said, panic in her voice.

According to her, she'd been sound asleep when I'd presumably gotten out of the bath and lay down next to her. She woke up, and swears she saw me floating—like, levitating—about a foot off the bed, rising like a hot-air balloon, gripping her hand like I was trying to take her somewhere.

"We're leaving . . ." I mumbled, rising up, still half in whatever state I'd been in.

Yeah, you read that right. Levitating. Less than a foot, but still—I was on my way up, people! I'm just telling you what Heidi told me— you'll get the full story in her book, I guess.

To this day, I have no idea what actually happened that night. Did we both have some kind of hallucinatory out-of-body experience? Was my consciousness actually trying to ascend to another dimension?

Either way, those were trippy times, to put it mildly.

I had a few theories about what may really have been going on. Were Heidi and I deities? Uh, no.

Were we insane? (Which is what a lot of people assumed upon watching Season 6 of *The Hills*.) No. We weren't insane. Stressed? Definitely. Concerned for our safety at all times? Totally. Traumatized? Absolutely. But actually mentally ill, no.

Here's my other theory. What I'm about to suggest is speculation, not fact, but the pieces fit together in a way that's hard to ignore. For months, Hugo, our spiritual bodyguard, had been spraying me with his "essential oil blend" multiple times a day. "For protection," he'd say, misting me like I was a houseplant. Looking back, I wondered if we may have been microdosing LSD without knowing it, walking around LA in a constant state of altered consciousness. If when MTV cameras showed up, they weren't just filming Spencer Pratt—they may have been filming *Spencer Pratt on acid*. Which tracks, according to what people tell me about Season 6.

The show was pushing us toward a specific narrative. They wanted the villain edit cranked to eleven, turned up so loud it would blow out the speakers. And when you're already paranoid, and maybe (unknowingly) high, playing the villain becomes Method acting. I couldn't turn it off. I was just this simmering, crystal-carrying prophet of doom, terrified for my life at all times.

People had started showing up at our house, harassing us. The FBI had contacted us about credible threats. There were names, addresses, specific plans. I was continuing to stockpile weapons and ammunition among the crystals and biblical texts, like we were preparing for a siege. Now Hugo was dropping hints about wanting to manage our careers.

"You know, Spencer," he'd say during one of our portal-opening sessions, "I could really help optimize your brand while maintaining spiritual integrity."

My bullshit detector—which had been mysteriously offline—finally started beeping.

"Nah, bro," I told him. "We're good."

We were nuts, but we weren't *that* nuts. When he started asking to see our MTV contracts to check for "negative energy attachments," the paranoia kicked into high gear again—who could we trust?

Looking back, that period was obviously one of the most intensely ungrounded times in my life. Some people took advantage of us; we learned how predators operate in spiritual spaces, targeting people at their most vulnerable moments. But it was also one of the most expansive times we've ever experienced.

We discovered a world of energy and frequency. We started learning how reality is far more flexible than maybe we're taught to believe. That's the real juice—being open to the unknown, being willing to explore. Question everything. Reality, space, time—none of it is linear, nothing is what it seems on the surface. Once we began being okay with that, life seemed to feel a lot less frightening, somehow.

Hollywood had always wanted us locked into one reality—villains, jerks in their scripted dramas. But those were just masks. And masks can be swapped, edited, destroyed. The storylines, the fights, the meltdowns—they were just shadows on the wall. Puppet versions of us projected for ratings. What mattered most now was learning to decipher what felt honest. And that search, as wild and chaotic as it may have looked from the outside, was one of the most transformative journeys we ever took as a couple.

We weren't losing our minds; we were finding ourselves. Our real selves. And if we frightened or exhausted the people who loved us during this time—I'm sorry. It ain't easy, being trapped inside a completely manufactured reality. You'll grasp for anything that feels solid, anything that doesn't dissolve under the harsh light of day, and you'll cling to it with both hands. Whether it's a crystal, a prayer, or the person you love.

Everything else? Just illusion.

CHAPTER 22

SWAT TEAM SERENADE

From Chart Flops to Cop Raids

January 11, 2010

I burst into the kitchen where Heidi was making her morning smoothie, my phone still in my hand, panic written all over my face.

"Babe, we have a problem," I said. "A big fucking problem."

She turned off the blender. "What now?"

"*Superficial*. Your record. It . . . it came out."

She blinked. "What do you mean it came out?"

"I mean it's out. Like, released. Today. People can buy it right now. On iTunes."

"But we didn't . . ." She looked confused. "We didn't do any promotion. No interviews, no radio, no—"

"I gave *Us Weekly* those quotes." We'd put out a few quotes saying that the record was better than Michael Jackson's *Thriller*, but that was about the extent of our prerelease promo. "We didn't even announce it."

"I know."

"Why is that, Spencer?"

"Um. Because we got busy?"

It was just us and the Orchard's distribution system, which was basically a website where you uploaded files and picked a release date. It must have been me, just randomly selecting a date on some distribution form, maybe high on Hugo's spray, clicking buttons and forgetting what I'd done five minutes later.

We stared at each other for a long moment, the weight of our complete and total fuckup settling between us.

"So what are we supposed to do now?" she asked, her voice getting smaller.

"I don't know," I said. "I honestly have no idea."

I pulled her close, and she buried her face in my chest.

"Four years," she whispered. "Four years and two million dollars, and we just . . . spaced?"

Yeah, the problem with going on a vision quest while simultaneously trying to manage an entertainment career is that it's . . . kinda distracting. You're so busy ascending to the fifth dimension, opening portals, and battling demons that you might actually forget to check in with what's happening on Earth.

Six hundred and seventy-two. That's how many copies her album sold in its first week.

I didn't even know about those sales numbers until years later when people started throwing it in our faces. "Oh, what? It sold that many?" I'd say. "I had no idea." Because honestly, 672 copies sounded like a lot to me. It's actually a miracle it sold any at all.

Those 672 people who bought *Superficial* got an incredible pop album. They got songs written by future Grammy winners, produced by hitmakers, sung by someone who David Foster said had the voice to be a star. They got $2 million worth of music for $9.99. The other three hundred million Americans just never knew it existed. That's not failure. That's invisibility. Which, in the music business, might be worse.

Heidi was devastated, of course. This was her life's work, her biggest dream. *Superficial* was supposed to be our great pivot, our evolution from reality TV caricatures into legitimate artists. This wasn't some vanity project—this was our retirement plan.

But the failure of *Superficial* to register on the cultural landscape was just another message from the universe that the game was up. Everywhere we looked, the signs were unmistakable. The Speidi show was at a tipping point. The walls were closing in from every direction. Whatever wild ride we'd been on, we were about to get kicked off.

Two days after the catastrophic *Superficial* release, on January 13, 2010, our security had just brought Heidi home from a follow-up appointment at Dr. Frank's. She was wearing a veil, not feeling much like getting papped in her fragile state. Well, I guess one of our neighbors must have seen a woman in a dark veil being escorted into our property by men in security uniforms. In retrospect, I can see how that might have looked . . . concerning.

I was in the shower, taking a bong hit, when I heard it—helicopter blades cutting through the morning air. Low and close, shaking the bathroom window.

Then a voice, amplified and authoritative, booming from a loudspeaker.

"COME OUT OF THE HOUSE, NOW!"

Surely they can't be talking to me, I thought, standing there naked and stoned in my own bathroom.

I crept over to the shower window and carefully moved the blind back just enough to peek out. There it was—a police helicopter hovering directly over our house, close enough that I could see the pilot staring right back at me.

"YES, YOU IN THE WINDOW!"

This was every stoner's absolute worst nightmare.

I scrambled out of the shower, threw on whatever clothes I could find, and grabbed my phone with shaking hands. Was this it? Was this how Spencer Pratt's story was going to end—arrested while high, just out of the shower and still dripping wet?

"This police helicopter is circling my house," I said into my flip camera, a little handheld. "This is crazy. Why is the police helicopter circling my house?"

The sound was deafening—that mechanical thunder that rattles your windows and makes your four fluffy dogs lose their minds. It had been circling for what felt like forever, low enough that I could feel the vibrations in my chest.

With the chopper hammering overhead, I was frantically speed-dialing my lawyers, who immediately referred me to a criminal attorney. This guy wouldn't even take my call until I wired him ten grand on the spot—apparently, that's what it costs to get legal advice when helicopters are circling your house.

There I was, one hand clutching the phone, trying to explain this surreal situation to some high-priced criminal lawyer, while with the other hand I'm flushing thousands of dollars' worth of primo weed down the toilet.

Then I saw them through the window—police officers with guns drawn, moving up our front steps like they were storming a terrorist compound. Our sizzle-reel editor, Jackson, who worked for our production company and lived in the unit below us, was being marched up the side stairs at gunpoint, hands behind his head.

Sorry, Jackson! Wrong place, wrong time. (Jackson was not accused of any wrongdoing.)

My phone started exploding with notifications. TMZ had already picked up the story—"SWAT TEAM SURROUNDS SPENCER PRATT'S HOUSE." The entire neighborhood had been cordoned off like a crime scene.

The texts started flooding in: "Dude, why is SWAT at your house???" "Spencer, there's like fifty cops outside your place!" "WHAT DID YOU DO?!" "ARE YOU OKAY??? TMZ says there was a 'possible kidnapping!' at your house?!"

Through the front window, I could see the street completely blocked off. The helicopters were so low my meditation crystals were vibrating off the coffee table.

LAPD was at our door, pounding. With my camera still rolling—always document, always have evidence—I called out through the door: "You cannot come into my house."

Heidi, trembling with fear, was on the phone with 911, trying to explain their mistake, her voice cracking with panic and pain.

"I don't appreciate this harassment from the police!" she shouted. "You are harassing me. Do you understand? In my own home, in America, you are harassing me, sir!"

I tried to sound calm through the door, professional, buying time: "Our criminal attorney will be here in five minutes, sir, and then we'll all come in the house. We just want our criminal lawyer!"

Maybe if they knew who we were—not criminals, just reality TV's most hated couple—they'd realize how insane this was. "Yeah, it's just my wife and me. It's just the two of us. Heidi Montag. Spencer Pratt. Married. Happily in love. Just got home."

The absurdity of it all was making me manic. I went full California spiritual: "I love LA. I love LA. I want no problems. I was just meditating, doing Kundalini yoga, straightening my feminine spirit, and now I got a helicopter circling my house."

The cops were still screaming at us, banging on the door.

So when the yoga angle didn't work, I pivoted to hospitality—maybe I could kill them with kindness. "Please, sir. Everything is fine. Wait, the lawyer will let you in, we'll all come in and talk. I have some German chocolate for you, sir. We'll give you some German chocolate. But I just cannot let you in legally because you don't have a warrant and we didn't call you. This is a prank call, sir, and we don't open our door for prank calls."

Heidi was crying. I turned to her, trying to keep my voice steady. "Please sit on the couch, babe. In the middle with your hands behind your back."

One more attempt at reason. I yelled to the cops outside: "Look, if you're LAPD, we know you're just doing your job, sirs. Thank you for being such honorable police officers. We know if there was a true emergency and somebody wasn't wasting taxpayer dollars, then this would be a great situation."

I grabbed one of our two Pomeranian puppies, Rainbow, holding her up to the window like a shield of innocence. "Look, I'm holding a dog right now. A cute little puppy. What are you doing to us, officer? All I'm doing here is holding a puppy!"

But they kept yelling at us to open the door. I knew I had no choice. With my whole body trembling, I made the call. "All right, sir, we're prepared to let you in consensually. Do you mind if we videotape your search? Is that all right? If we keep our lawyer on the speakerphone and we videotape your search, we have no problem with you seeing if there's a hostage situation in our house."

My hands were slick with sweat as I reached for the door handle. "Thank you, here we go. I'm putting—I'm gonna open the door." My instinct was to drop to my knees immediately—show submission, don't get shot.

About fifteen guns swiveled in my direction.

Time slowed down. I could see each individual weapon, each finger poised on each trigger.

"Stand up. STAND UP!" the officer barked, his voice like a drill sergeant's.

"Oh, standing up, okay! Sorry, my brain doesn't work when there's guns on me," I babbled, my words tumbling over one another. There were so many guns. So many fucking guns pointed at us from every direction—rifles, pistols, tactical weapons I couldn't even identify. And they all had their fingers on the triggers. Basic gun safety 101—you never, ever put your finger on the trigger unless you're ready to shoot. But I was seeing fingers on triggers everywhere I looked. These weren't cops preparing to de-escalate—these were cops preparing to fire. We were surrounded, outnumbered, and apparently considered dangerous enough to warrant an entire SWAT team with their safeties off.

Then Heidi snapped. The woman who'd just endured ten surgeries, who could barely stand, found the strength to scream: "Why do you have a gun? Why do you have a gun on my husband?"

"On the ground now!" the officer commanded.

Watching them push her around, knowing every movement was agony for her, I felt helpless rage. "She just had surgery, don't push her, please!"

"Who else is in the house?" they demanded, still treating us like we were harboring some imaginary victim.

As they stormed through our home, I was on the ground. "Please, please do not step on our camera. Watch the dogs. Don't let the dogs out. Please watch the puppies. They're little puppies."

Initially, they told us there was a hostage situation. Once we were in handcuffs, they started asking why we had so much ammunition stored in our house. The ammo was stacked right next to all my designer suits—racks and racks of YSL next to cases of bullets. When they questioned the quantity, my response was simple:

"Did you see how many suits are in there? I buy a lot of whatever I buy."

I explained that we went to the LAX gun range three times a week—Monday, Wednesday, Friday, 10 a.m. to noon—and when you're shooting that much, it's just more economical to buy ammunition in bulk. Basic math.

After they finished tearing through our house and confirmed there was no hostage, no threat, no actual emergency—they just left. No apologies, no "Sorry for the confusion," no acknowledgment that they'd terrorized us based on what turned out to be a neighbor's misunderstanding. They packed up their weapons and walked away like nothing had happened.

"Thank you for your swift and vigilant service," I said weakly.

Looking back, that was probably another lawsuit I should have filed. But at that point, we were so exhausted by the constant battles that we just wanted them gone.

In the cops' eyes, the equation was simple: Veiled woman plus armed household equaled full tactical response. They showed up ready for war—only to find two reality TV kids from *The Hills* cowering with four puppies and a whole bunch of crystals.

No one ever gave us a straight answer about why they rolled so heavy, but we weren't clueless. They must have known I'd been stockpiling ammunition and weapons. They also must have known I'd been spending time with King Casey's crew, some of whom, you'll remember, had ties to the Rollin' 60s. Connect the dots, and suddenly Spencer Pratt looks like he's running guns for gangs.

Twenty-four hours earlier, we'd been worried about album sales. Now we were processing what it felt like to have a SWAT team treat us like legitimate threats to public safety. We'd always known people hated Speidi, but we'd never imagined that hatred could manifest as a militarized police response.

Lord, let this nightmare end, we prayed that night.

Our deliverance was closer than we knew.

CHAPTER 23

HEEEERE'S SPENCER!

Our Last Days on The Hills

By 2010, Season 6 of *The Hills*, the writing was already on the wall. *Jersey Shore* had smashed onto MTV like a tsunami—cheaper to produce, raunchier, and pulling in blockbuster numbers almost overnight.

Its debut season averaged more than 2.7 million viewers an episode, with the infamous "Snooki punch" clip going viral before "viral" was even a thing. Basically, Nicole "Snooki" Polizzi was calling out a random drunk at a Seaside Heights bar, getting in his face for stealing their vodka shots, and this asshole fully socked her in the face, sending her tumbling to the floor.

The shocking clip exploded, news outlets everywhere ran with it, and overnight, Snooki became a household name and *Jersey Shore*'s ratings exploded, sealing MTV's shift away from the expensive, scripted gloss of *The Hills* toward the cheaper chaos of fistfights and GTL—gym, tan, laundry.

Yup, MTV had found their new golden goose—raw, messy, unfiltered—and we were yesterday's scripted-reality news. Our viewership had already slid from a peak of over four million during *The Hills* Season 3 to barely two million by Season 6. Even Tony DiSanto, then head of programming, had warned me off camera: He was over *The Hills*, over the ballooning production costs that made us the most expensive "unscripted" show on the network. *Jersey Shore*, by contrast, was shot in a rented beach house with unknown kids who worked for next to nothing when they began—and it was outpacing us in ratings week after week.

The only reason anyone was still tuning in to *The Hills* by Season 6 was to watch "Psycho Speidi" spin out like a flaming car wreck. The producers knew it and leaned in hard, cutting my storyline to look more unhinged by the week. Hell, *Vulture* even compared me to De Niro in *Cape Fear*—the lunatic clinging to the bottom of the boat, grinning as it sank.

In one episode recap, they wrote:

"We . . . couldn't help but see a freaky similarity between De Niro's crazed revenge seeker and Spencer Pratt—it's all about simmering rage, of which Spencer has an abundance . . . you could see the anger rising up from his taut neck into his pale face like a cartoon tea kettle about to blow off its lid."

And honestly? They weren't wrong. That's exactly how I felt. Not because of whatever bullshit storyline the producers were trying to force-feed the audience, but because of real life—and how completely overwhelming it had become.

Heidi had gone no-contact with her mom after that post-surgery ambush—their estrangement would drag on and on, punctuated by Darlene's public "open letter" to RadarOnline, melodramatically titled "It's Time for Us to Heal." Because obviously, the best way to reach your daughter is through a tabloid.

Her mom had shown up at our actual house, uninvited, in May 2010. Darlene sat in our driveway, like a paparazzo with a grudge, and simply refused to leave, despite Heidi's repeated requests for space. Darlene called Heidi's phone over and over, insisting she was there to perform a "welfare check." Heidi begged her to go, pointing out that her welfare was deteriorating with every second Darlene remained camped out in our driveway. In the end, our security called the cops. Darlene made the cops go in and do the welfare check. Which they did, only to find Heidi fine and well.

Meanwhile, House Pratt was living up to its reputation as the most dramatic family in the Palisades. Stephanie had already gotten popped for a DUI in late 2009, driving home from Heidi's birthday party with too much wine in her system. (She accused the producers of calling the cops and snitching on her.) There was so much tension at home, especially between my mom and Stephanie, things that aren't my business to share here, but all I'll say is, sometimes I wondered what Skip and Janet did in a past life to deserve us. They were fun-loving, normal people who liked barbecues and beach days, and somehow their DNA created . . . *us*. Two human tornadoes, constantly fighting, constantly spiraling, turning family dinners into episodes of *Jerry Springer*.

The producers? Please. They lived for the drama. They just leaned forward, grinning, and kept the cameras rolling like they'd hit the jackpot.

In Season 6, MTV had me and Heidi "living" in a rented Hollywood Hills mansion that wasn't ours. In one episode, production made it look like Heidi was staging a full-blown birthday party at the house for our "neighbor's kid," a little boy named Enzo—who in reality was the son of the family who actually owned the house we were pretending was ours.

That party was largely designed to showcase Heidi's out-of-touch extravagance. Heidi wanted balloons, petting-zoo lambs—even an elephant ride—for a seven-year-old she barely knew. It looked less like a child's birthday and more like *Scarface*'s wedding scene or one of Gatsby's blowouts—an overstuffed, glittering set piece that screamed "LOOK AT ME!" and was meant to symbolize just how far gone she was. Spending a fortune to stage a spectacle that had nothing to do with the kid and everything to do with the performance of excess.

When they staged Enzo's birthday party as a storyline, I played it like a cartoon villain—some deranged mash-up of *American Psycho* and Heath Ledger's Joker when he crashed Harvey Dent's fundraiser in *The Dark Knight*. Petting farm animals, cracking sinister one-liners.

"This is the first time I've been at a party where there aren't people I want to muuuurrrrdddeeerrrr," I announced while stroking a lamb.

Then I pointed at a kid making machine-gun noises and said, "I'm going to send him after Darlene [Heidi's mom]."

There's a scene at our so-called Hollywood Hills home where Heidi's sister, Holly, tries to square up with me, defending their mom like she was Joan of Arc. Holly, who'd sat next to her mother during the humiliating post-surgery encounter, suddenly wants to play protective sister?

Please.

> Spencer: *"Holly, this is my house. You keep defending her and I'm going to ask you to leave."*
> Holly: *"It's my mom."*
> Spencer: *"Well, you can defend her off our property in about five seconds."*

The producers wanted their *Here's Johnny!* villain shot, and I gave it to them. By then I had no filter, no patience, and no problem screaming *"Get off my property!"* to Heidi's sister, outside on a property that wasn't even ours to begin with.

In the next episode, Heidi and Kristin finally shared a storyline over lunch. But the media coverage wasn't about the plot—it was about Heidi's body. Every outlet treated Heidi's post-surgery body like a sideshow. Calling her sad, disturbed, an alien with giant breasts and an abusive husband. Actual words.

The producers told us to show up at Kristin Cavallari's housewarming party. The thought alone made my skin crawl. I was already so over this show, and now they wanted me to play nice in front of people I could barely stomach?

We showed up, with a housewarming crystal gift, prepared for the worst. Everyone giving Heidi the side-eye over her new body—even though she was happy, they couldn't even pretend to be happy for her. Me making fake small talk with Brody—we still hadn't had a real, off-camera conversation since our falling-out.

Then, on camera, it looked like I went nuclear on Stephanie out of nowhere. One minute I was standing there, the next I was in full rant, telling my sister I wished she'd never been born. That's what the viewers saw. But off camera? I'd already been dealing with weeks of drama around the conflict between Stephanie and my mother. I'd tried to talk to her about it earlier, but by that point, I was done. Over it. I didn't want to be around her anymore. So when she walked up to Heidi and me—eyes watery, lip trembling—I lost it. The rage boiled over.

"What are you crying about, Stephanie? What the fuck are you crying about? That's why you're not in my life, you crazy bitch! 'Cause you come to barbecues and just start crying. I was just enjoying myself with my wife and I get crying sisters in front of me?!"

Reading the words now, it comes off vulgar. But if anyone knew what we were dealing with behind the scenes, it might have made more sense. What I was having wasn't a storyline—it was a fucking breakdown, broadcast for ratings.

Anyway, that's what *The Hills* had become. Every episode, they tried to squeeze a little more blood from the stone—more fights, more meltdowns, more bridges burned. If I didn't give them a spectacle, they'd poke until I snapped. And sure enough, I always gave them what they wanted.

Later, in a club scene, I blew up at Audrina, too—"You're the lamest fucking girl in this club!"—and Brody jumped in, getting in my face about it. Another train wreck to keep the ratings afloat.

I had been trying to cope with the pressure by leaning in to crystals, leaning in to my spiritual growth, my rock-solid relationship with Heidi, convincing myself that, somehow, we'd survive all this. But by this point, even that strategy was collapsing. The crystals didn't hum the same. The healing didn't protect us anymore. Like my good buddy Charlie the surfer said, somewhere in Season 6: "I don't think your crystals are working, 'cause you're fucking hyperventilating over here."

He was right.

Something inside me was broken. I knew, deep down, that if we didn't walk away, there might not be anything left of us to save.

Producers and directors in Hollywood have been dehumanizing their talent since the dawn of cinema. Hitchcock starved his actresses. Bertolucci conspired to humiliate Maria Schneider in *Last Tango in Paris*. Weinstein—disgusting.

Plenty of these producers and directors have since been called out for the psychological damage they inflicted. People asking if the means always justified the ends. So why is it that in reality TV, the same tactics still get a free pass when the emotional wreckage they left behind is just as real? Lauren, Heidi, me, Kristin, Audrina—none of us escaped unscathed from *The Hills*. We were all victims of the same divide-and-conquer strategy, a game that made other people a lot of money while hollowing us out in the process.

One of the executive producers on *The Hills* was a woman the cast had nicknamed the Collector. Her real name is Sara Mast. It seemed like her specialty was pushing buttons. Saying whatever it took. Whispering the line that would unravel you. To me, it felt like her job was to dismantle us psychologically, piece by piece, until she collected the shot. Hence her nickname.

I know it was the 2000s. Different time, different rules. The ethics around entertainment were still fairly nonexistent, everyone was running plays from a book that had long since lost its humanity. Years later, in a keynote to her alma mater, Sara framed the behavior as though she was doing us a favor. *"They felt like we were ruining their lives, but at the same time they were making money and becoming stars. They're brands now."*

That was the moral high ground some reality TV producers like to take: *Hey, you thought your life was being ruined, but look at the brand opportunities!*

By Season 6, I had already demanded that the Collector be barred from set whenever Heidi and I were filming because of a prior incident with Heidi. But there she was again, back on set. I was just low-hanging fruit at that point. An easy mark. Knowing how mad I was at Steph, she sidled up to me with that smile. "You know what would make great TV?" she said.

"What?"

"You should punch your sister in the face. It worked for Snooki."

"Are you fucking kidding me?" I said, my voice rising. "You want me to hit my sister?"

She just stood there, still smiling, like she'd asked me to pass the salt.

That's when something broke inside me—but not the way they wanted. Not the way they'd been trying to break me for five seasons.

I walked off that set, and I knew, with absolute certainty, that I was done. I would never be on *The Hills* again.

According to the story MTV later put out, I was about to literally unalive Sara Mast on set. That's obviously not what happened. If I had, the security that was outside would have arrested me.

They issued a statement to the press about an "altercation" on set, and told me I'd have to complete six weeks of anger management or we wouldn't see a dime of our season's pay. That was nearly a million dollars.

Anger management? Hell no. That would have been an admission of guilt. And I hadn't done anything wrong. MTV's response was swift and predictable: After Episode 4 of Season 6—no more Speidi. We were gone. Cut out. Erased. Like we'd never existed.

"You owe me all my money," I told them flat out. I brought in our attorney Peter Lopez, and together we started building a case to sue Viacom, MTV's parent company, for every cent they owed us for Season 6.

If they wanted to play hardball, fine. We'd play harder.

The show limped along without us for the rest of the season. No villain to drive the drama. No Spencer and Heidi to generate hate-watching.

The series finale aired to . . . tepid numbers. Not terrible, but not great either. Meh. Forgettable. Part of me wanted to feel vindicated. *See? You needed us. You built this whole empire on our backs and then tried to discard us when we demanded some respect.*

But the truth was, they didn't need us anymore. *The Hills* was ending anyway. It felt like they'd already extracted everything valuable from us—our reputations, our relationships, our dignity, years of our lives—and now they were moving on to the next generation of disposable reality stars.

We weren't irreplaceable. We were just run through.

Obviously, we weren't invited to the series finale party, a big farewell bash at the Roosevelt Hotel in Hollywood. So I booked out suites around the pool where the party was being held and brought in backup—an off-duty sheriff's detective we called Big Kahuna, a guy who now runs security for A-list movie stars and has billionaire clients. (Heidi, who was fully over the drama, sat this one out.)

My plan? Go full incognito. I hired one of the top prosthetic makeup artists in Hollywood to transform me into an old man, complete with liver spots and wrinkles. Backpack on, change of clothes inside. I was "spotted" by Perez Hilton on the sidewalk outside the hotel (yes, that video is still on YouTube).

Once I was inside, the hotel figured out what was happening and started canceling my rooms. Old Man Spencer made it to the far end of the lobby, lurking like the exact psycho-creep the show had always painted me to be.

The producers lost it. They actually called the cops. Two LAPD officers came charging in, shouting, "*You! Up against the wall!*" But before they could lay a hand on me, Big Kahuna stepped in, flashing his badge. *"Both of you, stop right there. What are your grounds for talking to my client like that?"* Just like that, it was over. They couldn't arrest me at their big, glossy finale.

I didn't ruin the party, but I definitely messed up at least the first round of drinks.

Revenge is so very sweet.

CHAPTER 24

THE GOLDEN BACKPACK

Why a Trail of Dead Bodies Made Us Pack Our Crystals and Run

The second *The Hills* ended for us, we flipped straight into survival mode. First priority: Cook up a spin-off. And because Speidi are master manifesters armed with the most powerful crystals in all Christendom, that's exactly when the phone rang with what sounded like salvation.

That's when VH1 came calling. Jeff Olde, head of programming over there, said he wanted to give me and Heidi our own show, probably because we were still hated enough to be relevant.

Yes, even though we were planning to sue Viacom—VH1's parent company—for a mil, he wasn't aware of that yet and was ready to offer us more money. Because he, like everyone, knew one thing for sure—Speidi means guaranteed ratings. He didn't care if America loved us, hated us, or wanted us deported to a remote island with no Wi-Fi. He cared that people watched. And they always watched.

I felt that old electricity again. That sense of vindication. Getting offered another show felt like a sign from God, the universe. It was a resurrection. A reminder that, yes, we were Speidi, the most compelling villains in the reality ecosystem.

"This is perfect timing," I told Jeff. "But you gotta drive out to our new place in Malibu first. You need to see this operation we've got going."

"Spencer, I'm offering you a television show," he said. "Just come into the office."

"Obviously yes, but you need to come out here first! The entourage, the crystals, the armored cars—it's insane."

"I'm not driving to fucking Malibu, Spencer. Do you know what the PCH looks like at five o'clock?"

"I'm telling you—you need to witness it firsthand, feel the vibes, understand the energy we're living in. Then you'll know exactly what you're buying."

"Spencer, I don't need to 'feel your energy.' I need you to come in and have a meeting like normal talent."

But I wasn't normal talent. And I really wanted him to walk through my front door and just . . . witness the spectacle of my life.

Picture the setup—we'd just moved into a new house right across from Zuma Beach, next to Nick Nolte's place. (The lease on our house in the Palisades was expiring, and we still felt flush enough with cash to make the jump to a Malibu compound renting for $75,000 a month, owned—no joke—by the Russian mob. On the day we toured it, tatted-up guys with attack dogs walked us through the property. Instead of thinking, *Run*, I thought, *This is it. I'm an actual Prince of Malibu.*)

We'd had new Japanese toilets installed, plus all our crystals strategically positioned for maximum spiritual protection alongside our weapons cache. Out front sat my armored car, plus white-and-black matching Cadillacs. My entourage at the time included Goose Blackfinger—my old weed-dealer-turned-assistant—our three recon Marines (Venom, Vader, and Panther), our kung fu master Sifu, and Big Kahuna, the sheriff's detective. They were always around, keeping watch, protecting Speidi. I felt like a warlord.

That's why I needed Jeff to see what I saw every morning: the crystals glowing in the sunlight, the ex-military guys patrolling like we were guarding a foreign embassy, the armored fleet shining in the driveway. If he saw all that—if he really felt it—he'd understand this wasn't just another show. This was going to be the greatest project he'd ever worked on. Full chaos. Goose arguing with a Marine about chakras, Sifu doing slow-motion sword forms in the yard. Part *Entourage*, part *Ancient Aliens*. Speidi cinema. A metaphysical circus.

But for some reason, Jeff really, absolutely did not want to drive to Malibu. He kept refusing our invitation, over and over, until one day, he stopped calling. And that was that. The development deal fell through.

But if he had made that drive? He would've known. Our show would've been insane—incredible—unforgettable. The greatest unscripted television since *The Osbournes*. Maybe. Honestly? Probably better. Certainly historic.

WHATEVER.

We didn't need VH1.

I had other irons in the fire, projects in the pipeline—like *Tower 69: Malibu Beach Patrol*. Yes, I was in development with a *Baywatch*-inspired movie comedy featuring my bodyguard in the lead role. No A-listers, just a warehouse of beach babes and my entourage.

I had a USC film school student shoot a sizzle, and to me, it had this early-1960s cinema verité flavor that I was sure my fans would appreciate. RadarOnline had some fun with it when they found out: "*Watch-out* [sic] *James Cameron . . . Spencer Pratt has released the trailer for his first 'feature' film!*" they teased.

(I'd been wanting to make a lifeguard movie since I was a teenager, starting with "Bite Me," a script I cowrote with Dave Chernin right before *The Princes of Malibu*. He'll probably deny it to this day, but trust me, it existed. The pitch was simple: *Baywatch* meets *Jaws*. Imagine the slow-mo lifeguard runs, the swimsuits, the beach romance—except instead of saving tourists from riptides and jellyfish stings, they're fending off a massive, bloodthirsty shark terrorizing Malibu. Dave Chernin and I thought we were making the next great cult classic. Our own *Sharknado*, if you will.)

Anyway, Adam Sandler's partner Jack Giarraputo—one of the most famous comedy producers in history from Happy Madison—loved my *Tower 69* lifeguard sizzle reel so much, he had me meet with the president of Columbia Pictures over at Sony. I had real studio interest in my beach comedy. Still, though, in the absence of an actual project—a show, or getting a movie green-lit, which *Tower 69* tragically wasn't (I dropped the sizzle on YouTube for free instead)—we'd need to ensure our names remained in the media, maintain our relevance, and cash in on our little tabloid sideline.

We cooked up a story that ran in *In Touch* magazine, in which we presented ourselves as hoarders, me lining the windows with crystals to "trap Heidi inside" and a random Marine living on our couch. Of course, that whole storyline was completely staged. We piled stuff around the living room, and leaned into the narrative because chaos sells better than reality. To the outside world, it looked like we'd gone feral; to us, it was just another fun plotline about Crazy Speidi we'd produced ourselves.

Oh, and we decided to get divorced. I mean, we'd already gotten married, so there was only one relationship card left in the deck, in terms of media coverage. And that was breaking up.

So on May 19, 2010—literally the day after I'd quit *The Hills*—*People* ran a story claiming Heidi had hired a divorce attorney and was looking to move out.

I WONDER WHO TOLD THEM THAT?

Heidi filed for legal separation in Orange County on June 8 with photographers in tow. One of our entourage, whose mom was a divorce attorney, helped Heidi file the papers, did us a solid. By now, TMZ and the rest of the pack were eating it up. There was, of course, speculation that we were just trying to get more publicity.

WHO, US? NEVER!

On June 22, I allegedly hacked Heidi's Twitter to send a flirty message to Justin Bieber: *"now that I am getting divorced I think you and I should do a photo shoot together! Cutie ;)! I'm closer to your age."*

Blogs went insane over Heidi hitting on the "Baby" singer, and she fired back: *"I didn't write that thing about Bieber my fame hoer x husband hacked my Twitter and wrote that he is so lame!"*

Then she twisted the knife deeper:

"Let me be clear! I had nothing to do with it! He is the famewhore!"

I clapped back in *People* magazine, saying our breakup was because I was choosing fame over my wife: *"We love each other, but I'm a famewhore and I'll never grow out of it. Heidi knows that and doesn't want that."*

By July 30, Heidi went nuclear, amending her petition and filing for actual dissolution of marriage.

And on August 22, she blasted me with the tweet heard round the tabloids:

"@spencerpratt F U!!!!!!!!!!!!!!!!!!!!!!!!!!!!!!!!!!!"

By then, the press had me shopping a Heidi sex tape to Vivid and drafting a tell-all about our marriage. The public saw chaos, betrayal, and divorce papers.

But behind the scenes? Heidi and I were still thick as thieves, scheming side by side, laughing at how easy it was to keep the world guessing and the checks coming in.

At twenty-four and twenty-seven, we were young and famous, having the most fun you could possibly have while allegedly getting divorced. And the public? People ATE IT UPPPP.

Even Lauren Conrad reached out to Heidi directly, calling her to see if she was "okay."

I'll let Heidi decide if she ever wants to share the details of that conversation, but my feelings about it are complicated. On the surface, sure, it looked sweet—former best friend rushing in to show support during the divorce-rumor frenzy. But in my opinion, LC never made a single move without calculating the upside.

My read? If the divorce was real, she saw her opening—swoop in, play the loyal friend, turn Heidi's frustration against me. It was the perfect play: LC as the heroine riding back in, me as the villain who'd finally gone too far. (When our house literally burned down, did we hear from LC? Not a word. Why? I think it was because there was no camera-ready angle in it for her. No drama to leverage, no narrative where she could paint herself as either the victim or the hero. Just two people dealing with an actual crisis—and that held zero strategic value. She stayed silent.)

Anyway, we put real creative effort into our divorce. The way some couples throw themselves into saving their marriage, we threw ourselves into ending ours. We needed the money, the headlines, the endless "will they, won't they" suspense to keep the Speidi circus alive.

We weren't broke, but our overhead was still insane, and our lawyer Peter Lopez was still grinding away trying to get us paid for Season 6 of *The Hills*. Without those *Hills* checks coming in—our bread and butter—we needed that lawsuit fired up ASAP so we could actually get paid and keep the gravy train rolling.

The afternoon of April 29, 2010, Peter and I had talked strategy for our case over the phone. He seemed completely fine—calm, focused, invested in getting us a positive outcome, like always. The next morning, my phone rang. It was Kevin Carlson, our security guy who also worked for Peter. (Kevin handled security for Dr. Dre, and since Peter had worked with Dre, they'd developed a close working relationship.)

"Spencer, it's Kevin." His voice was flat, different than usual. "Peter's dead."

The words didn't compute. "What do you mean, 'Peter's dead'?"

"He shot himself this morning. In his backyard." Kevin's voice cracked slightly. "I'm sorry, brother. We're all in shock."

I couldn't process it. *Peter had taken his own life?*

I understand that people contemplating suicide don't always show warning signs, but Peter literally showed none. At all. He'd seemed like his usual happy, cheerful self. He had two daughters, a beautiful wife—Catherine Bach, Daisy Duke from *The Dukes of Hazzard*—and one of the most successful entertainment law practices in town. He was wealthy even by lawyer standards.

The official story was a self-inflicted gunshot wound in his backyard. But my conspiracy brain went into overdrive. Peter was, after all, one of those people who genuinely knew where the bodies were buried in this town. He was behind the scenes with the heaviest hitters in the business. If anyone carried Hollywood's secrets, it was him. So when he suddenly turned up dead, my brain couldn't accept the "suicide" line. Call me crazy (you wouldn't be the first), but it felt like a hit to me. And if someone like Peter could be erased, then nobody was untouchable. Definitely not Speidi.

I couldn't sleep. Nights were spent sitting upright in our Malibu mansion, pistol holstered on my hip, my two Pomeranians and two Maltipoos standing guard like furry little soldiers, my eyes glued to the security monitors. I was rattled. I was heartbroken. And I was REALLY getting concerned about money, now that Peter was gone and we had no one fighting on our behalf to get us paid by Viacom.

Thankfully, Kevin Carlson decided to become a one-man collection agency on our behalf—the real-life Ray Donovan, picking up where Peter left off, but with different tactics.

"I'll get you that money, Spencer," he said, grimly. "It's what Peter would have wanted."

I told him he could keep 10 percent of whatever he managed to get out of Viacom. Like a regular agent would have. (Our agency, WME, should've been the ones pushing hardest to get us paid, but we weren't exactly at the top of their call sheet.)

Kevin's tactics were simple. This magnificent man, used to protecting rappers, who looked like he'd break your jaw for breathing wrong—suddenly became the world's most persistent telemarketer. He started calling Viacom business affairs like clockwork, every hour on the hour.

Ring ring.

Then, in that deep, street-hardened voice: "Hey boss, I'm just checkin' in about Spencer Pratt's money he's owed for Season 6 of *The Hills*. Not ready yet? No problem, player—I'll hit you back at five p.m."

Five o'clock rolled around.

Ring ring.

"Yoooo, it's Kevin Carlson again, circling back on behalf of my client Spencer Pratt. Still no million? Cool cool, I'll check in tomorrow morning. Don't trip, I got nothing but time."

He kept the pressure steady—morning calls, midafternoon reminders, last-minute check-ins right as the accountants were shutting down their computers for the day. A polite but relentless drumbeat: *We know what you owe, and we're not going anywhere.*

Eventually, they must have gotten so sick of hearing his voice that they wired us our money. The full million dollars. Not because Viacom was scared of me—because they probably couldn't survive one more "*Just circling back!*" call from our six-foot-four rapper-protector.

We dropped the lawsuit since MTV paid us the money (without admitting wrongdoing). Afterward, our agents at WME of course sent over their invoice for 10 percent. No way was I cutting them a check. When I teased our agents about our bodyguard doing a better job than them, they understood. That's the dance in Hollywood: you need the agency for access—they can get you opportunities you could never reach alone—but sometimes you need muscle, persistence, or your own hustle to make sure you actually get paid.

But still, it felt like a hollow victory. We were reeling from the loss of our friend Peter, whose death didn't make sense to us. Catherine Bach later told *Entertainment Tonight* that she'd been stalked in the weeks around his death. It was so serious that the police even considered whether the fatal gunshot hadn't been self-inflicted at all but meant for her—and Peter was the one who paid the price. Like us, she couldn't reconcile the "suicide" narrative with the man she knew. "He was very happy with his family and very proud of his girls," she told *ET*. "We had a deep love... we were together. We were very happy for nineteen years."

Her words only deepened my sense of persistent unease.

Then, just a few months later, on August 16, 2010, another tragedy. Another Hollywood death that made no sense. Dr. Frank Ryan—Heidi's plastic surgeon—crashed his Jeep off the Pacific Coast Highway in Malibu and died on impact. He was just fifty years old.

He'd been tweeting about his dog—*"Border collie Jill surveying the view from atop the sand dune"*—right before his Jeep veered over the cliff. The dog was in the car at the time but survived with head and paw injuries.

The California Highway Patrol launched an investigation, and in the end they chalked it up to "unsafe turning." But in our heads—after losing Peter and now Frank—the tragedies didn't add up, even though I had no proof. Two pillars of our world gone, back-to-back, in ways that felt implausible as hell.

Even with all our security, Los Angeles no longer felt safe. The overwhelming feeling was GET US THE HELL OUT OF HERE. Even with enough black tourmaline to hold back hell itself, it felt useless. Whatever was happening felt way above any crystal's pay grade. When the Four Horsemen are circling the damn block, it's time to hit the Four Seasons.

Yes, Costa Rica was where we'd escape to. The same place we'd practically clawed our way out of on *I'm a Celebrity . . . Get Me Out of Here!* just a year earlier. But this time, no jungle. No ants, no producers, no Frangela or Torrie. This time, we'd head straight to the Four Seasons in Papagayo, and stay there.

That same night we found out about Dr. Ryan, I went to our safe and spun the dial. Five hundred g's in gold maple leaves right there. My dad had taught me well. *Gold is the only currency that matters when everything collapses,* he always said. I didn't know much about Costa Rican currency, but I knew gold was universal. Gold was safety. Gold would buy us our way out.

One by one, I loaded the coins into a matte tan military backpack. Then I stuffed my Glock 19 and my Colt .380 in a duffel bag. Meanwhile, Heidi was in full mom mode, laying out sparkly collars and leashes for our four dogs. Our little fur angels were coming, too—nonnegotiable.

I made sure to carefully wrap and pack all my tektites and my Lemurian seed crystals—chunks of quartz with distinctive markings into which the Lemurians, who were the most spiritually advanced civilization ever, supposedly encoded all their wisdom before their society was destroyed. Since they allegedly contained all the sacred knowledge in the universe, I figured they might come in handy while we were trying not to get assassinated, Star Whacked, whatever.

"Spencer, I'm scared," Heidi said. "Grab my Birkins."

Our four dogs watched this chaos with confusion, their pure spirits unable to comprehend the interdimensional warfare happening around us. One kept bringing me his favorite toy, like maybe if we just played fetch, everything would return to normal.

"Buddy, it's okay," I told him, feeling his innocent energy. "We're going on an adventure."

The plan was simple: We'd all escape together—guns, gold, dogs, some crystals in tow—and start fresh on a beachfront ranch in Costa Rica. A new Eden, away from this hell called Hollywood.

Bye.

Speidi OUT. We never liked you anyway.

END SCENE.

CHAPTER 25

THE SOUND OF SILENCE

How We Went Broke in Paradise

NUFORC—that's the National UFO Reporting Center, basically the government-adjacent hotline where regular people log sightings—has thirty-five separate reports from the same stretch of Malibu beach alone since 2005.

That's not one drunk surfer seeing Venus. That's orbs over Point Dume, cigar-shaped crafts over Decker Canyon, peach-colored lights hovering over Zuma, whole diamond-shaped things splitting the sky. People pulling over on PCH, snapping photos, filing the reports. It's all in the database. Malibu isn't just beaches and celebrities—it's straight-up *Nope* out there.

That's why we shouldn't have been *too* surprised when, on August 22, the day before we bolted for Costa Rica, Heidi and I saw a massive white orb floating over our house in Malibu—smooth, silent, glowing, moving fast. Out of nowhere, two F-18s came screaming after it. All of nature froze. Birds stopped midsong. Even the ocean seemed to hold its breath.

It wasn't just us who saw it. Vader, our security guard, freaked so hard he walked straight into a sliding glass door and dropped. Drivers on PCH pulled over, climbed out of their cars, staring up like the world was about to end. It felt like *Independence Day* come to life.

My tinfoil hat firmly on, as always, I couldn't help wondering if maybe there was a reason.

Was it us?

"Spencer, we have to get the hell out of here," Heidi whispered, her nails digging into my arm.

The next morning, before the sun even thought about rising, we said goodbye to Malibu. Locked up the house like we might never see it again, slid into the car, and tore down PCH toward the airport. The freeways were empty, but overhead the sky kept flashing like it wanted to remind us we weren't escaping clean. At one point, a shooting star—massive, green, flaming—ripped across the horizon right in front of us. Heidi gasped, and I swear it didn't look like a star at all. It looked like a signal.

By the time we touched down in Costa Rica, the universe doubled down. We came in hot through a lightning storm so violent it felt biblical. Bolts split the clouds in every direction, rainbow-colored lights flickering like they were alive, darting back and forth between the thunderheads. I thought, *This isn't weather, this is communication.*

Then—boom. After we got to the hotel a lightning strike nailed the generator, killed the power completely. For days we sat in the dark, no lights, no Wi-Fi, just rain hammering the roof while the sky above us kept dancing with impossible colors.

Eventually, the storm broke. The sky cleared like a curtain lifting, and for the first time in days we could actually breathe. It was like whatever dark force had chased us down here had finally given up, burned out in the clouds. There was something in the air in Costa Rica—charged, almost holy—that wrapped around us and said, *You're safe now.*

The Four Seasons was supposed to be temporary, a hideout until we found a house of our own. But temporary has a way of stretching. Days of "just looking at properties" melted into weeks. We fell into a rhythm: wake up to crashing waves, stroll the grounds like they were our private kingdom. My beard grew wild like a prophet's. I stopped wearing shoes to stay grounded to Earth's frequency.

Oh, and room service. Three times a day, minimum. Sometimes four.

The staff learned our quirks fast. I'd call down and order entire chef-made meals for the dogs, because we hadn't brought dog food. "The grilled salmon is for Rainbow," I'd tell them, dead serious. "No seasoning, please. She likes it plain." And they'd deliver it on a silver tray, white linens, the whole thing.

By this point, the press had figured out that we were not, in fact, getting divorced, even though we thought we'd choreographed the Costa Rica trip pretty well: Heidi would "arrive" in Costa Rica first, I'd follow after, and one of *our* guys would be there to pap the "will they, won't they get back together" reunion.

But we got outplayed. Splash News—the Navy SEALs of the tabloid world—nailed us when we checked into the resort on August 23, before our own hired pap could even uncap his lens. They caught us smiling, hauling luggage, looking way too honeymoon-fresh for a couple allegedly mid-divorce. Those shots went everywhere, and overnight our "tragic split" read more like performance art. After that, we cut a deal with Splash. If we were going to keep hustling the tabloids, better to run with the one slick enough to beat us at our own game.

But the house hunting was, alas, a joke. We'd roll up to these viewings, me sweating under the weight of my backpack full of gold coins like some wannabe pirate—only to be told we were paupers. "This property is listed at five-point-two million," the Realtor said, waving his hand at a house that looked like a concrete shoebox with windows.

"For *this*?" I barked. "You're kidding me."

He gave me this patient little smile. "A nice gentleman from Chicago actually owns all four homes on this stretch of beach, perhaps you know him?"

"No, sir, I have five hundred grand in gold coins, that's it. What luxury homes can you show us in that price range?"

"Unfortunately, Mr. Pratt," he said, still trying to stay polite, "the Costa Rican market has appreciated significantly . . ."

I cut him off, yanking open the zipper of my backpack so he could see the stacks of glinting coins. "GOLD! Five hundred K, right here. Real money." He sighed and shook his head.

"Your little bag of coins might have worked in 2000, sir. Not in 2010."

Dammit.

Yep, the property boom in Costa Rica was already fully popping. We should've flown to Honduras or Nicaragua—our pirate's loot would have stretched way further. But we didn't know that. We didn't know anything. We were making this whole thing up as we went along, as we always had.

A month into our Costa Rican exile, the fantasy of owning a jungle palace fell apart. Every property we liked was too expensive, and meanwhile, the Four Seasons bill was bleeding us dry. The dream was dead. Time to cut our losses and retreat to Malibu—back to the land of UFOs, demons, and whatever other forces were waiting for us.

I booked a private jet home—a Cessna Citation X business jet, the fastest we could get. It was September 11. We packed up our gold, our puppies, our guns, and set off for the airport. Maybe because it was 9/11, security at San José airport seemed much tighter than when we'd arrived. They opened my bag, pulled out the two guns I'd been carrying the whole time in Costa Rica, and suddenly the vibe shifted.

"Señor, estas armas . . ."

The dogs were barking, Heidi was trying to distract security while pretty much wearing a bikini, and I was standing there with my hands up while Costa Rican police went through my bags.

"I have permits," I said, knowing damn well my California concealed carry meant nothing here. "I'm a public figure. Death threats. I need protection."

I was never put in handcuffs, but they took me to a holding area while Heidi waited outside in the courtyard with the four dogs. A guard told me I was looking at *three hundred days in a Costa Rican jail*, minimum. I was stunned. No one had cared when I *brought the guns in*, but now it was a federal case when I was trying to take them out? It wasn't like I was boarding a public plane. It was just me, Heidi, and four dogs—we weren't going to hijack *ourselves*. But logic wasn't getting me anywhere, and I could see the timeline splitting: In one version, I was headed for a Costa Rican jail cell. In another, something else was about to happen.

That's when HE appeared.

Clean-shaven, khakis, the most American-looking dude I'd ever seen. He flashed some kind of badge, and spoke rapid Spanish to the officers. The guards' whole demeanor changed instantly, like someone had flipped a switch in their minds. Suddenly, my weapons were being carefully repacked, and I was getting apologetic nods and smiles.

"Have a safe flight, Mr. Pratt," the mystery American said.

"Who are you?" I asked.

"I'm your new best friend," he said.

"I have gold, should I pay you something? Or them?"

"No, sir. You should catch your flight now." Then he walked away. He was gone so fast it was like he'd stepped into a portal, disappeared.

"Who was that man?!" Heidi asked, clutching my arm.

"I have no idea."

To this day, I don't know if he was CIA, State Department, Obi-Wan Kenobi, or something else entirely. Maybe he was an alien friend of Hugo's, doing us a solid. I mean, they say Costa Rica sits on ancient ley lines, that it's a portal point between dimensions. Maybe we'd been called here to complete some ritual. Maybe we were bait. Maybe we were being protected by white hats in a spiritual war. Whatever it was, after that mystery American intervened, we were free to leave.

Still, when we landed in San Diego, things weren't exactly smooth sailing. Because I'd been detained in Costa Rica, US Customs came on board our jet, running checks, making sure everything was legit. I have video of it—officers combing through the cabin like we were drug lords. And yet, weirdly, Heidi and I were in the best mood. Costa Rica had been a bust—no house, no paradise—but it had taught us something: There really is no place like home.

• • •

The second we walked into our Malibu house, our jaws dropped. The place had been *trashed*. Even the Japanese toilets we'd imported and had custom-installed were ripped out of the ground. It looked like a frat house after the apocalypse.

The culprit? One of our so-called security guards. While we were gone, he'd been throwing ragers in our house, acting like he owned the place. He even went so far as to change his driver's license address to ours. (Later, he graduated to full-blown professional squatter—when Realtors tried to sell the house, they literally couldn't get him out.)

That's when it hit us: There was no way we were ever seeing our security deposit again. Seventy-five grand, gone down the drain . . . or it would've, if there'd actually been any toilets left to flush. With the Malibu lease up, and no Costa Rican palace waiting for us, we had to face facts. The Four Seasons had drained our account dry, and suddenly—there it was—we were homeless.

Homeless. Speidi. Who would've thought?

So we made the call nobody ever expects to make after years of reality TV fame: "Hey, Mom and Dad . . . mind if we crash at yours?" And just like that—after all the chaos, the headlines, the fake divorce and photo ops—we were moving back in with my parents, headed to their beach house in Santa Barbara, hauling with us a caravan of puppies, crystals, guns, and gold coins like it was the Oregon Trail.

Our first morning there, I leaned on the balcony, hoodie up, watching the sun rise over the Pacific. The sky went cotton candy, the Pacific was glass flat, and for a minute the world felt like a screensaver set to "peaceful." The sun climbed higher, burning off the marine layer, and the crystal around my neck caught the light, throwing tiny rainbows across my chest. For the first time in months, my brain felt quiet—not the manic faux-clarity of paranoia, but the soft click of something lining back up.

It felt good, being away from Hollywood.

It felt good. This thing. This sound of silence. Of something close to peace.

PART THREE
NEW DAWN

CHAPTER 26

CRYSTAL VISIONS

Manifest, Receive, Release

Once we were back with my parents, we were living check to check. But honestly, that had always been the case. Ever since I'd met Heidi, every dollar that came in, we'd spent right away. That's just how we rolled. No savings account, no backup plan, just direct deposit and vibes. Because what's money, really? Just energy moving in and out of your life. We'd always had faith that the universe would drop the next opportunity, the next check, right into our laps. And when it did, we'd spend it. That was our rhythm: manifest, receive, release. A cycle as predictable as the tide. (If my sons are reading this as adults, I don't advise this financial strategy for you—or anyone, by the way.)

After *The Hills* and Costa Rica, we never went bankrupt, despite what people may have said. Feel free to check the government records, my friends. We were just . . . you know. Flying by the seat of our pants, as always. Manifesting hustles and opportunities.

Yes, the Hermès binges, the expensive crystals—those days were over. But weirdly, losing all that excess felt like a kind of cleansing. We weren't pretending to be ballers anymore; we were just inhabiting this new version of us, stripped down and almost human. It was refreshing. Weird how our "bottom" was starting to feel a lot like freedom.

Abundance rolled back into our lives again when Heidi scored *Famous Food*—this VH1 reality show that dropped July 2011. The pitch was as follows: Ryan Seacrest (who else?) brings together seven "celebrities" who have no business running a restaurant and makes them open one in West Hollywood. Perfect. The cast comprised a *Housewives* villain (Danielle Staub), two rappers from Three 6 Mafia (DJ Paul and Juicy J), the call girl from the Eliot Spitzer scandal (Ashley Dupré), a disgraced Bachelor (Jake Pavelka), a mobster from *The Sopranos* (Vincent Pastore) . . . and Heidi Montag. Basically the most random dinner party guest list ever assembled, arguing over menu fonts and pasta specials like they're Wolfgang Puck.

Heidi was filming the show one day and I was just, like, alone. For the first time in forever. So I decided this would be a good moment to finally meditate with this monster chunk of moldavite I'd just bought. Moldavite, by the way, isn't just some casual crystal. Google it—it's the fast track to spiritual acceleration. It's supposed to blow open your heart and your third eye at the same time, trigger insane downloads of information, melt away whatever's fake in your life. They say it rearranges things for the better, even if it's not exactly a smooth change—relationships implode, jobs vanish, you suddenly find yourself moving across the world. Moldavite doesn't care about your comfort zone. It's not here to soothe you, it's here to rip you out of the simulation and drag you straight to whatever the universe actually intended. Ready or not.

I sat cross-legged on the floor with the moldavite in my lap, its jagged green edges humming against my skin. I closed my eyes, drew in a deep breath, and tried to empty my mind. At first there was static, like always—stray thoughts, scraps of headlines, little anxieties buzzing like flies. But then I locked in.

I pictured white light rising through me. At the base of my spine: a red spark, pulsing like lava. It spread up, glowing orange, rippling like a sunrise on water. Higher—yellow, burning bright in my stomach. My chest cracked open into a flood of green, heart blooming, vines wrapping every inch of me. My throat was sky blue, a flowing river I could almost hear, then indigo seared across my forehead, a third eye burning itself open. Finally, pure white, blinding, a beam shooting upward until I felt like a lighthouse, signaling into the heavens.

And then all boundaries dissolved and I wasn't sitting in a room anymore—I was in some endless grid of light, time falling away, colors folding in on themselves, shapes unfurling and disappearing. It was like being plugged into something. Like the universe was downloading a whole new operating system straight into my soul.

I opened my eyes and looked at the clock.

Whoaaaa!

FOUR HOURS had vanished in a blink. I looked around. Everything seemed sharper. I felt changed, somehow. Stripped bare. New again.

That night, after Heidi wrapped shooting, I turned to her and said, "I want to go back to school."

"To USC?" she asked.

"Yes. I want to finish my degree."

It had been ten years since I first enrolled at USC. The next morning I picked up the phone, called the registrar's office, and asked if I could come back and finish my political science degree. They said yes. I enrolled for classes starting in the fall 2011 semester.

Fast-forward to day one of school. I woke up groaning, already regretting my decision.

"Heidi, I don't want to do this. What was I thinking? I'm really gonna drive from Santa Barbara to downtown LA three to four times a week just to sit in undergrad classes? With a bunch of kids staring at me like I'm some washed-up reality star?"

I was only twenty-eight at the time, but I felt like I'd lived about a thousand lives since I'd last sat in a classroom.

"Yes," Heidi said, gripping my hand. "You are. And I'm coming with you. Someone's gotta make sure you don't cut class. Come on, I'll help you take lecture notes. It'll be fun!"

My heart swelled with love for this angel who kept showing up, no matter what. She was my anchor, my teammate, my fiercest believer. More powerful than any moldavite, truth be told.

We drove together. On the way, though, I got pulled over for speeding. At first, I thought, *Okay, bad omen . . . maybe this really isn't a good idea.*

But then the cop leaned down, ticket in hand, and noticed Heidi in the passenger seat.

"Wait—are you Heidi Montag, the actress?" he asked her.

She smiled and said yes.

The cop looked at me straight-faced.

"Hand me that," he said.

I gave him back the ticket, and he took out a pencil and drew a line straight through the speeding part. Then he waved us on.

Heidi looked at me. "It's a sign. You're doing the right thing. You're meant to go back to school, Spencer."

Walking back onto the USC campus after ten years away was surreal. The whole place looked the same—red brick, palm trees, kids rushing to class—but I felt like I was stepping into an alternate universe. I'd left here chasing fame; now I was coming back, trying to recover what pieces of myself remained, stitch myself back up again.

Before heading to class, I decided it would be funny to swing by my old frat, the Beta house off the Row. The minute I saw it, my brain—being my brain—started spinning out a reality show pitch: me, the washed-up TV villain, now the "house dad," running the fraternity like some deranged dean. *Beta House: Pratt Edition.* Tell me that wouldn't have been fun to watch. Tommy Lee had just gone back to college and was making a show about it, so why not me?

We knocked. A kid answered, squinting at me.

"Hi, I'm Spencer Pratt, I'm a Beta," I said confidently. "I'm back!"

He looked me up and down, not having a clue what I was talking about.

"What's your pledge number?" he shot back.

"Uh, I'm not sure. But I was in the Secret Society of Beta," I told him.

"Uh, never heard of that," he said flatly.

"Well," I told him, "it was a *secret* society. Our code name was Stumpo's Raiders."

A couple more brothers came to the door. They basically told me the house didn't honor Stumpo's Raiders, a rogue underground organization that had been forced to cease formal activities or face suspension of people affiliated with the group.

"Jeez, well, what do I have to do to be recognized by you guys?" I asked, already flashing back to the feral horrors of hazing.

"To be a Beta," one of them said, "you need a four-point-oh GPA. Bring us your transcripts and we can reassess you if you want to re-pledge."

I stared at him. Revenge of the nerds, in real life.

"Uh, yeah, sure, I'll do that," I said, walking away and off to class, so mad, intending never to return unless it was to TP the place.

"Kids today sure are serious," I muttered to Heidi as we left. "When I was rushing, they wouldn't let you in if you had a high GPA."

"Well, times change," she pointed out. "Maybe it's not the worst thing if these kids are a little more serious now."

"Whatever," I grumbled, still salty. "A frat without chaos? That's just . . . student housing."

True to her word, Heidi came to every class with me, sitting in lectures, helping me take notes, keeping me from ditching. There we were, side by side in a classroom, learning together. One day it was Rousseau on the social contract, the next it was Hobbes insisting people were basically animals who needed a strong hand to keep them in line. I'd be scribbling in the margins, thinking, *Wow, maybe* The Hills *was just Thomas Hobbes with better lighting.*

Meanwhile, we were surrounded by kids who'd watched me on TV when they were in middle school. Some professor would be unpacking Locke's ideas about natural rights, and the girl next to me would be live-tweeting about how she was sitting next to "the villain from *The Hills*."

One of my professors at USC, Mark C. Marino—he taught Writing 340—was genuinely fascinated by me and Heidi. He didn't see what we were doing as just reality TV trash; he saw it as performance art. Marino was known in academic circles, and thanks to him, I finally had a new vocabulary for my own life. He described our media presence as "manufactured reality." Every tweet, every staged paparazzi shot, every "candid" moment wasn't just entertainment: It was performance. We weren't merely on a reality show—we had turned our whole existence into one. In many ways, Professor Marino understood what we were doing better than we did. To him, Speidi was less trash TV and more avant-garde. Not art by standard definition, but a performance in the Warhol lineage—fifteen minutes stretched and looped, self-parody elevated into spectacle.

Most people thought we were just fame-hungry idiots. And we definitely were that. But he thought we were also experimenting with the mechanics of fame in real time—manipulating it, testing its limits, bending reality TV into something more self-aware, playing inside the fracture between fact and performance.

Now, years later, the culture has finally caught up. People like me and Heidi, Paris and Nicole—the so-called celebutantes of the 2000s—are being reevaluated as pioneers of a certain kind of internet-age celebrity economy: empty and yet magnetic. Lindsay Lohan stumbling out of clubs, Kim Kardashian pre-billionaire status, Britney with a Frappuccino—our every move was branded "trash" at the time. But in hindsight? We were just beta-testing a system everyone uses today. Living content. The Kardashians built an empire on it. Influencers are making millions doing the same thing with ring lights and Amazon hauls. Back then we were mocked for being shallow, unserious; now they call it strategy. It warms my black heart, I'll admit, to see people viewing us not as jokes but as prototypes of the new attention economy.

• • •

One day, I needed to get notepads and school supplies (I was a student, after all), so we stopped at a Staples down the street from Don Antonio's, after our regular taco pit stop.

As I'm walking in the bathroom, coming out of a stall is none other than Adam DiVello.

"Spencer . . . what are you doing in here?" he asked, clearly startled.

"Going to pee, how about you?"

"Why are you peeing *here*?"

"Uh, because I'm getting notepads? Why are YOU peeing in here?"

"Oh, this is a better bathroom than the one in our production office next door."

Ah. So he was going number two.

He still looked like he thought I'd been lurking outside the stall, ready to O.J. him. No, Adam. This was just cosmic coincidence. I'd been meditating with moldavite every day. Of course the universe would put me in front of Adam DiVello, fresh off the toilet at Staples. The question was, what did this mean?

I wasn't sure yet.

Once Adam realized I wasn't there to assassinate him, his fake producer smile flickered on like a faulty light switch.

"Wow, well . . . how are you guys?"

"Doing great, Adam. And you?"

I locked eyes with him, steady, not blinking. He couldn't hold my stare—his gaze slid away instantly.

"Doing good," he muttered.

I didn't stop smiling.

Adam washed his hands and hustled out of the bathroom, head down, desperate to get away from me. Of course, I followed him.

"Heidi, look who I found!" I called out to my wife, who was waiting in the hallway.

Heidi's eyes widened. Then, with razor-edge sweetness in her voice, she said, "Adam! So good to see you here at Staples. Are you stocking up on stationery so you can finally write us that apology?"

I'd forgotten how savage Heidi can be when she decides to be.

DiVello kept moving, quickening his pace like the floor was on fire. He couldn't get out of there fast enough. We just stood there, laughing at him. And that's when it hit me—why the universe had staged this absurd little scene and brought us face-to-face with our enemy in the most random way imaginable.

For years, in my head, Adam had been "DiVello the Devil"— puppet master, executioner, shadowy double agent who'd gotten rich by using all of us, by scripting me as Hollywood's villain. But standing there under that buzzing fluorescent light, with the chemical tang of printer ink in the air, that mythology dissolved. He wasn't the devil. He was just a guy—flustered, embarrassed, rushing out of a Staples bathroom because he didn't want to look me in the eye, let alone apologize or say anything even remotely sincere. He was still tethered to the machine, he hadn't tasted what it was like to slip the leash, to step outside the narrative entirely.

And that was the revelation: The devil only looms large when you're stuck inside his script. The moment you start authoring your own, he shrinks back to scale. Even if I said everything I'd wanted to say to him over the years, it wouldn't have changed anything. This guy was never going to change. But even knowing that, I'll admit there's a part of me that still wishes I'd put his head down the toilet and flushed it.

CHAPTER 27

RULE BRITANNIA

Speidi in the Shire

I'd just finished my USC degree in 2013—thank God I only had to do two years, since my old credits still counted—when Speidi signed on for *Celebrity Big Brother* in the UK. One minute I was turning in term papers, the next I was packing for London to move into a house full of strangers under 24/7 surveillance.

At the time, *Big Brother* was still a cultural juggernaut over there—massive ratings, front-page tabloid coverage, must-see TV. And we were ready. Everything we'd learned on *The Hills*—every ambush edit, every producer manipulation—had been training us for this exact moment. We knew the assignment: Stir the pot by saying the things no one else had the guts to say. Tell the truth people didn't want to hear, then sit back as it detonated. Of course, we demanded a paycheck that reflected the value of what we brought to the table. Five hundred thousand pounds, please. About $750,000 at the time, for about a week's work.

When the network head, Richard Desmond—billionaire owner of Channel 5, *The Independent*, and *OK!* magazine—found out how much we were getting paid, he supposedly called Simon Cowell and asked, *"Who the fuck is this Speidi I'm paying through the nose for?"*

Simon's reply: *"Write the check. It'll be worth it."*

Desmond himself was something out of a movie. He'd built his empire from scratch, starting with adult magazines (*Penthouse, Asian Babes*), then pivoting into mainstream publishing by buying the *Daily Express* and *The Daily Star*. His *OK!* magazine, which was all about celebrity weddings, babies, and glossy exclusives—was the kind of place where Speidi belonged. He was brash and outrageous, a throwback to the kind of media barons who didn't care about rules—just ratings. There are plenty of stories about him losing his temper in boardrooms, banging the table, swearing, threatening lawsuits. Very *Succession* energy.

Made Adam DiVello look like a puppy dog.

Apparently, his order to the producers was simple. *"Make sure they earn every last penny."*

Hey—fine by us. We were used to feeling tortured in the name of entertainment. People think reality stars are having fun out there? Hell no. Being on reality TV SUCKS. It's brutal. It rips open your fears, your insecurities, your weakest spots, and then broadcasts them to the world so everyone can laugh. It's a gladiatorial arena. An experiment in feeling a form of psychological torture designed to break all but the strongest. Luckily, by this point, we were seasoned masochists. We were Russell Crowe as Maximus Decimus Meridius, commander of the Armies of the North, taunting the crowd in the arena:

"ARE YOU NOT ENTERTAINED?"

The show dropped us in this British sampler pack of supposedly famous randos we'd never heard of. A talent show runner-up, a pop princess weeping into her tea, a shirtless ex-footballer spoiling for a fight, an actual jockey among them. And us, the American villains—a double-headed live grenade, dropped into a teacup.

They hated us.

On day one, we were banished to the basement because our instant nemesis, Rylan—this malfunctioning Ken doll and *X Factor* reject who looked like the spray-tanned love child of Liberace and Spock—banished us there. The house was divided into the "luxury" upstairs crew and the "basement" crew, which meant no beds, no hot water, no comforts.

"How are you enjoying your visit to the UK so far?" *Big Brother* asked us.

"The dungeon is quite lovely," Heidi said in her best Queen of England voice.

"We're having a blast, I'm ready to starve in the basement," I said.

Thankfully, we were given the opportunity to cut off the hot water upstairs. I said something along the lines of how if it were up to me, they wouldn't just be showering in cold water—they'd be tied up in a closet in their underwear.

Our furious fellow housemates then slapped us with ten nominations to be evicted (which we of course weren't). I didn't care; I was sipping champagne, having the time of my life. "I'm probably going to win this thing," I said in the diary room. "It's just how the universe works for me. My British superfans are going to keep saving the day, and I can feel it in my bones."

GOD SAVE THE QUEEN!

The other housemates were mainly awful at first. Except Gillian Taylforth, this British soap legend—we loved her. But the rest were kooks with zero clue how to play the reality game.

"They're all actresses," Heidi explained in the diary room. "They're all playing. We're reality stars, we're actually real. We've played the fake game, and we're done with that."

"Even our fake reality game is one hundred times more real than their reality game," I added.

Most of these people had spent their careers hiding behind scripts or characters, thinking they could "play" reality like another role. But you can't fake endurance. You can't fake what happens when you're stripped of privacy, sleep, food, and dignity, and the world still expects you to be entertaining. Ultimately, they could NOT handle their emotions, because mentally, most of these people were just . . . children. Completely unprepared for the psychological mindfuck of reality TV.

Things got a little scary when our housemate Neil "Razor" Ruddock—this four-hundred-pound ex–pro soccer player—lost it and came at me like a runaway bus. I swear my life flashed before my eyes.

"If you wanna get nasty, I could be the horriblest cunt to you in the world," he said, lunging for me.

Whoa, whoa, whoa, fella! Do you not realize THIS IS A GAME? Big guy was really taking things to heart. Our nemesis, Rylan—bless him, and thank him for this—had to physically hold him back.

We demanded our lawyers at that point. We were ready to walk. We're not trying to compromise our actual safety, ever. Neil was reprimanded for threatening and aggressive behavior, and things settled down.

If you go back and watch the footage, it's interesting how little we had to actually do in order to create fireworks in that house. We weren't scheming. We weren't acting. We were just speaking our minds—unfiltered, straight to the point. It was healing, in a way. Our first reality experience that actually felt . . . real.

We placed second. Yep, we nearly won that show, even while being the most hated people in that house. The British public were rewarding us for being authentically entertaining people, and we'll forever love them for that. Rylan wound up winning. Was I surprised? Not really. Rylan was methodical, a warlock who studied this show like his life depended on it. Me and Heidi? We were never supposed to win. We were the plot twist that made the show worth watching.

That's fine. Let him have his little trophy. History will show who actually carried that season—and it wasn't the guy with the teeth so white they needed a dimmer switch.

When we got out of the house, we were "the biggest stars in England since Posh and Becks," according to bossman Richard Desmond. "Stay in London, I want to launch a show with you!" he told us. "I'll put you up wherever you want."

Wherever we want?

"How about the Dorchester?" I said, without missing a beat. The Dorchester is where royalty goes to feel fancy. So bougie that the doormen have doormen. After three weeks in *Big Brother* hell, we were ready for a little pampering.

When we got there, all we had were bags of filthy clothes—weeks of *Big Brother* house grime stuffed into duffels. I dumped them at the front desk and told them we needed laundry done. A few hours later, my phone rang.

"WHAT THE FUCK, SPENCER?" Richard Desmond yelled. "Why do I have a seventy-eight-hundred-pound dry-cleaning bill? Are you MAD? I would have bought you new clothes!"

Later, he sent his Rolls to fetch us, and we were chauffeured across London to his penthouse overlooking the Thames. The guy who picked us up—Desmond's right-hand man—looked like a British mob enforcer cast by Guy Ritchie. Silent, menacing.

In the elevator I tried to break the tension.

"Man, that's so cool that Richard's got his own Oddjob!"

The guy stopped dead, turned, and snarled in my face: "DON'T YOU EVER CALL ME ODDJOB AGAIN. HEAR ME, SON? I AIN'T NO ODDJOB."

We remained silent for the rest of the elevator ride.

Penthouse doors opened. Marble floors, skyline view, Desmond looking like a kingpin.

"Listen, kids," he said, leaning back like he owned the skyline. "I made Posh 'n' Becks. And I can do the same for you two. We'll whack together a pilot for Channel 5. We'll call it 'Something Speidi.' You'll sell papers, you'll shift magazines, you'll be stars."

Heidi and I locked eyes—*Holy crap, yes! A thousand times, yes!*

Desmond jabbed a finger at us, grinning. "Only thing is, keeping you two at the Dorchester's costing me a fortune. Why don't you sack it off and move in here? I've got bedrooms, staff, the full monty. Much better than a hotel."

I nodded. "Sounds baller."

Heidi's smile froze. Later, back at the Dorchester, she turned to me and said, "I don't feel comfortable living in that man's house. He's too much. I want to stay here."

So, to Richard Desmond's intense irritation, we ended up living at the Dorchester for three glorious weeks, on his dime. Every day he'd summon us to lunch or dinner, puffing on these skinny Cuban cigars like he was Tony Montana. Naturally, I ordered the fattest Cubans on the menu, just to compete. "Bloody hell, Spencer," he wheezed across the table one night, smoke circling his head in a cloud. "That's not a cigar, that's a tree trunk."

I leaned back, grinning. "Size matters, Richard." Heidi just rolled her eyes.

By week two, Desmond was pitching us new formats over every course. "Picture this: you two in a farmhouse, middle of nowhere. Milking cows, mucking out the pigs. Like *The Simple Life*, but it's Speidi." I was in immediately. *Yes!* Two famous Americans terrorizing a small English village. Chickens scattering as I roll up in designer wellies. Me trying to drive a tractor like it's a Bentley. I could already see the poster. Heidi just stared at him, not smiling.

Later, she told me, "Spencer. I am NOT living with pigs. And I'm definitely not letting us get wrapped up in some producer's weird vision for us. We already did that once, okay?"

She was right. For the first time in our lives, we were starting to think strategically instead of just blindly following every check waved in front of us. *Speidi in the Shire* was dead. No hobbit hideaway, no more farm exile. The English fairy tale was finished because we'd finally decided we weren't about to hand over our identities to someone else ever again. That was the trap of *The Hills*, and we'd escaped it. If we were going to play characters again, we'd be the ones writing the script.

CHAPTER 28

PRATT DADDY

Wait, People Actually Like Me?

In 2014, we signed on for *Celebrity Wife Swap*. For Heidi, spending three days in Seattle—stepping into former Olympic athlete Amanda Beard's life, taking care of her two kids—flipped a switch. She was packing lunches, reading bedtime stories, wiping peanut butter off little faces. Her maternal instincts kicked into gear, and by the time the show ended, she couldn't stop asking when we were going to start a family of our own.

Whoa, whoa, whoa. Hold your horses, baby!

I wasn't sure I was ready. Not yet. I always wanted to be stupid rich before I brought a kid into the world, and we were still living at my parents' house, trying to save up for a home of our own. Despite the forward momentum in our careers, I always felt like we were one bad decision away from free fall. I didn't want my little prodigy born into that kind of volatility.

But there was something else, too. Something I'd never really acknowledged out loud. A feeling I was carrying around. Like, what would my kid say when people asked what Daddy does for a living? *"He's a TV asshole. Everyone hates him!"*

Shame. That's what that feeling was.

Listen, being a villain is easy when the shrapnel hits only you. But being a father means that shrapnel might land on someone else, someone who never asked for it. I couldn't stand the thought of a little mini

Pratt being teased on the playground because everyone hates their papa, because their mom was on Team LC.

One night, I confessed my fears to Heidi. She listened, really listened, the way she always does when I'm opening up. Then she said, "Spencer, kids don't care what the world thinks of you. They care about how you treat them. If you love them with everything you have, that's all that matters."

Deep down, I knew she was right. But there's a difference between knowing something in your head and accepting it in your heart. Admitting I was ready—or worthy—of becoming a father meant confronting parts of myself I'd spent years avoiding. It demanded a new kind of inner work. I wasn't sure where to begin, to be honest. There weren't any "daddy confidence" crystals on the market that I knew of.

Speaking of which, Pratt Daddy Crystals was booming. I'd teamed up with the same guy who'd sold me that huge chunk of moldavite, and we were selling my crystal healing kits online, containing moldavite, black tourmaline, and Herkimer diamond, aka the Disruptor, the Protector, and the Amplifier. A recipe for blowing up your old self, shielding you from the fallout, and then tuning you in to a higher frequency. "Rebirth in a box," if you will.

While researching new marketing tools, I stumbled onto this quirky little app called Snapchat and decided to start selling my crystals there, too. At the time, Snapchat felt like a gimmick, a place for disappearing selfies. But they had just rolled out this new feature called Snapchat Stories, where you could post little videos that lasted twenty-four hours. That clicked for me immediately. It wasn't just a way to show off the crystal kits—it was a stage. A place I could talk about moldavite and tourmaline, hype their power, and actually connect with people one snap at a time.

Snapchat was a direct line between me and a new audience. I didn't have to go through producers, editors, or network executives in order to reach them. For the first time in my career, I wasn't handing my story over to someone else—I was in control. I was the narrator. And that shift—tiny as it seemed then—would change everything.

Before long, I started creating content beyond the crystals. I'd snap myself eating Mexican food. I had a waterproof phone case and would snap myself swimming out in the ocean chasing seals. Filmed myself making my coffee, going to the health food store, getting juices, going to jiujitsu. I just filmed every single thing I did. I obsessed, the way I always do when I throw myself into a project. Most people would post one little snap video; I went full *Truman Show*—wake up, snap all day long, then go to bed.

The algorithm likes it when you post regularly, and before long, the numbers were wild: millions of views a day. Seven-point-seven million views a week. Twenty-two million a month. It was like *The Hills* ratings all over again—actually, much higher—except this time, it was just me and my phone. The term *influencer* may not have even been coined yet, but looking back, that's exactly what I was becoming.

What I loved the most was that my audience (which was 91 percent women) wasn't tuning in to boo me. It seemed as if . . . they actually *liked* me? They weren't mad at me for talking about crystals, or making coffee, narrating tabloids, or just . . . existing. For the first time in a decade, I experienced what it felt like not to be hated. I was just Spencer being Spencer. And that person was weirdly likable, apparently. Strangers were stopping me on the street to say, "*Oh, Spencer Pratt? I love you on Snapchat.*" Not once did they mention *The Hills*.

Social media felt so much more real than reality TV, back then. Of course, it would later become more and more staged, riddled with inauthentic "image crafting." But in its infancy, we were living in an age of innocence. And this new medium, this new frontier, was allowing me to experience something I'd never felt before from an audience: being loved.

Maybe I AM someone worth rooting for, I thought. *Maybe I AM someone who could raise a little Pratt, after all.*

In 2016, Heidi came off her birth control. Less than a month later, we were pregnant.

The day we got the positive pregnancy test, we'd just gotten back to the house and were in the yard when something flew straight into my face. A hummingbird. I'm serious, it flew straight INTO my face. Not since that day in my pool with Brody had I seen a hummingbird that close, never had one just kamikaze into my head like that.

"What the hell?" I said, watching as the little thing zoomed into a bush nearby. When I looked closer, I saw this tiny nest no bigger than a golf ball. Inside were two eggs the size of Tic Tacs.

Something about seeing those impossibly small eggs and that fierce little hummingbird mama who would have kicked my ass to protect them sparked something in me. It all felt fated, somehow. Like our stories were running side by side.

I spent the entire day googling "symbolism of hummingbird nests," "spiritual meaning of hummingbird eggs," "pregnancy signs from nature." The internet confirmed that hummingbirds were symbols of joy, resilience, and new beginnings. Now that Heidi was pregnant, I knew I was about to enter a whole new phase of my experience with love. I was ready to defend, to nurture, to love more fiercely and more completely than anything I'd ever loved before. Those hummingbirds weren't just pretty little birds in my backyard. They were a part of my story.

That night, the weather report warned of a massive rainstorm. All I could picture were those fragile eggs, no bigger than jelly beans, being swept from their nest.

"I can't let the babies die!" I told Heidi. "I have to do something!"

I spent the next few hours building an entire tent fortress around the tree, engineering an elaborate system to keep the rain out while still allowing the mother bird to fly in. Of course, filming all of it on Snapchat. My parents' neighbors probably thought I'd completely lost it, watching me out there with tarps and poles. But it worked. The eggs survived the storm.

Once the babies hatched, I installed a camera in the tree, just to watch them grow. Every morning I'd check the footage, watching these tiny featherless babies slowly transform into birds that glimmered like opals.

One day, I looked at the monitor and my heart dropped. There was only one baby left in the nest. I rewound the footage and there it was, at 3:47 a.m.—a fucking rat hanging upside down from the branch, eating the other baby. He never even had a chance.

I called animal rescue immediately, practically screaming into the phone. "You need to come get this nest right now! Once a predator knows where it is, they'll come back for the other one!" The rescue people probably thought I was insane, this grown man having a breakdown over a hummingbird baby, but they came.

We carefully moved the surviving baby to their facility. "When he's ready to fly, do you want us to release him back here in your yard?" they asked.

"Absolutely. Call me the second he's ready."

Months later, they called. "Just so you know," the woman warned, "people always get disappointed. We release them and they just fly away, never to be seen again."

"I don't care," I said. "Bring my hummingbird home."

They brought him back, opened the little carrier, and that bird— I'd named him Allen—flew straight to the bush where he was born. But he didn't fly away. He just landed on the branch where his nest had been and sat there, looking at me. I walked to the bush, and slowly extended my finger. Immediately, Allen hopped on. From that day forward, I would walk outside and Allen would always find me. I'd hold up a tiny syringe filled with sugar water and he'd hover there, drinking from it.

I have videos that still blow my mind—this wild hummingbird who, for some reason, chose to be my friend during those quiet months in Santa Barbara, when Heidi was pregnant with our first son, Gunner. I still think about him a lot.

It was bittersweet when we finally left my parents' beach house and moved into a place of our own. Things were picking up again. We were moving forward. And that meant we had to move back to LA, back into the center of the hustle where we belonged.

Our new house was in the Palisades, directly across the street from the house Heidi and I had lived in during *The Hills*. Literally, directly. From driveway to driveway. The street was called Chautauqua, four minutes from my childhood home by car, twenty minutes if you walked slowly. Same neighborhood, just up the hill instead of down by the ocean where my parents lived.

This was the place we'd raise our family, right next to our favorite hiking trail. Our dream home, paid for in the strangest patchwork of ways: the deposit covered by those gold coins I'd stashed away, the monthly mortgage and bills carried by whatever money we'd saved from reality gigs and now, improbably, from Snapchat and later TikTok LIVE, where I'd figured out how I could make thousands a day just by battling strangers online.

Still, leaving Allen and my hummingbird garden behind broke my heart. That little sanctuary in Santa Barbara had been more than a stopgap—it was where I learned how to sit still long enough to feel the world, where I'd begun to understand love in a new way, to see nature not as backdrop but as teacher. Those lessons from the quiet, from the birds and the trees and the pause in the madness, I'd carry them with me. Back home. To my beloved Palisades. Where I would begin again.

At the new house, I started with one hummingbird feeder. Just one, to see what would happen. Within a week, I had dozens of hummingbirds. So I bought more feeders. Then more. Soon I had sixty or seventy feeders, a hummingbird airport in my backyard, with birds constantly coming and going.

My first real connection at the new place was with Tiki—the most beautiful hummingbird I'd ever seen, with feathers like liquid ruby. I could walk outside, raise my finger to the sky, and Tiki would appear from nowhere to land on it. No food needed. Just pure trust.

People always asked me how I did it, how I got them to trust me. The secret was dedication bordering on insanity. I made fresh nectar every single day—four cups filtered water, one cup white cane sugar, specifically the C&H in the pink-and-white bag. Had to be that exact brand. I cleaned the feeders with boiling water daily. And what the hummingbirds really gave me in return was meditation.

I'd always struggled with sitting still, with quieting my brain.

But to get a hummingbird to land on your hand, you have to become a statue. You can't even blink. Your breathing has to slow until you're barely moving air. One twitch and they're gone.

I'd stand in my backyard for hours, especially during those long days when Heidi was out and I was alone with my thoughts. I'd just stand there, breathing, waiting. It was the deepest meditation I'd ever experienced. My mind had no choice but to stop. To stand still in my backyard, waiting for tiny birds to trust me enough to use me as a perch. Learning how to be patient. How to be present. How to exist in a moment without needing to fill it with drama.

The hummingbirds were my teachers. They showed me the final lesson I needed to learn before becoming a dad—that real love isn't about performance. It's about presence. About creating a space safe enough for something fragile to land, and trust it will be cared for.

For the first time in my life, I was ready to be that space. A human bird feeder. A sugar daddy to a thousand tiny babies with wings. And then, finally, to another angel. On October 1, 2017, the hummingbirds met the first Baby Pratt.

Our son, Gunner Stone.

• • •

After Gunner was born, Heidi and I were in one of the happiest stretches of our lives—our full-blown triumph era. We loved our home and being back in the Palisades. I'd turned the backyard into a hummingbird sanctuary, and the living room into Pratt Daddy Crystals HQ, complete with a staff running orders and fulfillment. Snapchat was peaking—eight million people a week tuning in just to watch me eat burritos and talk about crystals. Various networks were circling us again, and it seemed like we might be on track to getting our own show. We had our baby, I was training jiujitsu and had just won the LA Open in the purple belt division. Our parents were doing well, and Stephanie was off living in England, building a new life on *Made in Chelsea*—a setup I helped broker that conveniently neutralized a whole lot of potential family drama. No beef, no chaos, everyone was thriving.

Everything was up, up, up: the numbers, the vibes, the birds.

Yeah, 2017 through 2019. That was peak magic. Everything felt possible. Like, *Oh—we can do* anything.

Oh, and I found a brand-new obsession: Taylor Swift.

It started the day the single "Look What You Made Me Do" from her forthcoming album dropped, August 24, 2017. This record was Taylor's big comeback after 2016, when she disappeared from the spotlight in the wake of what people now call the "snake backlash." Some beef between her and Kanye West and his ride or die at the time, Kim Kardashian. A beef that seemingly framed Taylor as a liar.

The mob piled on. This was the birth of "cancel culture," and before long, the hashtag #TaylorSwiftIsOverParty was trending worldwide. The hate was cruel because it wasn't just about disliking a pop star—it was the whole world ganging up on a young woman.

After going through that deeply traumatic experience, Taylor came back swinging with *Reputation*. Instead of denying the snake label, she'd owned it—snakes on the album art, snakes towering over her stage, snake rings on her fingers. Songs like "Look What

You Made Me Do" flipped the hate into power, one of the great pop F-you's of our time, taking all that public humiliation and turning it into empowerment.

When I hit play on that song, it felt like someone had cracked open my skull and started reading my diary out loud. It sent me straight back to the sex tape rumors, to the fallout after LC stood by her version of the story and let the world unleash its full fury on us, turning us into the punching bag of Millennial pop culture.

The role you made me play of the fool.
No, I don't like you.

Sure, we'd monetized the backlash, we'd made lemonade out of being America's most-hated couple, but hell—it wasn't easy. It hurt. And we still bore the scars. I really felt for Taylor, all while relating to her on a very deep level. The track was like our entire *Hills*-era backstory disguised as a pop song.

For a full year, every single morning, I had the same ritual: pull a shot of espresso, hit play on "Look What You Made Me Do," and post it on Snapchat. Rain or shine, didn't matter—I never missed a day. My followers probably thought I'd joined some Taylor Swift cult, and honestly, they weren't wrong. But that's what great art does—it takes something deeply personal and somehow makes it universal. Taylor's words were her story, but they echoed mine, and probably millions of other people's, too. Anyone who's ever been misunderstood, lied about, judged, or misrepresented could listen to that track and think: *Yeah, that's me, too.*

One day, in May 2018, I got a call from my good friend and manager Kyell Thomas, saying, "There's a package here from Nashville." Now, everyone knows that anything from Nashville *has* to be from Taylor Swift.

I drove all the way to my manager's office just to open this box. Inside was this insane mock-up of a stadium, all decked out in the *Reputation* aesthetic, with snakes and chrome and drama. Tucked inside was an invite to the show.

May 19, 2018, me, Heidi, and baby Gunner in protective headphones rolled up to the Rose Bowl, thinking maybe we'd scored decent VIP, a little lanyard action, something like that. At will-call, I ripped open the envelope and the tickets said Row 1, Seats 1 and 2. I looked at Heidi, eyes bugging out. *"Wow, Heidi . . . are we literally front row?"*

And sure enough—we walked in, and boom. Dead center. Front row. Practically leaning on the stage. I swear I could see the rhinestones on Taylor's mic sparkle before the lights even hit. The whole thing was insane—giant animatronic snakes wrapping around the stage, the bass shaking the stadium like an earthquake, fireworks blasting out of nowhere.

All of a sudden this woman walked up to us. I didn't get it at first—I wasn't yet a full-blown Swiftie who knew all the lore. I didn't realize this was Tree Paine, the GOAT of publicists, Taylor's PR. "Taylor wants to see you guys backstage," she said.

Next thing I knew, we were backstage with Taylor and her mom, who was thanking me for being such a Taylor supporter in the wake of her daughter's lowest moment. Taylor held Gunner in her arms like it was the most natural thing in the world as she chatted with us, warm and genuine. She even let me snap a photo of her cradling him, for Snapchat.

That moment felt ceremonial, like my samurai initiation, my Jedi knighting. Except instead of Luke Skywalker handing me a lightsaber, it was Taylor Swift handing me something even more powerful. *Credibility.* Or at least some semblance of it. Suddenly, the entire Swiftie galaxy knew my name. From that point on, the fandom (at least on Snapchat) embraced me.

I'm not saying Taylor gave us her official endorsement or anything. She was just being herself—sweet, generous, real. But this felt like the first time ANY famous person had EVER genuinely wanted to be seen with us, just for the fun of it. Most people probably worried about what standing next to us might say about them, thanks to all the stories that had been spun about Speidi. That we were crazy, that we were toxic, that we were liars. But Taylor didn't care about that. Maybe because she understood the same truth we did: Don't believe everything you read. Or see, even. Because things aren't always as simple as they might appear to be.

CHAPTER 29

BRING BACK *THE HILLS*

Reunions, Regrets, and the Confession You'll Never See

Shortly after I became a Snapchat master, a pitch began developing at MTV: a new reality show built around my new life—featuring Pratt Daddy Crystals, my hummingbird sanctuary, the whole cosmic circus. Just me and Heidi, unfiltered.

It could have been perfect.

Until, in one of the all-time dumbest Spencer moves, I blurted out: "*Let's bring back* The Hills *instead!*"

Why, Spencer, whyyyyy?

At the time, it felt smart. MTV had just successfully rebooted *Jersey Shore*, and I thought if I hitched my wagon to a franchise, I'd guarantee more seasons, more money, more longevity. What was I thinking? One or two seasons of a Spencer show about crystals and hummingbirds would've been *heaven* compared to slogging through multiple seasons of *The Hills* again, trapped with the same cast and all that baggage.

The Hills: New Beginnings felt like a toxic family reunion where half the cousins showed up and the other half pretended they didn't get the invite. Heidi and I signed on, of course—but Lauren and Kristin wanted no part of it. So instead, we had Audrina; Brody; Stephanie; Justin Bobby; Jason Wahler and his wife, Ashley; Frankie and his wife, Jennifer; and then, out of nowhere, Mischa Barton—yes, the actual star of *The O.C.*—wandering into our world like a crossover episode nobody asked for. (Later they swapped her out for Pamela Anderson's son, Brandon, and Caroline D'Amore, the DJ and Pizza Girl.)

It was messy, it was weird, and it was never going to hit the cultural high of the original, but I'll be real: I was excited at the thought of being Spencer Pratt on *The Hills* again. Older, wiser, happier. Plus, I was genuinely thrilled about reconnecting with Brody. Enough time had passed that I thought we could finally put the past behind us. Maybe we could move on.

Alas, our first reunion was painfully awkward. His partner at the time, Kaitlynn Carter, made it pretty clear she wasn't a fan of mine, and that set the tone. Instead of slipping back into easy brotherhood, it felt like I was constantly on probation in my own friendship with Brody—one wrong word, and I'd be benched again.

It was disappointing.

Equally disappointing was the fact that no one wanted to bring their A game, apparently. I honestly thought my old castmates would have appreciated the opportunity for a *Hills* reboot. I thought they'd come back hungry, ready to make another hit, but *authentic* this time. That's what I'd always wanted us to be, like the *Jersey Shore* crew—messy, chaotic, committed to real entertainment.

Instead, my castmates seemed guarded, image crafty. It felt like every scene was them trying to polish their brand, not tell the truth.

DAMMIT.

I knew from day one of shooting that this show was going to suck. Everyone was talking like robots—so scripted, so full of agenda, like they'd practiced their lines in the mirror. I thought throwing Mischa Barton into the mix would have made things more interesting. But no. She did a scene with Heidi and me and said, all prim and proper, "I'm not drinking wine while the cameras are rolling." The cameras cut, and boom—she downs three glasses like it's a frat initiation. I was so pissed.

JUST BE YOUR BEAUTIFUL, CHAOTIC SELVES. BE AUTHENTIC. THAT'S WHAT MAKES FOR GOOD REALITY TV.

But no. Why would anyone want to do that.

The one saving grace was that MTV actually brought in a legit heavyweight to produce the show: Alex Baskin, the producer behind *The Real Housewives of Beverly Hills*, *The Real Housewives of Orange County*, and *Vanderpump Rules*. For the first time, we had a producer who believed in shooting the truth. His mantra was simple: *If it happens on camera, it's going in the show.* That should've been a blessing.

Instead, it worked against us, because this cast wanted pampering, edits that protected their "brands," producers bending to their image-control demands. Lauren Weber, an amazing showrunner, committed to documenting reality, had to deal with the cast staging a mutiny against her after Brody's partner, Kaitlynn, decided she didn't like how their relationship was coming across.

By the time Season 1 wrapped in 2019, the cracks in Brody and Kaitlynn's relationship were already obvious. And sure enough, right after the finale aired in August, the split went public. That was the same week Kaitlynn was photographed making out with Miley Cyrus on a yacht in Italy, and suddenly her and Brody's breakup became headline news around the world.

Best thing about Season 1, to be honest.

Once Brody realized he was done with Kaitlynn, the mood between us lifted. In the final scene of the *Hills* reboot—which didn't air—Brody apologized to me on camera and said, "I should have never taken LC's side. You were my best friend, we had a great real thing." Now Brody and I are friends again.

At his fortieth birthday at Nobu, in front of everybody and his mom, he made a whole speech and repeated everything he'd said on that *Hills* finale.

Unlike LC, I'll forgive *and* forget.

The other life-changing moment to come out of the *Hills* reboot—another moment no one ever saw—was when Jason Wahler had a conversation with us about the rumors that had destroyed us.

Heidi and I met Jason at Café Gratitude, cameras rolling. If you've never been there, it's this temple of positivity disguised as a restaurant—every menu item is an affirmation. You don't order a kale salad; you declare, "*I am fulfilled.*" It felt apt. We were about to have the most illuminating conversation of our lives in a place where the menu promised enlightenment.

Jason showed up looking nervous. From where Heidi and I were sitting, here's what we heard. We started with small talk, but Heidi couldn't hold it in. Ten years of carrying this weight, and it all came pouring out. Her eyes filled with tears as she told him what it had cost her. The years of being called a liar, a backstabber, a monster. The way the media had chewed us up and spit us out. With no one stepping up in our defense.

"We aren't liars," she said, her voice breaking.

I watched Jason's face carefully, wondering how he'd respond.

Then he spoke.

He said he'd been too sick back then, too lost in his own addiction and spiral to speak up when it mattered. That he should have said something—anything—but he'd been too messed up to do the right thing. He apologized.

"What can I do now?" he asked. "How do I make this right?"

"You already did," Heidi said quietly.

The apology didn't magically rewrite history or erase a decade of hate. But it did something we hadn't expected: It validated us. Someone who'd been there was finally acknowledging what Heidi and I had gone through, as a result of the stories surrounding those rumors.

We closed out the meal with wellness shots, toasting to health and maybe a little healing. Heidi glanced at her phone—we needed to get back to Gunner—so we hugged it out and left. I can't speak for what Jason remembers about that conversation or what he meant by his apology. I can only tell you what it meant to us.

We all knew MTV would probably never air this footage. This conversation we'd waited for would most likely end up on some cutting-room floor. Which is exactly what happened. It's there, somewhere in MTV's vault. We have the production notes from that scene, detailing exactly what was said. But the footage has never seen the light of day.

I hope someone at MTV is brave enough to just drop the raw footage one day—the pieces of reality that actually meant something. Imagine that: reality TV saving itself by finally being honest. What if authenticity became the storyline? What if truth was the cliffhanger?

People would watch that show, I think.

The *Hills* reboot was never destined to last, and the global pandemic drove the final nail into its coffin. March 2020 hit, and the entire world shut down. Suddenly, shooting reality television became nearly impossible. The whole premise of our show was built on social interaction—parties, dinners, clubs, manufactured drama over bottles of expensive wine. But now? Everyone was wearing masks. Restaurants were closed. Nightclubs didn't exist. You couldn't even go to the beach without risking a fine of up to a thousand dollars—but somehow hiking was fine, because apparently COVID understood the difference between sand and dirt.

We tried to keep filming. MTV wanted content. But how do you capture authentic reality TV when reality itself has been suspended? We'd meet up for "socially distanced" conversations in backyards, sitting six feet apart like we were strangers at a bus stop, not people who'd spent years of our lives on camera together. The crew wore masks. We wore masks. Everything felt staged and sterile—which is ironic, considering reality TV is supposed to be staged anyway, but at least it's supposed to *feel* real.

The show needed energy, conflict, and life. The pandemic had drained all of it. By the time production officially shut down, no one was surprised. Season 2 limped to its finale, and that was it. *The Hills:*

New Beginnings ended not with drama, but with a whimper, suffocated by a virus none of us saw coming.

But losing the show wasn't even the worst part. Pratt Daddy Crystals—our business, our actual empire—was destroyed.

Let me put this in perspective: We'd been making a quarter million dollars a month selling crystal jewelry. We had fifteen employees working out of our house in the Palisades, packaging orders, managing inventory, handling customer service. This wasn't some side hustle I was doing between reality TV gigs. This was a legitimate operation. We had a warehouse system set up in our garage. We had processes. We were scaling. I genuinely believed we were going to have the most successful crystal jewelry business in the world.

And then the government decided we weren't essential.

Let that sink in for a second. We operated entirely online. Our customers ordered from their homes. Our employees worked in our home. There was no storefront, no physical retail space where the public could congregate and spread disease. We were literally the model for pandemic-safe business.

But none of that mattered. California's lockdown orders were sweeping and absolute. I wasn't allowed to have employees in the house. Period. Packaging orders? Not essential. Shipping crystals to people who wanted them? Not essential. It didn't matter that we'd built something from nothing, that fifteen people depended on these paychecks, that our customers were waiting for their orders.

The government shut us down, and just like that, our quarter-million-dollar-a-month business became zero.

So what did we do?

We learned how to live small. We got really good at making cocktails at home—not by choice, but because there was literally nowhere else to go. Thankfully, we had a backyard. We bought two planters and started growing vegetables like we were homesteaders in 1885. Tomatoes. Peppers. Herbs. I'd stand there watering them in the morning, thinking about how I used to manage fifteen employees, and now I was nurturing basil.

I wasn't Snapchatting much during this period. My fans would ask where I went, why I was so quiet. The truth? Life was that depressing. What was I supposed to post? "Hey guys, watching my business die in real time while the government tells me I can't work! #Blessed"? Nobody wanted to see that. I didn't want to *be* that.

Heidi and I just tried to survive it. We told ourselves it was temporary. Once things reopened, once the madness ended, we'd rebuild. Pratt Daddy Crystals would come roaring back.

Except it didn't.

When California finally lifted restrictions and I was allowed to bring employees back, I genuinely believed we'd pick up where we left off. We'd banked all this goodwill, we had our customer base, we had the systems. All we had to do was turn the lights back on.

But I didn't realize that the pandemic had fundamentally rewired how people spent money. The customers who used to drop $200 on crystal jewelry without blinking were now pinching pennies. The cost of living had exploded—gas prices, groceries, rent, everything. People were scared. Their priorities had shifted. A beautiful crystal necklace wasn't essential anymore. It was a luxury they could no longer justify.

During all this chaos—the pandemic, the business dying, the world falling apart—Heidi and I were trying for a second child.

We'd always known we wanted more kids. Watching Gunner grow up only made us want another baby more. We were young, healthy, ready. How hard could it be?

Turns out? Incredibly hard.

We tried for two years to get pregnant with Ryker. Two years of hope and disappointment, of timing everything perfectly and still seeing negative pregnancy tests. I wanted another child so desperately. Heidi did, too. We'd talk about baby names, imagine what Gunner would be like as a big brother, picture our family complete. And then another month would pass, and that future would feel further away.

At a certain point, we broke. Not our marriage—our grip on the outcome. We'd been white-knuckling it for so long, trying to manifest a pregnancy through sheer force of will, that we'd made ourselves miserable. So we stopped. We surrendered it to God. We let go.

A month later, Heidi was pregnant.

I'm not saying I understand how that works. Maybe it was the carnivore diet she'd started—beef, eggs, and organ meats, the diet that some fertility specialists swear by. Maybe her body finally relaxed once we stopped treating conception like a second job. Maybe it was just timing, the universe's dark sense of humor finally deciding to smile on us.

Or maybe it was God. Maybe that's what surrender actually means—making space for something bigger than yourself to work.

Ryker Stone Pratt was born on November 17, 2022. Seven pounds, six ounces. Perfect.

The business was gone. The show was over. But holding our baby, none of that mattered anymore.

CHAPTER 30

WHEN THE PALISADES BURNED

Our House Went Up in Smoke, and Heidi Went to Number One

The year 2024 brought us yet another twist in our wild, improbable saga. Out of absolutely nowhere, Heidi's music started blowing up in China. We're talking billions of streams. Billions with a capital *B*.

Her song "I'll Do It"—a track she'd recorded years ago, written off as a relic of the Speidi era—suddenly became the soundtrack to an entire culture. On Douyin, China's TikTok, people were using it for dances, transitions, memes—you name it. Overnight, it turned into a viral phenomenon. And then the checks started coming. Big, juicy checks. You know how I like those.

I remember sitting at my computer, staring at the streaming numbers like they were written in ancient Sumerian. I reached out to our distributor, asking where those checks were coming from. How the hell did the album that sold 672 copies in America in 2010 suddenly blow up in China? The same songs that US radio wouldn't touch with a hazmat suit and a priest's blessing were now soundtracking millions of videos of Chinese teenagers doing synchronized dances in subway stations.

Really, there was no explanation. No strategy. Just pure, inexplicable virality. Funny how you can spend years trying to launch something and fail, then lightning strikes and suddenly, you're global.

"Maybe this is it," I told Heidi one night in early January. "Maybe we were just born in the wrong country. Maybe China gets us."

"Spencer," she said, "China gets us—but America should, too."

Then, holding up her phone to show another royalty deposit, Heidi grinned. "Actually, we should just rerelease everything. The anniversary's coming up."

She was right; the fifteen-year anniversary of *Superficial* was January 11, 2025. We went full throttle, planning this whole anniversary rerelease—remastered tracks, unreleased songs. I was coordinating with producers who answered my calls out of morbid curiosity, reaching out to distributors.

To make those new mixes, I tracked down Jason Joshua, who'd worked with us back then. Guess how many Grammys he has now? SEVENTEEN. He mixed all of Beyoncé's *Lemonade*. And he was happy to help us out, too, giving us a great deal because we had history.

The *Superficial* anniversary edition was locked and loaded. Everything was in motion. Fifteen years after being laughed out of the American music industry, we were praying for one last laugh, this time for us. Just one. We'd earned it.

Which is exactly when the universe took out a flamethrower, looked directly at us, and said, "Watch this."

The morning of January 7, four days before the album release, I woke up exhausted—Gunner had had pneumonia all week with a temperature of 104, so we'd been up all night long, every night, caring for him.

Our nanny came over that morning—since Gunner was so sick, we'd needed someone to help watch two-year-old Ryker, and she had taken him out on the hiking trail near the house. Everything seemed normal otherwise. Yes, we'd had some extreme winds in the days preceding, but that morning, the winds were low. Just another beautiful morning in the Palisades.

I was just getting into my regular morning ritual—making an espresso to the sound of "Look What You Made Me Do"—when I looked out the window and saw our nanny come running back down the hill, pushing the stroller, holding Ryker in her arms. It was around 10:35 a.m.

She burst in the door and said, "The workmen up the street said there's a fire on the hill!"

Heidi immediately started throwing our kids' stuff into bags: baby monitor, diapers, pajamas, matching teddy bears (Little Brother and Big Brother). We tried to stay calm. Fires near the Palisades weren't new—we'd been through this before. Usually, it meant a few days of evacuation, then back home once the smoke cleared.

Heidi took the boys to my parents' house down in the lower Palisades. No fire had ever made it all the way down to the beach. For their place to burn, the entire town would have to go up in flames. So on paper, it seemed like the safest spot for Heidi and the kids to wait it out. Meanwhile, I stayed behind at our house to document, never thinking that the fires would actually reach us.

Here's what we didn't know then.

Six days earlier, just after midnight on New Year's Day, a fire ignited on Lachman in Topanga State Park. Investigators would later allege that a man named Jonathan Rinderknecht had started it with a lighter (at the time of writing, Rinderknecht was pleading not guilty and his lawyers were vigorously defending against the charges). The fire was extinguished that night—declared "dead out" by crews who left the scene.

But in the aftermath, we'd learn the truth: It wasn't out. Deep below the surface, in the root systems beneath the soil, it was still smoldering.

Within days, there was a warning of an "extreme weather event." "Watch out for damaging northeast winds," they said, upgrading the situation to an extreme fire condition. Even with that being the case, there were no fire trucks sent to the location of the fire that had *supposedly* been put out, days before, in Topanga State Park. No thermal imaging of the area where the fire had been.

Well, guess what happened?

January 7, extreme wind events reignited the fire in overgrown brush in Topanga State Park and it spread, becoming the Palisades fire. The fire the construction workers had warned our nanny of. The first 911 calls started coming in around 10:30 a.m.

The fire could have been manageable, were it not for the fact that neither of the reservoirs accessible to our neighborhood—including the Santa Ynez Reservoir across the hills and the Palisades Reservoir next door to our house—had any water in them for some reason. So what you have now is extreme winds, a fire, and no water.

Hydrants in the Palisades were close to being empty, since there was no water in the reservoirs. Fire department helicopters were forced to fly all the way to Pepperdine in Malibu and Encino in the Valley to get water, spending two-thirds of their time going to get water rather than fighting the actual fire.

So there I was, up on the hill Snapchatting, showing my followers how far back the fire looked. It felt distant, almost cinematic—planes buzzing overhead, dropping water. I felt confident. This wasn't *our* fire. Not yet.

Then, just as quickly, the planes left.

Where the hell did they go?

I stood there staring at an empty sky, refreshing my feed, waiting for the sound of engines. Nothing. Two hours without air support. Two hours when the fire had the run of the hills. And in fire time, two hours is an eternity.

I watched it with my dad—this *thing* wrapping and curling, gaining speed, eating its way closer. Fire moves like it's alive, like it's hunting. My dad and I didn't even have words. We just stood there, watching the monster come down on us.

Heidi got the call from my older sister, Kristin: "You need to evacuate Skip and Jan's house NOW. It's crossing Temescal Canyon. It's coming."

That was the moment it stopped being abstract. For the first time in all the years we'd lived in the Palisades, firefighters themselves were saying the unthinkable: *"This one's going to the ocean. No one can stop it."*

After getting the call from Kristin to evacuate my parents' house, Heidi packed up the boys and fled to my parents' beach house in Santa Barbara. Meanwhile, I was still in our house, trying to load my BMW with everything I could fit. My Noah's Ark moment. Let me tell you, I will never again live without a pickup truck. Trying to save your life in a BMW is comedy and tragedy at the same time.

I called 911 one last time, begged them for one fire truck to be stationed on the hill above us. I knew the spot. If they hit it with water, it would break the chain, maybe save the whole neighborhood. The answer was flat: *"No assets are available."*

That was the moment I knew for sure. Our house was going to burn.

My dad was out there with nothing but a garden hose, spraying down the yard like it was going to make a difference, while the biggest flames I'd ever seen came roaring down the block like a wall of hell.

"Dad, we have to get out of here!" I yelled.

It was sometime between 4 and 5 p.m. when we finally left.

Because we'd waited so long to evacuate, the Palisades was eerily quiet. The gridlock traffic from before was gone. I was driving, watching the security camera footage from our house, and I saw the flames coming up, around the house. In the house. Then, flames in the shape of a heart, burning through Gunner's bed. Then the power went out.

We can rebuild. We can acquire new possessions, I thought. Followed by: *They knew this was going to happen.*

Like my parents, and many of our neighbors in the Palisades, we'd gotten dropped from Farmers Insurance earlier in the year because they knew this was coming, and they knew this state did nothing to protect this town. Farmers, State Farm—all the real insurance companies—realized they couldn't risk insuring anyone in a town surrounded by forty years' worth of dry brush that no one was maintaining.

We'd all been shoved onto the California FAIR Plan, the so-called safety net. Expensive, bare-bones stopgap coverage. I'd later learn all they'd cover would be cement pilings so any new foundation would be up to code. Under the FAIR Plan, if your house burns to the ground and you can't live in it, you're still on the hook for the monthly mortgage, as the plan doesn't cover payments. Traditional policies usually cover temporary housing if you're displaced. The FAIR Plan? Usually not, unless you tack on additional policies. It doesn't include things like liability, theft, flood, or most personal property unless you add expensive extras.

Victims get hit twice: first by the fire, then by a financial system that leaves them paying a mortgage on ashes with no meaningful safety net. That's why so many survivors end up bankrupt or forced to walk away—it's not that they didn't "have insurance," it's that the only insurance left to them seemed designed to fail.

In 2024, Pacific Palisades paid $700 million in state taxes. Shouldn't we have been protected, somehow? Even a fire break, where they cut back dead brush, would have cost $200,000 and a day's work. But just like in Hollywood, governments—in this case, state and local—can make just as much money in a crisis, in a disaster.

I'd had maybe twenty minutes to grab what I could. Twenty minutes to decide what mattered from a lifetime of material accumulation.

You know what I grabbed? Some crystal necklaces, Heidi's *Superficial* merch shirts, some pairs of shorts, and some socks. Everything else went up in flames.

• • •

Back in Santa Barbara, while trying to wrap our heads around what had just happened, I was still getting emails about Heidi's rerelease.

In my naive mind, I thought, *Maybe this will help us to buy a new house.*

"We just lost everything in the fires," I posted on my socials. "Heidi's album drops in three days. Please buy her music. Stream it. Share it. It's all we have left."

People responded. TikTok blew up with support. People were buying albums, sharing posts, sending messages of support. The internet was rallying around us. Heidi's streaming numbers went vertical—not just in China anymore, but everywhere. Americans were buying an album they'd ignored for fifteen years.

I was lying in bed, scrolling through my phone. *Superficial* was climbing the iTunes charts. Not just climbing—soaring. Past Taylor Swift. Past Olivia Rodrigo. Past every artist who hadn't just lost their house.

By morning, it was number one on iTunes.

"Heidi," I said. "Look at this."

She stared at the phone screen, at her name sitting above every other artist in the country, and started crying. Not sad tears. Not happy tears. Just . . . tears.

The interviews started immediately. "How does it feel to have the chart-topping album?" they'd ask, like we'd achieved it through traditional means. It was hard to know what to say, impossible to unpack what these feelings were. Gratitude, mainly. I guess.

The album stayed at number one for three days. Longer than our house had been on fire. The music had survived. Heidi's voice, the thing everyone had ignored—it was still there, streaming around the world, unchanged by fire or time or the opinions of people who never understood it anyway.

Billions of streams later, it brought us $150K. Which was incredible, don't get me wrong. But when I'd hyped Heidi with "*This is going to buy the new house,*" she just gave me that look. She knew better.

What it bought us wasn't a house—it was proof. Proof that even when everything else turns to ash, at least some things can still survive. Dreams, music, the truth. Those things are fireproof, at least.

CHAPTER 31

TRUE CRIMES

When the Villain Has Receipts

As I write this, my skin is covered in welts, still healing from a staph infection I developed a few months ago from crawling through the toxic ruins of our house, rolling around in the debris without one of those white hazmat suits everyone else had on. Guess I didn't realize the literal ashes of my life were pure poison. That ash got into my skin, into my system, and next thing I knew, I was on three months of antibiotics just trying to kill the infection. Which, in turn, destroyed my gut health. Cue the eczema. Then came the sixty pounds I packed on from grief eating. Now I'm choking down probiotics, guzzling kombucha, doing the whole "wellness starter pack" routine, trying to claw my way back to balance.

Fun times.

But that's kind of been my whole story, hasn't it? Diving headfirst into disasters I thought I could outsmart, only to get burned, infected, scarred—then turning around and posting about it anyway. Call it self-destruction, call it survival, call it Speidi. Whatever it is, it's the only way I've ever known how to live.

We've been using our California FAIR Plan insurance money to rent my parents' house in Santa Barbara while they're in a two-bedroom condo they're renting in Santa Monica—Dad still grinding, still drilling molars so his son and family can have somewhere to sleep, and Mom not doing good, grieving the loss of her home and a lifetime of possessions and memories. She didn't get a single thing out of her house.

I'd begun digging into what really happened with these fires. And you know how I get once I lock into a project—I'm relentless. I filed FOIA requests to find out why the firefighting planes vanished when we needed them most. I started chasing down why the reservoirs in the Palisades—literally next door to our house—were bone-dry, leaving hydrants useless. I pored over city budgets, state reports, anything I could get my hands on. What I found was as shocking as the flames themselves: years of neglect, mismanagement, and flat-out indifference from the very people who were supposed to protect us.

Remember the big fire aid concert that raised over $100 million? Streamed live on twenty-eight platforms, starring icons like Lady Gaga, Billie Eilish, Joni Mitchell, Green Day, and Nirvana's surprise reunion? Proceeds were matched dollar-for-dollar by Steve Ballmer and his wife, pushing the total well beyond the seven-figure mark. The organizers laid out plans: $50 million for immediate needs (housing, food, case management) and additional grants to support long-term recovery.

Here's the catch: Six months later, residents who lost everything hadn't seen a penny. Journalists like Sue Pascoe highlighted how most of the money had gone to nonprofits—not direct assistance to families like mine. Congressmen are calling for DOJ investigations, noting that many of those organizations had no clear ties to local fire victims.

It was the same playbook I'd already seen in Hollywood: the *death economy*. But now I see the *disaster economy*. The *homelessness economy*. Entire industries built not to solve crises, but to monetize them.

Meanwhile, the city and state are trying to turn our ashes into a land grab. They're out here rezoning scorched earth for "affordable housing"—translation: high-rise apartments jammed into one of the most fire-prone canyons in California. A neighborhood already on life support, where the roads can't handle an evacuation, the hydrants ran dry, and the power grid dies every Santa Ana.

They call it compassion. I call it opportunism. It's disaster capitalism 101—turning a tragedy into leverage while the smoke is still in the air. And the kicker? Some of the same politicians who left us to burn are the ones pushing this through. Smiling, holding press conferences, talking about "resilience" while quietly redrawing the map to suit their donors.

Not on my watch.

So I turned my socials into a war room. Receipts, names, clips. Why were no assets pre-deployed when the winds had been forecast for days? Why did California State Parks not inspect its properties, post a fire watch, or use thermal imaging to ensure there were no embers or hot spots remaining in the vegetation from the Lachman fire? Why was the FAIR Plan—the state's joke of a stopgap—the only insurance left to us? Why are Palisades residents paying millions in taxes only to be abandoned?

Then the office of California Governor Gavin Newsom—aka Mr. Hair Gel—clapped back, calling me a "C-list reality star" on X (formerly known as Twitter), accusing me of spreading misinformation. Excuse me? I'm a fire victim. A constituent. A taxpayer whose house just burned to the ground. Instead of leadership, I got condescension. Instead of accountability, I got a cheap burn.

Which leads me to the plot twist no one saw coming: The Department of Justice flew me to Washington, DC. Me. Spencer Pratt. The guy branded for life as a reality TV villain. Suddenly I'm in a suit, briefing federal investigators about corruption in California disaster relief. I sat there, laying out my 3 a.m. Google rabbit holes, the PDFs, the numbers, the money trail—and people actually listened. The irony wasn't lost on me. The villain was now delivering testimony. Because the villain keeps receipts.

Trust me, I never wanted to be playing this role—any more than I wanted to be Spencer Pratt, reality TV villain. Both were parts I got cast in, whether I liked it or not. The difference is, back then, it only served me: attention, checks, headlines. This time, it's not just about me. It's about people who got burned, literally and figuratively, by a system that abandoned them.

So here I am. Fire victim with an iPhone. Not glamorous, not lucrative, still ongoing. Who knows how many seasons it'll last before everyone's ready to move on to the next thing, a fresh character, a new narrative. But honestly? It's probably the only role I've ever played that's actually worth a damn. The one I'll keep playing until I get as many people as possible the justice they deserve. You don't even want to know the tricks I still have up my sleeve to make that happen.

EPILOGUE

HOLLYWOOD ENDING
The Director's Cut

I've talked a lot about villains in this book. No surprise—being "the villain" is what made my name. For years, I bought into the hype. Thought I was the shark in *Jaws*. Big bad. Apex predator. Cue the theme music.

But the older I get, the more I see the truth: I was never the shark. I was Nemo, that little guy. Lost. Swimming in circles until I finally found home.

The real sharks? They wear suits. They run networks. They promise you "protection" while cashing checks off your pain. They don't show up with mustaches or Darth Vader music. They don't hiss in corners. They shake your hand. They call themselves "friends," "leaders," "producers." Still. They don't bother me like they used to, because I'm not playing the same game they are anymore.

Spencer, out.

You want to know what I learned from twenty years of being Spencer Pratt, villain for hire? That fame is just expensive loneliness. Yeah, I found something way better than fame: the ability to stand still—like those hummingbirds taught me—and let life happen without trying to produce, direct, and star in it.

Heidi's sleeping next to me while our boys dream in the next room. My parents still love me after forty-two years of beautiful disasters. The hummingbirds will find me wherever I build the next sanctuary.

That's the real prize. I guess you could call it love.

So what's next for Spencer Pratt? Honestly—idk. Maybe I just keep making TikToks about government corruption until they figure out how to ban me. Maybe Heidi drops another album. Best-case scenario, my kids grow up proud that I stood up when it counted.

Meanwhile, I'm sitting here at 6 a.m., writing the last page of a book I never thought anyone would want to read. About a life I never thought would add up to anything except scandal and spectacle. Turns out there was a story here after all. Not the one narrated about me. Not the one I expected. Just the messy, complicated, sometimes beautiful truth of what it costs to become yourself.

Sure, I'm still the same guy who leaked that rumor, said those terrible things—but also the guy who learned that love matters more than being right. That home matters more than headlines. That being nobody to everyone is fine, as long as you're somebody to the people who count.

Is that a Hollywood ending?

Probably not—and I'm good with that.

They usually save those for the hero, anyway.

ACKNOWLEDGMENTS

To God—for the plan I couldn't see, but somehow followed anyway.

To my wife, Heidi—you're my ride or die, my guardian angel, my ultimate reward. Thank you for being the heart of this story.

To my sons, Gunner and Ryker—thank you for turning me into a man who actually deserves you. You are my greatest teachers, my reasons for everything.

To my loving parents, Skip and Janet; Nana Joan in heaven (don't worry, Nana, I'm going to get even more famous after this book); my older sister, Kristin, a peacemaker who has always had my back; Kristin's dad, Andy (rest in peace), who said "If Spencer was a stock, I'd buy it" when I was a kid; and my younger sister, Stephanie, who's always kept me entertained—you're the original cast, and what a wild season it's been.

Endless thanks to my editor, Molly Gregory—without your vision and unconditional support, this book would never have been possible—and to the brilliant team at Simon & Schuster for believing there was more to this Millennial "reality villain" than met the eye. Huge thanks to Carolyn Levin for her legal expertise. High fives to Matt Attanasio for his enthusiasm and support.

To Caroline Ryder, my brilliant ghostwriter—from day one, you understood the deeper frequencies of this journey and transformed my chaos into something real and true. You're a master of your craft, and I couldn't have asked for a more empathetic copilot for this intensely personal process. (Publishers, take note: She's the real deal. Let's get Heidi's book done next.)

To my manager, Kyell Thomas—thank you for being here through every peak, valley, and plot twist.

To one of my earliest reps, Adam Gelvan, happy to have you back on the team.

To my agents at WME: Rich Gambale, for taking the swing to bring us back in; and to Eve Attermann, for manifesting this deal like a pro.

To our first agent, John Ferriter. Rest in peace.

To Rickson and Rockson Gracie for bringing martial arts to the Palisades and for training me.

To my childhood friend Alex Jackson, who would always take my calls and never lead me astray.

To Brian Rapf—thanks for being born next to me and still being part of my life forty-two years later. Thanks to Brian's mom, Lucy, for prophesying my marriage.

To Charlie Smith, who was the only person brave enough to film next to me on camera during the darkest days of *The Hills*.

To all the people who have never watched *The Hills*—please don't.

Brody Jenner—you always believed in me.

Wander—thanks for getting me out of Brazil alive.

To David Foster, for letting me follow you around your mansion, film you yelling at us, and for always being Speidi's champion.

To Linda Thompson, who always supported me.

Brant Pinvidic—thank you for being a consistent ally in this crazy industry for so many years.

Peter Chernin—thank you for taking me seriously and for making me an executive producer, despite my purple shirt.

To my brilliant friends in entertainment journalism: Peter Grossman, thank you for years of friendship and making tabloid fan fiction with me. Janice Min, Dan Wakeford, Perez Hilton—you are absolute geniuses who shaped how we talk about celebrity culture.

Rest in peace, Peter Lopez. We'll always miss you.

My legal team, Dan Black (I'm sorry!) and Ann Clark—you're the best in the biz.

ACKNOWLEDGMENTS

Alex Baskin—one of the only genuine, honest reality TV producers on earth.

Thank you, Henry the Alien, for putting me on the crystal path.

Taylor Swift—thank you for holding our miracle baby, Gunner, and changing my reputation.

Stumpo's Raiders, rest in peace. Nerds may not recognize us, but we know who the real USC OGs are.

To the Pacific Palisades—thank you for everything you were, the home I grew up in, the place I never wanted to leave.

To my hummingbird friends—thank you for reminding me that stillness is a superpower.

And finally, to everyone who picked up this book—you looked behind the curtain. And for that, I'll be forever grateful.